THE DICE ARE OUT

by

Robert S. Fuller

Jones Harvest PUBLISHING

ISBN: 978-1-60388-102-9
1-60388-102-6

Introduction

If you are one of the fortunate souls to have picked up this book, you are in for a real treat. Do not let the title "The Dice Are Out" fool you. It is a book about much more than gambling. This book is one man's honest recollection of what our world has been like for a good part of the last century. We are fortunate that Bucko is still alive to share the past with us. All good stories portray the greater conflict by revealing the true souls of a few individuals within that conflict. This book recalls a real American experience through the life and times of a few characters. All of these persons contain the essence of one character, namely, the author. Interpretive dream psychologists tell us that everything in ones dreams are a part of the dreamer themselves. Indeed, Bucko Bob Fuller has much to tell about his American experience.

I have read the unedited version of this tale, as Bucko has become a new acquaintance of mine. I have stood next to him at the craps tables many times now. Craps is a game that mirrors life in many ways. We are alike in that respect, because we love the game. All of us take a chance every time we cross the street, and in that sense we are all gamblers; however, one does not need to be a craps player or gambler to enjoy this book. There are many aspects of the book that all Americans can enjoy. How many US citizens are still alive that actually served in the armed services in WW II? It is a rapidly dwindling number. My father would often tell the stories of the WWII conflict from the fight with Germany in the Atlantic. Bucko's tale recounts the nature of our war with Japan. Indeed, he had many close calls, and he admits that it was his faith in the Lord that pulled him through. The book goes on through many experiences with his younger schooling days, accidents, women, business ventures, and the like. One gets the sense from his writing, that the Lord has always been with him, no matter the good or the bad experiences in his life. Bucko is the kind of man that sees the bad parts for what they were and makes no apologies. It was this positive outlook, as well as faith that helped him through those experiences.

I would hope that the editors would not "clean up" Bucko's writing too much for grammar or syntax. One gets the "feel" of being on Grandpa's lap, being told a story. The deeper meaning comes together when one realizes that Bucko Bob, never complained about his predicaments. He took what he was given, and "made it better."

It is the colloquial way it is expressed, like a Faulkner novel, that makes it so real. It is non pretentious and all-American in its scope. It's the perfect novel for today's youth as well as us "baby-boomers" that sometimes get tied up in the material world and forget where we live. Most Americans today, feel somewhat entitled. This book will tell you why it is great to be an American, and why we should not take that good fortune so lightly.

It was no small feat to complete this book, and I would like to personally congratulate "Bucko" on his achievement and thank him for his service to our country as well.

Dr. Jack B. Zito
Mathematics Education, Ph.D.
Administration & Supervision, Ph.D.
Thomas University
Thomasville, GA

Acknowledgments

Everything in this book has been a gift to me from God by giving me the gift to remember things in my past that could be brought up to date and put on paper. To fully understand this statement you would need to read my first book titled "Bucko". In that autobiography, I took my readers on a truthful journey through exciting events of my life. In this new book I was able to enhance all my incidents from the past and make it a work of fiction. Places in this work are real, but persons and incidents are used fictitiously.

The Lord has placed inside of me an eagerness that provided the ambition to do this work of fiction. I cannot type and I had lost the sight of one eye 60 years ago, but where there is a will, there is a sustaining way.

I wish to thank World Book and Globe Devise for many facts from our history and topics of interest. I wish to thank the U.S. Navy and its Amphibious Branch for making a man of me and giving me my first good home. To my fellow shipmates and dice partners I thank you for your encouragement and support.

I wish to thank my family for supporting in my struggle in bringing this to a conclusion. Especially to my wife of 60 years, Connie, who was so helpful in daily writings, and a special thanks to my lovely daughter in law

Barbara Fuller for giving of her time to full editing of this manuscript.

Robert S. Fuller

Chapter 1

His Christian name was Garston Alphonso Savino, later nicknamed Gar, sometimes Gassy, from the three first letters in his name. Only his friends were allowed to use the latter.

He was only 15, but life had been hard for Gar. He had been on his own since he was four, the year that both of his parents had been killed. They had been to a party, and left Gar with a baby sitter. When they were driving home, it had started to rain, then turned into sleet and freezing rain. Their car slid into the path of a tractor-trailer. They didn't survive the impact.

Since there was no one to care for Gar, the State placed him with Social Services, then into an orphanage. He had several opportunities for adoption, but each time it was about to happen, or if Gar didn't like his potential new family, he would find a way to scare them away. He had perfected different little tantrums. The one that seemed to be best was acting as though he was crazy, yelling loudly while tossing books or anything that he could get his hands on. This always worked, but the repercussions were very bad for him. He would have to go without eating and lost all of his privileges for two days, but not until he was made to lay across a chair, while the director gave him several whacks with a leather strap.

As the years slowly passed by, the beatings became more violent. Finally, all potential families were told that Gar was not a good candidate for adoption, and he was passed over. It was no surprise that the state viewed him as a hopeless case. This did not bother Gar. He was just waiting for the day that he would turn 18 and would be able to walk out and kiss this place good-bye.

Then something happened that altered this plan. When he was 15, he ran away from The Hickory Home For Children for the last time. He wandered into the garage at the Langwell Hotel in Elmira, NY with the intention of finding one of the cars with a set of keys, still in it. As he came through the doors, he heard voices coming from the rear of the garage. As he got closer he heard phrases like "Come on, Little Joe!" and "Whoopee, he sevened out!". Gar had never seen a crap game before. The fascination, was overwhelming. He got as close as he could, trying not to be seen. There seemed to be boys his age there, along with older ones. What caught most of his attention, was that pile of green money laying in the middle of this ring of guys, and after some more yelling, some one would reach down and take it all, or else they would divide it up again.

After watching for a long time, inching closer and closer, someone noticed him, and yelled, "Hey, who's that guy?"

The biggest guy, Ray, turned to Gar, and said, "Who are you and what do you want?"

Gar was big for his age, but he wasn't about to take on five or six guys, and draw attention to himself, while he was on the run.

Gar was defensive, saying, "Sorry, fellas. I was just passing by and thought I heard friendly voices, so I thought I would see what's going down. I meant no harm."

"What's your name?" Ray asked

"Gar's my nickname."

Then another guy said, "Do you know how to play Craps?"

Gar says, "I think so. I've been watching you guys for a while, but I sure would like to learn more." Gar said.

"Ya got any money?"

"No," said Gar, "but I do have this special jackknife that is worth a lot."

"Let's see it'."

Gar handed it over and they all took a good look. "Say, that is a beauty. Where did ya steal it?" someone said.

"Hey, I didn't steal it. It was handed down from my grandfather and I don't like your reference to me being a thief," Gar said stiffly.

"OK, OK, don't get your balls in an uproar! Just kiddin'," Then he asked "How much ya want for it?"

Gar was not prepared to do any trading, but he needed money and those dollar bills that they were passing back and forth were making his mouth water. He had stolen the knife, a long time ago and he knew anyone could buy one any place, for probably one dollar. He wanted so badly to get in this game and feel that money, those green bills. He might even win some to pay someone to help him steal a car and get out of this city, so it was time to bluff.

"Well, if you guys will teach me how to play this game, and no cheating, I will sell it to you for fifteen dollars and I know my Dad will kill me when he finds out that I no longer have it."

"Hey, what do you take us for, nutty? That knife ain't worth nothing like that! But I'll tell you what, I'll put a value of ten dollars on it and you put it in the center, and you can try to shoot the dice for it, every one will *fade* you, two dollars a piece, making it ten dollars that you will be shooting for, how's that?" offered Ray.

"That's okay by me. Run the rules of the game by me one more time," said Gar.

"It's simple. Just roll the dice, making sure they bounce off the back board. If a seven or eleven comes up on the first roll, you win. If a two, three, or twelve comes up, you lose. Any other number that comes up, will be your point number. Then you just keep rolling until you roll the point number again. If you do, you win, but if you roll a seven before the point, you lose," Ray said.

Gar placed the knife in the playing area and picked up the dice, while the five guys all put two dollars each in their positions.

"Okay, hot shot!" they yelled. "Roll! And remember, you must hit the back stop so the dice stay in front of it. If the dice go over or beyond it, it's a "no-roll," and you have to throw again."

Gar tossed the dice, and after they bounced, back 5-1, or a 6 was showing.

"His point is 6!" yelled out one of them.

"Do I keep shooting?"

"Of course, stupid! We told you before, keep tossing, try to make the six again, before the seven."

Gar picked up the dice again, tossed a four, then an eight. Then he rolled two threes, the hard way six.

"Whoopee!" he yelled. "I... I win!" and as he reached for the money, one of the players grabbed his wrist.

"Not so friggin' fast, jerk. The rules are that the winner has to let everyone get even," said a ruffian. "Otherwise, we break your arm now!"

Gar certainly didn't need to get into a fight and five against one was not in his favor. He saw that some diplomacy was needed.

"Hey, you guys never told me that before, but sure, I'm willing to shoot again. I'll just put the money in my pocket, and you try to win the knife again."

"Hell, no!" yelled Ray, followed by a chorus of nays, from the rest. "You can pick up the knife, if you want, but the dough stays in the game!"

"Well, okay," he said as he put the knife back in his pocket. "I'll shoot the ten," and he grabbed the dice.

Every one looked at each other, and they finally each put two more dollars in the center.

"Okay, you're faded again, so throw the damn dice!" Ray said.

Gar tossed the dice against the backboard, and out came a natural 6-5, eleven.

"I believe I win!" He stared into their eyes, slowly reaching for the money.

"Hold it, Buster," demanded Ray. "You have to win three times in a row before you get to keep it."

Just then a hotel customer drove through the front doors of the garage and tooted his horn.

Robert S. Fuller

Ray said, "I'll have to check this car in before we can resume this game. In the mean time, you guys keep this guy, Gar, here and make sure he doesn't try taking the dough. I will be right back. Then we'll see if he still thinks he can walk out with our money."

It finally dawned on Gar that these guys would never let him get out of there. Even if he won the money, he desperately cased the garage, trying to figure out how he would ever get out of here alive. If he did win, and boy, does he ever need that money. He had never owned twenty dollars in his life. He couldn't see anything that he could use as a weapon except the two by six board that was being used as the craps backboard and the table that their pot of coffee sat on.

Ray came hustling back. "I'll park that car later, right now, I'm more interested in seeing if our jerky friend here thinks he can win our hard earned cash."

Now or never, Gar thought to himself, as Ray and his buddies all got back down on their knees, with big smirks on their faces, winking to each other. He quickly grabbed all the green bills. Before they could react, he snatched the backboard and swung it hard, catching Ray flat on the side of his head, putting him out cold. Then he grabbed the hot pot of coffee, and threw it in the faces of the rest of them. He scrambled for the garage doors, as the players were screaming in pain, yelling, "Get that bastard!"

As he realized that he just might make it out, he saw the car that Ray was supposed to park, and made a dash for it, hoping the keys were still in it. "Yes, they're still in the ignition!" he thought. In desperation he started the car, slammed it in reverse and burned rubber all the way

6

into the street. It was close to midnight, so there was no traffic. He pulled it in drive and shot down Main Street.

"I made it! I made it!" he kept yelling to himself.

Now he must be careful for he had never really driven a car before. He had sat in one and gone through the motions and had read all about them. A neighbor kid near the orphanage had let him drive his go-cart a couple times, but this was for real now.

The car was a two-year-old, '39 Ford Coupe, all black, a thing of beauty and Gar was in a state of euphoria. He was free, money in his pockets, driving this beautiful car. He glanced at the gas gauge and saw that it was full of gas.

He needed to decide where to go. Getting away from the orphanage was the main objective a little while ago, but now he must decide on a plan for how he would survive. He realized that he would have to give up the car. The police would be looking for him and the car, no doubt. He quickly decided that time being of the essence he would try going south, crossing the border into Pennsylvania, maybe to a large city where he might not be noticed. The border was only about 15 miles, or even less, south on Route 14.

He sped up, gaining more confidence in his ability to drive every minute. The clock in the dashboard read 12:45 AM, and with no traffic, he let the car fly him to better times. His confidence was building at the same speed. He flipped on the radio, turning to Gene Autry, bellowing out You Are My Sunshine.

"Hey, is this great, or what?" he boasted to himself.

Flying down one of the hills, he saw the headlights catch a reflection. He asked himself, what the heck is that? Before he could react, a big buck jumped into the road.

Chapter 2

The first thing Gar saw was a beautiful angel in a rocking chair, holding her child looking right at Gar. The angel kept asking, repeating over and over, "Are you all right? Can you hear me?"

Then he was flying through space again, as his eyes closed with heavy lids, but the voice is still with him softly asking him, "Can you hear me?"

When he opened his eyes again, he realized that he had been looking at a picture on the wall and someone in a white uniform was standing beside him.

"Where am I?" he asked.

"You are in St. Joseph Hospital here in Elmira," the nurse told him. "You were in a car accident and an ambulance you in unconscious. You do not appear to have any broken bones, but from the knot on your head you may have a skull fracture and we have been trying to bring you around for some time now. How do you feel?" Gar took his time, carefully examining himself.

"Okay, I guess, except for this awful headache," he murmured.

"Well, we will have to keep you under observation for a couple of days to be sure that there are no complications. By the way, you have visitor. A policeman has been here a long time waiting to talk to you. I'll send him in."

The policeman went through the usual question and answer routine, then informed Gar that he was under arrest for stealing a car from the garage at the Langwell Hotel and that the Orphanage was looking for him. He told Gar that he would have to be held in Juvenile Detention, until he appeared before the judge to answer the charges.

"Sir, can you tell me what happened? I can't remember a thing, except taking that car while running for my life. Those guys at the garage were going to kill me!" Gar said.

"That's not what they say," said the policeman. "They reported, that you snuck upon them, then hit the manager over the head, threw hot coffee in their eyes and stole a customer's car. The State Police called us out to Route 14, where you had hit a deer, then crashed into a tree, totaling the car. You must have hit your head because they told us you have been out ever since they found you. I'd say you are one lucky kid to survive that crash with only a concussion. Consider yourself under arrest. We will have your room watched until the Hospital releases you, at which time we will escort you to jail and up before the judge, so don't do anything foolish," he said.

Two days later, the Hospital released Gar, and the Police escorted him to the Juvenile Detention Center, where they gave him orange coveralls, some bed clothes and booked him in. The headaches had gone away and the little black and blue marks were hardly visible. The doctors had declared him fit and had all remarked that he was, indeed, a very lucky person to survive such a crash with minor bruises. Gar was happy that he wasn't sent back to the orphanage, but he did have a lot of anxiety as to what the Judge would do. His record at the orphanage was not in his favor, but he knew that he was too young to be sent to prison. So what could happen to him, he pondered.

He didn't have to wait long, for the next morning he was taken to Juvenile Court of Chemung County where the judge asked him if he was guilty of the charges of stealing the car.

Gar said, "yes."

Then the judge told him that since he had no home nor any relatives to care for him, there was no alternative but to send him up to "Industry." That was the Industrial Reform School near Rochester, NY.

"You will learn a trade and with good behavior, you could be released, provided that the State find someone to sponsor you until you turn 18," the judge said, "You will be taken by auto next Monday and until then, you will remain in Detention Jail."

Gar spent the next few days waiting for the transfer, trying to find out what it was like in Industry by asking anyone he saw, but everyone kept telling him that he would find out soon enough when he got there.

Finally, the day came and he was driven up to "Industry."

Chapter 3

He was taken to the Administration Office, where he received instructions on how he should behave, where he would be staying and asked if he had any preferences as to a trade or skill that he would like to learn. They told him to pick three from a list they handed to him and if he didn't pick, that they would pick for him, because he was here to learn, and he could either do it the easy way or the hard way. The choice was his to make. He was told that every one here lives in a Colony. Each colony had a husband and wife, who would be his Guardians.

"While at your Colony, they will set the rules and give you your duties. All of the Colonies have 20 to 30 boys each. All named after different Indian Tribes. You will walk to and from your shop every day except on weekends, when you will have chores to do. You will walk to a church of your choice along with others every Sunday. We don't have fences on our property, but if you run away, your time will double, plus you will be severely punished. Do not make a move or do a thing, without getting permission."

Gar thought to himself, in other words my ass belongs to you from now on as long as I'm here. Maybe I might just do something about that.

Chapter 4

"Industry" was situated approximately 30 miles west of Rochester, NY, and maybe 100 miles east of Buffalo and the Canadian border. Lake Ontario stretched across the borders to the north. At the hub of this self-sustaining complex was where all the important functions took place. It was comprised of the administration buildings, all the trade school buildings like the machine shop, barber shop, bakery shop, mechanics shop and various other trade shops, including class rooms for elementary. There were also churches of different denominations , and a diversified candy store. It was no wonder that this area was known and referred to as the Center.

On a hill, to the east , sat the Hospital, with its nurses and a doctor, who was always available, if you had permission to visit him.

From the Center , there were roads leading out to the various colonies, where the boys were housed and given parental guidance. These roads were like fingers, each leading back to the center. A few of these colonies were farms, where some boys worked full time and didn't have to attend other trade schools.

Every one going from one place to another always had to walk in groups, no stragglers. Each group would leave from one place or another, after permission from the guardian, guard or instructor. Showing up late, or tardy, without a legitimate excuse was against regulations and grounds for punishment.

Gar, was then was taken to the Training colony, named "Alpha," meaning beginning. How appropriate! This Colony was also situated at the Center, where new arrivals could easily be taken to the barber shop for a "skinhead" clip. They would also be taken to the Hospital for a complete physical exam plus a dental visit.

The Guardians were, Mr. and Mrs. Lang. Mr. Lang was waiting for Gar, as he approached. He told Gar that he must always enter the Colony from the basement and never come upstairs with his shoes on. Shoes are always left in the basement and he must always have his socks on. He told him to report to the guard in the basement, where he would be issued proper clothing and instructed as to the specific duties that he would be expected to do.

In the center of the basement was a long sink with faucets hanging down that sprayed into a sink, with soap ledges on each side, making it easy for several boys to wash at one time. Along the back wall were several pipes, at eye level running all the way back to the furnace and water heaters, which were situated in the left rear area. From the furnace to the right were several shower stalls, ending at the right wall. The wall was lined with tall metal lockers just like the ones that are seen in movies at school halls, almost to the steps leading upstairs. The shoes were to be kept in the bottom, hats and incidentals kept in the top, while coats, and other clothing would be hung-up in the middle. Any personal materials, could be kept there also as long as it was approved by the guards. A locker inspection could happen at any time. Anything found not approved would bring disciplinary actions. One favorite action was making the boy stand at attention, while facing that left wall with his head about two inches from those metal pipes. If he spoke, laughed, lost his balance, or moved anything without permission, the Guards relished in slapping the boy's head from behind, causing the head to bang against those pipes, making for an awful headache or even bruises. If anyone ever complained to Mr. Lang, the guards would make it tougher, next time.

This Colony had one boy that was permanently assigned there. His name was Tom Wysocki, and he was a big, polish kid. He had grown up on a farm and had developed big muscles. His duties were to assist Mr. Lang in seeing that each new boy that came there had the proper clothes and were instructed in whatever duties were handed to him. He was a favorite with the guards, for they could rely on him to keep them informed as to little secrets that the new boys had, bringing anything that he felt warranted their attention. It was a known fact by the other boys that he hated everyone. Any boy giving him any lip or asking too many questions was pushed and slapped around. He was always wanting the boy to fight him, knowing full well that he could beat any kid his age. For some strange reason, he particularly had a bigger hatred for Italians, so when he heard that Gar's name was Savino, he began to smell fresh meat.

Gar seemed to be impressed so far, by what he had seen and by the way this joint was being run. So far he hadn't been hit and maybe, if he learned a trade here, his future might take a different direction. He was starting to convince himself that he would give it a good honest try by keeping his nose clean and not cause more trouble for himself. But little did he know that someone was about to give his new impressions a real test.

When it came time for dinner, word would be given to the guard. After they had washed and combed their hair, they lined up in single file, without shoes, they proceeded up to the dining room. No talking allowed without permission. Then they would stand behind the chair of their appointed table and wait for the guardian to tell them to sit. Then he would lead them in unison, as Grace was said. The guardians would always have their meal at the same time, while being seated at the end of the room, where the boys could be observed at all times.

One strict rule at meal times was you could have seconds of anything on the table after everyone had had their first serving, but if you put it on your plate you had to eat it all. The meal tasted good to Gar, but he noticed a bowl of green peas, and he hated them. The people at the orphanage had tried forcing him into eating peas. This only caused him to almost get sick just thinking about it.

Tom, who was sitting across the table, noticed that Gar would turn colors, whenever the peas came near him, he would always refuse them. When he was almost finished with his meal, Tom put a big scoop of peas onto his plate. It happened so fast, Gar almost yelled out, but caught himself just in time. He stared first at the peas, then at Tom, with a sort of "why?" frozen stare. Tom had that sly smirk on his face, making sure to avoid looking at Gar.

About that time, Mr. Lang stood to make his usual inspection of their plates before dismissing the group. He was about to dismiss them when he saw all those peas on Gar's plate and saw that Gar wasn't eating.

"Mr. Savino," said Mr. Lang, "you are keeping us waiting by not eating the rest of your food. You were told that if you take food, you are required to eat it all and if you don't you will be punished. Are you going to eat all your food?"

"Sir, I'm sorry, but I cannot eat peas. They make me sick," replied Gar

"Then why did you put them on your plate?" asked Mr. Lang.

"Sir, I didn't put them there."

"Are you telling me that someone else at your table did it?"

"No, Sir."

Gar did not want to be a stool pigeon, even if he still couldn't figure out why Tom had done this.

Mr. Lang looked at all the boys and said, "Did any of you see someone put those peas on Savino's plate?"

All heads shook a negative answer.

Mr. Lang moved to the back of Gar's chair, grabbed his hair and twisted his head around, so they were face to face.

"Mr. Savino, I am only going to say this once, and I want you to fully hear and to understand what I'm about to say. I'm going to dismiss the rest of our group, then I will give you just three minutes to clean up your plate. Do you understand me"?

"Yes Sir, but..."

"No buts," stated Mr. Lang. He then motioned for the guard to have the boys return to the basement, then told the guard to come right back up to him. As the boys were leaving, Mr. Lang said, "Your time is starting now, Mr. Savino."

Gar realized that this was getting too serious, so he put a spoonful in his mouth. He began chewing and gagging at the same time. He wanted to eat the damn peas and deal with Tom later, maybe even kill the bastard, even if he *was* bigger. The reflux and gagging sensation was just too much for Gar to handle, and each spoonful seemed to be falling back onto his plate.

"Mr. Savino, I'm running out of patience with you. Eat all those peas now! *Now*, and be quick about it, or maybe you would like us to hold your mouth open and pour them down your throat!" said Lang.

Gar tried desperately to comply with these orders, but his stomach finally rebelled, and he vomited uncontrollably, all over the table and floor.

"What the? Hey! Stop that.!" screamed Lang. He turned to the guard, "Take Gar below to the toilet and get him cleaned up! Send Tom and two other boys up here to clean this mess up!" As they left, he yelled, "Then I want you to bring that pup back up here to me!"

The guard shoved Gar all the way down the stairs, held his head under the faucets at the sink and turned on the cold water full force, nearly drowning Gar.

Mr. Lang could be heard overhead, still yelling at the cleanup gang. The guard threw a towel at Gar to dry off. He said, "Sonny, *you* really did it. Do you know how much Lang hates having anything spilled on those hardwood floors? He detests wasting food and he can't stand a liar. I wouldn't give a plug nickel for your life now."

A few minutes later, Tom and his cleanup boys were done and as they returned to the basement, Tom glared at

Gar, saying softly, "Hey, Wappo, keep your mouth shut, or else!"

Gar turned to be sure that the guard didn't hear, and said, "I'll get you, asshole, and don't think I'm scared of you!" while following Tom with his eyes.

The guard escorted Gar back up to Mr. Lang, who was waiting for him. In his hand was a wide razor strap and said, "Mr. Savino, you have just committed three Cardinal Sins. First, you wasted food; second, you lied about it; and third, you threw up on my beautiful floor. Your punishment for wasting food is that you will go without eating any meals, all day tomorrow. For lying about it, you will receive five hard whacks across your buttocks, with this razor strap. Then you will put polishing cloths under your feet, and polish this dining room floor, until it shines like glass, even if it takes all night and you will do it with your arms folded across your chest. Now, lay across that chair. I will refrain from having you pull down your pants this time, only because you need to be able to polish this floor."

Gar did as he was told and received five painful blows to his bottom. He gritted his teeth and vowed not to cry, but it, oh, how that did hurt! He then waited for some boys to help him move all furniture off to one side, sweep the floor, apply wax from a large bar, then he had to put a 4"x12" wool cloth under each foot and march up and back like a good soldier. When that side was done, all the furniture was moved and the other side was waxed. By the time his punishment was completed to Mr. Lang's satisfaction, it was time for everyone to shower and change into their clean pajamas and march up to the dormitory.

Chapter 5

Each boy was assigned to an army type cot, and was responsible for keeping their bed clothes clean and neat. In the morning, each bed had to be made up with no wrinkles, all corners tucked in properly. Each cot was inspected in the morning after they polished the floor just as it was done to the dining room, by putting cloths under their feet and marching back and forth in a line, making sure it was always straight with no talking. Then if they all passed inspection, they were marched down to the basement where they washed and dressed for breakfast.

Once you entered your bed at night you could never get out, unless you asked the guard for permission. The guard always had a small reading light at his desk, making it possible to see almost all the room. The guard also had a large rubber flashlight and one of his favorite things to do, would be to catch someone talking or whispering and sneak up on them and thump them with it. If you needed to go to the toilet which was adjoining the dormitory, you would rise up in bed and say, "Guard, Sir?"

The guard would shine his light around until he found you and say, "What is it?"

Then you could ask him for permission to go to the bathroom, or permission to speak. Only one boy at a time was allowed to go to the bathroom.

Gar laid there, his bottom hurting, but hurting worse was his pride. The more he thought about the last five hours, the more his hatred was building towards Tom. What in the world was wrong with him, to do this to him? He stewed over how he would get even. He knew he couldn't go to Mr. Lang about it and complaining to the guards was futile, as they would surely take Tom's side. Besides he was no stooge. The first step would be to just confront Tom and see where things go from there.

At six AM the next morning, the boys were instructed to rise, sweep and wax the dormitory floor and make their beds. After inspection, they were marched down to the basement, where they washed and dressed for breakfast. Tom was always either at the head of every line to count the boys, dismissed early to help Mrs. Lang in the kitchen or to do special errands for Mr. Lang.

Gar made a point of timing his being at the sinks at the very same time as Tom and softly said, "Why did you set me up? Did I do something to you?"

"Get the fuck away from me, you grease ball. Yeah, you did something all right. You were born. I can't stand you, you freaking Wap!"

"Ok, if that's how you want to play. I'll get even with you and don't ever forget it. You may be bigger, but I'm not scared for one minute, you prick."

Gar returned to his locker and took a seat on the bench in front of the lockers. The guard came over to him and said, "Savino, you line up with the rest when we go up for breakfast, you take your usual place at the table. Your plate will be missing and you will sit there and watch the rest eat their food. Maybe you will think twice before pulling another stunt like last night!"

After they had their breakfast and finished waxing the floor once more, they were allowed a half hour in the recreation room. This room was right across from dining area. It had several round tables and chairs, and was carpeted. Anyone could write letters or play checkers or cards. It was a supervised place where the boys could relax, maybe read a book or study their lessons. Talking was allowed here along with clean jokes and sometimes laughter. Anyone could return to the basement if he had to go to the toilet, but only with permission. Going to the toilet was something that a shy person found to be embarrassing for the first few weeks. All the commodes were near the shower stalls, and no doors or partitions, just wide open spaces. Privacy no longer existed, but eventually, you simply had to get acclimated to it.

The next few days were spent by Gar and the other new boys getting all the basics taken care of, like getting his physical at the hospital and a visit to the dentist. Then he was talk to the Trade Supervisor about picking the trade that he would be pursuing. His first pick was the Bakery, which would be his very first class early in the morning from 8:00-9:30AM, then he was to take Machine Shop from 9:45-11:30, then to his home Colony for lunch and duties, returning to the classrooms at the school from 1:00-2:00. His final trade class would be from 2:15-4:00PM, but he had not finalized his choice for the last class. He thought he might try the Barber Shop, but wanted to wait until the mandatory visit to the barber, where all the recruits had to get their hair scalped. He wasn't to wait long.

The very next day, Mr. Lang and his boy, Tom escorted the boys to the Barber Shop. This was in the basement of the school. It was very clean, with four barber chairs. The first chair belonged to the instructor, Mr. John Mucci. He had been a barber for twenty years, he had owned his own shop in Rochester, but the State made him a fine offer to teach barbering at Industry, so he decided to sell his business and he enjoyed teaching. He commuted between Rochester and Industry every day.

When Mr. Lang brought fifteen new boys into the shop, Mr. Mucci greeted them with respect, and lots of laughing and joking. He immediately put the boys at ease, treating them as customers, not inmates. This impressed Gar and he felt lucky to have Mr. Mucci cut his hair, and they hit it off well. He told Gar that he would like to have him try Barbering. He said not everyone could do it, because it takes someone who can be friendly and courteous to the customers. When he found out that Gar was Italian, he told him that he could guarantee to make him a good barber. Gar told him that he would be glad to try it.

Before Mr. Mucci was finished with Gar, Tom, who was waiting to escort the boys back to the Colony, yelled out, "Mr. Mucci, after you cut that jerk's hair, we want you to shave his head also, 'cause he is a trouble maker."

At this, Mr. Mucci turned to Mr. Lang, "That right"?

"Of course not!" Mr. Lang answered. He turned and yelled to Tom," You just sit back in your chair, and keep those remarks to yourself! Carry on, Mr. Mucci."

"What was that all about?" whispered Mr. Mucci.

"It appears he hates me for no reason, but it would be best for me if we could forget about it."

"OK, I get you, and I will be expecting you for the afternoon class, as soon as you are approved by the Super."

"Oh, just one more thing," warned Mr.Mucci, still whispering, "Be careful around this guy, Tom, because he has been here before with other boys and they have told my barbers that he is trouble."

The next few weeks went by fairly fast and Gar somehow managed to stay clear of Tom. The routine of classes and the trades was finalized and he was looking forward to being sent to one of the Colonies that would be his future home for a while. He wanted to come up with an idea for pay-back to Tom. Gar had seen Tom occasionally would light up a cigarette when he was taking some of the boys to various classes. Smoking was not allowed, so Gar had been thinking on this for a few days. When ever Tom would throw the cigarette butt to the ground, Gar would keep his eye on it, and as he was usually at the rear of the group, he would pick up the butt as he passed by. He would only save the longest ones, putting them in his sock.

The night before Gar was to be transferred out to his designated Colony, which turned out to be the "Iroquois Colony," he envisioned an opportunity. Tom was taking his shower and he noticed that he had left his locker door slightly open. When Tom turned, facing the shower head, Gar opened Tom's locker and took out an empty cigarette pack. Tom had wadded it up to throw away, but hadn't done it yet, so there was a good chance that he wouldn't miss it. A plan was taking shape in Gar's head. This might be the only chance he will have to repay Tom. He could have told on Tom many times, but he detested a stooly, besides that would only continue the debacle. This had to be well planned and executed. As the call for lights out came, Gar settled in for a long wait. Making sure that he did not fall asleep.

As luck would have it, tonight's guard was the meanest of all the guards. He had a bad reputation from roughing up the boys, and Tom was not his favorite. It was after midnight when he heard,"Guard, sir,"

He recognized Tom's voice.

After shining his big flashlight around the dormitory, the beam focused on Tom.

"What is it?"questioned the guard.

"Permission to use the bathroom," asked Tom.

"OK, make it snappy," as he turned back to reading his book.

As Tom was getting out of bed, Gar carefully snuck out of his bed, keeping on his hands and knees. When Tom left the dorm, Gar very carefully crawled over to Tom's bed and placed the cigarette pack with three long butts inside, under his pillow.

Gar crawled back toward the hallway leading out of the Dorm and tossed a big butt down the hallway. Then he crawled back to his own bed but before he laid down, he threw a marble in the same direction. It startled the guard, who rushed out with his big light, as he grumbled, "what the hell is that?"

As he approached the toilet entrance, Tom rushed out and the two collided.

"What were you doing and what was that noise that I heard"? demanded the guard.

"Sir, I'm sorry for running into you, but I was only taking a leak."

"Why were you taking so long, and what did you drop to make that n—? Say, wait a minute, what the hell is this"? as his light spotted a cigarette butt at the entrance to the toilet.

"Looks to me you were having a little smoke, Tommy boy."

"No! no!" Tom said frantically, "I swear to you, I never saw that butt before."

"Well, if you didn't, who do you suppose did?" angrily demanded the guard.

"I do not know, but I *do* know that *I* did not do that!"

After going back and forth for some time, the guard said,"Enough of this! Come with me," and he grabbed Toms arm, pushing him back into the dorm.

Then the guard flipped all the lights on.

"Everybody up!"

With this jolt came confusion. They were rubbing their eyes, and there were sounds of murmuring amongst them.

"Shut up," he shouted, "I want everyone to line up along this wall, *now* ."

When he had them all lined up and at attention, he began pacing in front of them.

"I have here in my hand, a cigarette butt that one of you fags carelessly left in the toilet, and I want the guilty one to step forward. If he does not step forward now and admit his guilt, every last one of you will be punished. The punishment will be less severe if you admit it *now* !!"

The guard waited impatiently, but no one said a thing.

"This is your last chance before I call down to Mr. Lang and if he is brought into this, all of you will be in deep trouble."

Minutes quietly passed by and still, no one spoke up. In fact, they were so petrified that they hardly dared breathe.

The guard walked between rows of beds, stopping often to sweep the floor with the flashlight, making sure he looked under each bed. Then with disdain, he started going up each row removing all the bed clothes, inspecting each article. Then he saw the cigarette pack and the butts inside.

"*Hey*, what do we have here?" exclaimed the guard. "The person that has this bed come here *now*!!"

After it was determined that it was Tom's bed, he walked down to the guard and with a questioning stare said, "That is my bed, sir. Is there something wrong?"

The guard shoved the crumpled pack of cigarettes in his face, exclaiming, "Wrong? I'll say there's something wrong! You had these hid under your pillow, you have been smoking in the John, you lied to me about five minutes ago when I asked you about that butt on the floor, you tried to get these other boys punished for your damn bad behavior and I was about to beat the crap out of them, too. I am so mad that if I touch you, I'll probably kill you. What I should do is turn my back and let these boys beat your brains in. No, I'm taking you downstairs to Mr. Lang and he does not liked to be disturbed from his sleep. Go over to the hallway and stay there at attention!"

The guard instructed the boys to go back to their beds, replace the sheets and get back into bed. "Make it quick, because I'm in a hurry!" he yelled.

After they were all in their beds, he flipped off the lights, leaving only his small desk light on. "*No talking! Go to sleep!* ", he exclaimed. He grabbed Tom by the arm roughly, saying, "Now, Mr. Wysocki, lets take care of you. Mr. Lang will not enjoy this, *ha*, but you are going to enjoy it less!"

After repeated knocks on his door, Mr. Lang slowly opened the door.

"This better be important, mister. It's after one in the morning" flipping his front room and hall lights on. Then he saw the Guard holding Tom stiffly by the arm.

"I am sorry to disturb you, Mr. Lang," said the guard, "We have a serious problem that needs your immediate attention." Then the guard began to reiterate all of the circumstances that took place within the last few hours.

When he was finished, Mr. Lang, staring hard into Tom's eyes, said, "Tom, I want you to tell me why, after all the attention I have given you, and the fact that you were soon to be released back to your parents, did you pull such an idiotic stunt like this?"

"Mr. Lang, I know it looks bad, but I swear, I did not put that butt on the floor, nor did I put those butts under my pillow. Someone must have planted them there. It must have been one of those new kids that is mad at being sent here", exclaimed Tom.

"What? Even with the evidence found on you, you want to put the blame on others"?

"*Yes* , sir, I did not do it, I swear!" claimed Tom.

Mr. Lang shook his head in disgust, "OK, let's go to the basement. I think that we need to take a look in your locker. I know you keep it locked, so if we do not find more evidence there, you may have a better chance to convince me of your innocence."

When they were all standing in front of Tom's locker, Mr. Lang told Tom to use his combination and open the lock. Tom started to shake and little beads of sweat appeared on his forehead, as he took the lock in his hand. Impatiently they waited, as Tom continued to fumble with it.

"I can't seem to hit the right combination, Sir"

Finally, Mr. Lang's patience ran out, and he found a large hammer and said, "Stand-back!"

He then hit the lock with a crushing blow and it fell to the floor. When he opened the locker, he quickly tossed everything out, and hidden deep inside of a catcher's mitt was another pack of "Lucky Strikes" cigarettes.

"Well, well, imagine that, more cigarettes," reflected Mr. Lang. "I believe that you have just sealed your destiny with me, Mr. Wysocki. There is no room in my Colony for someone like you. Tomorrow I will ask our administrator to place you in another Colony, adding more time before they release you. They will inform your parents of this escapade. But before that, I have an obligation to fulfill. I want you to go over to the sink and bend over. If you stand up before I tell you, I will double your punishment."

Mr. Lang found his razor strap, and began to lay it across Tom's buttocks, each one getting a little harder. After the third one, Tom let out a bloodcurdling scream that carried clear up to the dormitory. Mr. Lang was careful not to break the skin and placed each strike in a different spot. He stopped at the count of ten.

"Now, I want you to go back up to bed, then after breakfast in the morning, I want you to report to me in my office, at 9 AM, now *go*!!!"

When he reported to Mr. Lang in the morning, he was told that arrangements had been made for him to spend some time at the P.C. Colony.

"The letters stand for a whole lot of things like Prisoner, Privileged, C-sucker, Punish, but for you, I think Prevaricator will fit nicely, since you are such a liar!"

At this remark, Tom started to reply, but Lang cut him off. "*Shut-up!* You will not speak again unless I give you permission!" Lang angrily shouts.

"You most likely will be digging ditches for a while, then you will spend the balance of your time here, in a different Colony. I regret that I made a mistake in trusting you. I always want the best for the boys that pass through my life. It is my desire that you use this punishment as time to reflect and use the good that we try to teach you boys to go into the world and make a difference. Now return to the basement, put all your personal belongings in a box or sack and someone from the Punishment Colony will be here for you very soon."

When Tom returned to the basement, the other boys stopped whatever they were doing. They just stared at him as he was gathering up his belongings.

"*Hey*, you assholes! I know one of you planted that butt and when I find out who it was, he's gonnna be dead meat!" yelled Tom.

"That's enough of that talk," said the Guard. "Everybody finish dressing."

"*Hey Tom!* We're sorry that you are leaving and only want to wish you luck," said Gar, with that same smiling smirk on his face, the one Tom had used on him.

"*YOU!!* It was *you,* wasn't it?" barked Tom.

"Oh no, not *me,* you did it to *yourself,* Polock!"

"All right, that's enough!" said the Guard as he pushed them apart, standing between them. "You guys get on with your business."

As Gar walked away, he could feel Tom's eyes boring into his back. He turned around and, still smiling, gave Tom the finger . They both knew pay-back had happened.

Chapter 6

The same day that Tom was sent to the Punishment Colony, Gar and three others were sent to Iroquois Colony. Mr. Lang instructed them on how to get there and told them to stay together. He also gave them his usual pep talk that he gave to all his boys and sent them off.

Iroquois Colony was about a mile from the Center on the eastern end of the complex. It was about a good twenty minute walk from the Center, crossing through alot of wooded area. At one part the road met another crossroad that turned to the to right. After one hundred yards was a road to the left that led directly to the Colony. The boys walking this every day soon found that instead of staying on the road and making right and left square corners, they could cut through the woods and save an extra few steps and minutes. Thus, the short-cut was used by all. Halfway through the short-cut was a very small pond. This was where all the fights took place by those who felt it was necessary.

The Colony was classified as a farm colony with beef cattle, not dairy. It had work horses, but no tractors. The usual farm chores and care of its properties were done by those boys who picked farming as their trade, under the watchful eye of its guardians, Mr. and Mrs. Bennett. They were referred to, with their permission, as Mr. B and Mrs.

B. Mr. B was a big muscular athletic- type person. A no-nonsense sort, but appreciated good clean humor. He allowed the boys to play touch football, softball, basketball and most outside games. In the summer, he would allow one of his farm boys to hitch a team of horses to one of the hay wagons and take those who desired to the large swimming pool at the Center on special days or on weekends. He promoted boys to try out for Industry's baseball team, one that had bragging rights at beating neighboring Prep-schools.

If any boys carried their arguments too far and couldn't come to a peaceful agreement, he made them settle it with the boxing gloves. However, if someone appeared with a bruised nose or a black eye, he usually ignored it. He figured that some things are just better left alone to take its own course. It was no wonder all the Iroquois Colony boys loved their guardians. It had the best record of all the colonies and no one had ever attempted to run away from it.

Mrs. B was a typical farmers wife. She was of a large body structure and never hesitated in handing out a hug to her boys, especially if they did their best at whatever they attempted. She was also a mighty fine cook. It was deemed an honor to have her ask you to help in the kitchen. She had her usual boys that were assigned to the kitchen at meal times, but occasionally she needed an extra hand and never failed to reward them with cookies or goodies. So it wasn't any wonder that she was loved by all the boys.

The daily procedures were very routine, consisting of. Wake up time was 5 AM for the farm boys and kitchen help, and 5:45 for the other. Sweep and wax the dormitory, return to the basement, wash and dress for breakfast. After breakfast, sweep and wax the dining room, retiring to the Rec. Room for any studying or writing that was needed, then wait as a group for permission to walk to classes.

At noon walk back to the Colony for lunch, then back to the Center for afternoon classes. Then they all would walk back to the Colony at 4:00 PM. All classes started at 8:00 AM, and ended at 4:00 PM. Before dinner, which was usually at 6:00, some had a few chores, others were permitted to go to the Rec. Room to study or play cards, etc. Everyone ate at the same time. Tardiness was not accepted. After dinner, if daylight they played softball, football or basketball or read. Gar enjoyed sports, participating in them all and occasionally, he would teach some boys how to play craps. This was a fascinating game to him.

From 7:30 to 8:00, everyone showered and changed to pajamas and went back to the Rec. Room before retiring to the dormitory at 9 PM, with lights-out at 10 PM.

On Sundays, everyone was required to put on a better shirt and pants and walk to the Center to the Church of their choice. Usually Mr. B would walk with them on those days. If it was raining, everyone put on a rain Poncho, and a ball cap. Gar enjoyed worshipping at the Methodist Church and soon was asked to join the choir. He accepted after he found out that the choir boys could stay a little longer and were treated by the preacher with ice cream occasionally.

On the first Sunday he went to church, he noticed that after most everyone had been seated with their respective Colonies, a group of boys entered last, and sat in the rear pews. They wore dark brown uniforms and on their backs was a large letter "P". Gar bumped his neighbor and asked who they were. He was told they were the boys from the Punishment Colony and the letter on their backs meant prisoner. Gar searched through them, and there in the back sat Tom Wysocki.

After seeing such a dejected Tom, Gar was asking himself if maybe the punishment was too harsh? Nah, he asked for it, he tells himself. He was often reminded of the statement that the Administrator had given when he arrived that first day, "You can either do it the hard way or the easy way, the choice is yours."

It was a true statement so far. Gar was beginning to see the light. I keep out of trouble and learn a good trade, maybe I have a good chance of becoming somebody. Maybe, just maybe there is a better life out there than what I've seen so far, he pondered.

The Machine Shop proved to be an interesting trade and he liked learning how to make different tools and learning to run those big machines, but better yet, he liked being able to keep the things that he made. Would this be the kind of trade that he could do for the rest of his life? I will have to wait to answer that, he thought.

The Bakery Shop also proved to be interesting. He liked how putting all those ingredients together into a hot oven produced such delicious tasting food. Food that everyone seemed to want. Was this trade be challenging enough for him? Same answer.

The Barber Shop was a totally different challenge. Here was a trade that required many things from its participants. Mr. Mucci was very good to each and every one of them. He taught his boys to be good at cutting many variations of cuts and styles plus how to shave with a straight razor, while at the same time being a good salesman, greeter, and storyteller. His shop not only cut hair for all the boys at Industry, but his shop was where all the male personnel were employed came for their haircuts as well. They, of course, had to pay Mr. Mucci for theirs.

It seemed that Gar took to Mr. Mucci immediately. In a matter of a few weeks he was very proficient in his new trade. Gar had not only found a trade that he was good at, but he had found someone who seemed to care about him. They were to bond very nicely. After a few months most customers, if Mr. Mucci wasn't available, would wait to sit in Gar's chair.

The classroom studies were not as interesting, but Gar realized that to make it in the big world you needed to be able to read well and be able to do the math. He was gaining ground on the books, not liking them, but he was trying hard to gather all the knowledge he could. He now listened to what each instructor tried to teach. His attitude was changing. The counselors had finally penetrated his thick skull and convinced him that he was lucky to be sent here. Sort of a blessing in disguise, as they put it to him. Here he was. learning different trades, getting an education and provided with food, clothing and shelter. For someone without a home or kinfolk, and facing a life of crime to pay his way, this could very well be his best break. Of course he would never have the luxury of being smothered with love and affection by his mom whenever he was hurting or when he needed protection from bullies or teasers. He would never have his Dad teach him to throw a curve ball or take him fishing or tell him how proud he was of him. Many a night was spent crying in his pillow. Many times he was punished at the orphanage for crying in bed. It wasn't any wonder that those conditions created a rebellious nature in a child who had to endure this and other inferior whims.

Chapter 7

The three other boys that were transferred to Iroquois Colony at the same time as Gar were finding their way around as well. One was Sammy Cross from New York City. He was one month older than Gar, turning 17 in about three more months. He and Gar seemed to become close friends and enjoyed each other's company walking together to and from most classes at the same times. Sammy was also taking Machine and Bakery shop, but instead of barbering in the afternoons, he was attending the Mechanic shop. They were about the same build and were lucky in that respect, for the smaller boys seem to always suffer the indignities from the bigger ones.

In any institution where only one gender is housed it is a known fact that acts of sex are taking place. Try as they may to set all kinds of rules, the enforcers are at a loss to completely control this ongoing problem. Industry was no different in that respect. There were always times when a guard could not see everything or know exactly where each boy was every moment. For instance when a group walked to or from classes which involved taking the short-cut through the woods and an altercation between two boys transpired and no one ever reported it, then the guard or the guardian never were concerned that they needed a guard to walk with them. Until a problem was reported, the honor system was effective. All the boys made sure that no one ever reported an incident and a squealer would never survive.

The boys that were permanently situated as the farm helpers were usually bigger and stronger. They were notorious for threatening smaller boys. They were a little braver than most, mainly because it seemed that Mr. B. favored these guys more.

One way that they trapped a smaller boy was to hear him ask to go to the toilet late at knight and when the Guard said,"OK", and turned back to his paper, the big guy followed the smaller one into the toilet, grab him and put his hand over his mouth and tell him if he yells out, he will break his arm or neck. He would then demand that the boy give him a blow-job. If after violent protests, the smaller boy refused, he was made to lean over the commode and the other's penis was shoved up his rectum. All the time reminding him that to cry out would mean sudden death to him. If that didn't fly, he was made to give the bigger one a hand job, with the promise that if he did a good job, he may reward him later.

One of the boys let it be known that he was for sale and anything asked for, he could do but he demanded payment first. His fees were five dollars or one carton cigarettes for a blow-job, four dollars, or eight packs of cigarettes for a rectum screw two dollars, or four packs of cigarettes for a hand job. This boy did very well for himself, but he had no friends and no one ever cared that he often would be seen with bruises on his face. The bigger farm guys took turns slapping this guy around if he demanded money.

Some boys couldn't bring themselves to violence for sex and self indulgence was a way to find relief to a natural craving. Gar never participated in violent threats and stayed away from gay guys, but he was all man and he had the same natural desires. Many a bull session with his friends were about girls and how much they waited with anticipation to their fist Lay. It was rare for a sixteen year old to have had sex, but it had happened to a couple of boys. They always had a big audience when they related their adventures.

Chapter 8

One Sunday after church and lunch, the boys picked sides for a football game Sammy and Gar were favorites and were usually on the same side. Sammy was a good Quarterback and his favorite target was Gar, who, with his speed, always found a way to be open. The game progressed along with the score tied and Mr. B called for a twenty minute break for water and rest. Most all of the boys went into the basement to take a leak and run water over their heads to cool off.

Gar told Sammy that he had some studying to do and to continue without him for a while. He was the last one going into the basement and most everyone was back out to the field. As he ran the water and toweled off he thought he heard someone, but didn't pay much attention to it.

"Hello, good lookin'," came a voice, "I've had my eye on you for some time but I hadn't had an opportunity to get you alone. I'm going to screw you in the ass or you are going to give me a good blow-job. Which will it be?"

Gar swung around to confront him and saw that it was Big Jim," the farm guy that handled the big team of horses. He was bigger and stronger than the other boys.

"Hey, you got it wrong, big guy. I don't do that shit," exclaimed Gar.

"Oh no, I got it right. I'm getting one or the other, *now* !!, If you yell out, I'll break you like a twig. I can lift a 150 lb. bag of feed like nothing, so come here." He lunged for Gar and grabbed him around the neck.

Gar's head and hair were still wet and he slipped out from his grasp, running to the other side of the sink. Jim pounced on him like a cat mauling a mouse. He slapped and punched him until suddenly, Gar saw his opportunity and kicked Jim in the balls. Jim doubled over but as he fell to the concrete, he pulled Gar down with him and twisted his arm behind him forcing him face down onto the floor. He rested all of his weight on top of him while the effects of the low kick faded.

"You damn near got me, Sonny, but now I got you," and started to bear down on Gar's back twisting his arm 'till it felt like it was about to break. The pain was unbearable.

"OK, you win!" cried out Gar. "I'll do it."

"Damn right you'll do it! You are going to suck my dick and you are going to love it or believe you me, I really will break both your arms, but I'm sitting here on you 'till I catch my breath, then you can do me."

Gradually, Jim let Gar rise only to his knees. Then Jim dropped his pants and his shorts. Gar saw that this guy was really hung like a horse and Jim's anticipation had given him a real hard-on.

"OK, Sonny, let's get this into your mouth. Ain't it a beauty?"

"Yeah, it sure is."

He grabbed for Jim's penis with his right hand and quickly grabbed his balls with the other. He squoze so hard, Jim screamed as he collapsed onto the concrete.

Gar put his hand over Jim's mouth, while Jim held his privates with both of his hands in agony.

"Now, I want to tell you something, big guy," Gar yelled at him, right in his face, "If you ever, *ever*, try this again, you son of a bitch, I will kill you and that is not a threat that is a promise. Do you understand?"

Jim was sobbing like a baby and didn't answer.

"I said, do you understand me?" yelled Gar.

"Yes," moaned Jim.

With that, Gar grabbed a bucket, filled it with water and threw it on Jim.

"Now listen up, Jimbo, I'm telling a couple of my best friends and if they ever see you alone with me, they will make you pay, remember that!"

The minute Sammy saw Gar strolling towards him he knew that something was wrong.

"Hey, Gassy, why the long face?"

"You're not going to believe this. That big guy Jim tried to make me go down on him, and he damn near succeeded, except that I was able to wring one of his balls before he almost broke my arms. He is going to be sick for a while. So I think I'm gonna need your help."

Then Gar related everything that has just taken place and Sammy agreed with Gar that they will have to watch each other's back from now on.

"I'm going to relate your story to Sandy Grimes, because he was telling me that he heard the same guy, Jim, has roughed up other boys before. Maybe we three can stick together on this for our own safety. You remember him, he was transferred out here with us."

"Yeah, that's a good idea!" exclaimed Gar.

Chapter 9

The summer passed into fall and the incident with Jim seemed to have become history, but not forgotten. The boys knew that Jim's eyes have been on them, but they were careful not to give him any opportunity to catch them alone.

All three boys had seen their 16th birthday come and go. By October, some of their worries faded away as Big Jim's parents come to take him home as he had either served his time or reached his 17th birthday.

Both Sandy and Sammy had parents to write to and would occasionally receive a package filled with candy and cookies, which they shared with Gar. They knew the story of Gar's past at the orphanage and tried to include him in any visits when someone came to visit them. Both Sammy and Sandy's parents lived in New York City area. Once they were acquainted with each other they would drive over together to visit the boys. They never failed to include Gar in their visits. They each were learning a trade and had realized that crime was not the option that paid well. Smarts was the key word now. They certainly were reminded of that often by their parents. Sandy was more interested in wood work and carpentry, while Sammy liked the tools and Machinery better. Gar liked everything, but the Barber Shop was a mix of everything and he liked the attention he received from customers who liked his hair cuts.

All three boys excelled in swimming and had been awarded lifesaving Diplomas by the American Red Cross. They were also on the school's baseball team. Gar had become popular as a fast ball pitcher and had the honor of never losing a game. They loved football, but tackle football was not allowed. The touch football was popular, but not the same.

A game that was fascinating, and also slightly dangerous was played by almost every boy in the place. It was called "mumblety-peg." It was a game in which a sharp jackknife is flipped so it sticks in the ground. The player had to apply the sharp tip to various parts of his body, starting with the fingers. Using one finger applied to the other end of the knife, which was standing straight up, you had to make the knife flip over in the air and the blade stick into the ground. If the knife was on a tilt when it was in the ground, you placed two fingers between the ground and the blade. If they cleared, it was OK, and the player continued. He had to do it on each finger and thumb on each hand, each elbow and shoulder, nose and chin. The last was on the tongue. The loser, or the last guy to not make it all the way would be asked "Pound or Punch." If he said, "Punch!" Then everyone in the game would give a hard punch on the shoulder to the loser. If he said, "Pound!" then a peg about four inches long and near the size of an ice pick, sharpened on one end and blunt on the other was pushed into the ground so that it stood solid. Then each player holding the knife by the blade, was allowed to hit the top of the peg only one time, driving the peg deeper into the ground. After each one had their hit, usually the peg could not be seen. The loser had to retrieve the peg with only his teeth. He was not allowed to use his hands. This game created many heated confrontations.

Soon the Autumn leaves were falling and the cold weather was increasing its chilly winds. The boys were issued coats, woolen hats, gloves and boots.

The radio reported the bombing of Pearl Harbor by the Japanese on Dec 7, 1941. The "Center" was buzzing with rumors about teachers and instructors joining up and what could be done to help the war effort. One of the instructors that had served in the Army, volunteered to teach the boys how to march and to do the rifle drills with fake rifles. It was not mandatory, but any boy that had aspirations of joining the service when he was released, was asked to participate in these drills. Gar, Sammy and Sandy were one of the first to volunteer for this training one hour after school, three times a week. They also figured maybe this would work in their favor when the time came to think about their release.

A few days before Christmas, the boys waited anxiously in the Rec. room for Sammy and Sandy's parents to arrive. They had received a letter previously that they would be there today and would be bringing presents for all three boys. Usually, the parents arrived by 10 AM on Saturdays, but it was now noon, so the boys ate lunch with the others. They became increasingly worried and they feared that maybe they had been involved in an accident on the wintry highway. However, soon Mr. B came and announced that their families were here and for them to bring them into the rec. room where they would have more privacy.

After the usual hugs and kisses, Mr. Cross explained that Sammy and Sandy's parents had received a request from the Administrator for a family talk when ever they next visited Industry. They had just now left his office and had some good news to report. The administrator said that if Sammy and Sandy keep up their good work and do not get into trouble, he would recommend that the State release the boys into the custody of their parents. The parents would be responsible for the boys behavior until they are age twenty one," reported Mr. Cross.

Another round of hugs were bestowed on Sammy and Sandy. They were all excited with the good news. Gar was patting them on the back and trying to put on the happy face like the rest were.

Suddenly Sammy exclaimed, "Hey, what about Gar? Will he be able to get out also?" Suddenly it got real quiet, before Mr. Grimes spoke.

"Gar, we did go beyond our bounds and asked the administrator if there was any way that the State could release you. I explained that you three boys had a close bond to each other and genuinely cared for each other's welfare. At first he told us that he couldn't discuss your case, but relented after he saw that we were sincere. He told us that they had seen a great improvement in Gar's behavior, but since Gar has no living relatives or someone that would be responsible for him, the State has no alternative but keep him until he is 18 years old. Even then, he would need a sponsor. Also, if he gets into further trouble or breaks the law again, he could easily be sent to prison."

Mr. Grimes put his hand on Gar's shoulder, as he softly said,"We are so sorry Gar, but keep your chin up. Mr. Cross and the rest of us have been discussing your case and maybe we can come up with something , but for the present, we do not have a solution to the problem."

The rest of the day was spent opening presents and eating cookies until it was time for the parents to leave. They all agreed that six months wasn't long and farewell hugs were given. Gar made a point in thanking them profusely for talking on his behalf and for the wonderful gifts.

After they were gone, the boys were trying to be happy about getting out but a dark cloud had appeared in the form of Gar's non-release. Both of his friends were consoling in their pledge to find a solution to the dilemma.

The winter and all the snow made the walking a little more trying, but the boys never missed their classes and since big Jim had left, the Iroquois Colony ran smoother. The classes with the drill instructor were held indoors for the winter with more rifle drills. Their was alot of talk amongst the boys about joining the different branches of the Armed Forces. The instructor was always helpful in answering all the many questions that the boys had. Since the US was involved in both wars, in the South Pacific and in Europe, there was a great demand for recruits. Before the Pearl Harbor attack, most of the conversation was centered around getting out and finding work. Now everyone was talking about what branch of the service they would like to enter when they got out. Both Sammy and Sandy expressed desires to join the Marines, while Gar felt more like going with the Navy.

"Probably the war will be over before I am ever going to be able to get out of here," stated Gar.

Chapter 10

Irving Grimes had been born and raised in the New York area. He had graduated from NYU and had studied hard to attain the title of "Architect." He had married his school sweetheart Mary. Their first born was Sandy, then 2 years later they had a daughter, Rose. Irving Grimes became employed at one of the busy architecture firms in Manhattan, designing for the future. He and Mary were very happy. Mary wanted to also go to work after the children reached 10 and 12, but Irving felt that his salary was enough for them and they had been putting a little in a savings account every month and he wanted her to be there for the kids. Eventually Mary won out by doing alot of volunteer work at their local hospital.

Sandy was a bright boy and had a fascination for automobiles. By the time he was 15, he could drive a car. It wasn't the family car. It was one that a gang member had. His Mom and Dad weren't even aware that he belonged to a gang, since their time was spent elsewhere. Sandy was starting to stay out later and when reprimanded about this, he began to invent lies.

His gang had started to steal cars and take them to Ace Body Shop, where the shop dismantled the autos, using the parts for wrecked ones or selling to other body shops. The gang worked in pairs, one boy watched for cops while the other shoved a metal stick down the outside of the door glass, dismantling the door lock, then cross-wiring the ignition, they drove it to the body shop.

One afternoon they picked the wrong car. It belonged to an off-duty policeman who just happened to be coming around the corner as the boys were trying to unlock the car. He immediately called for backup and as they started the engine, the policeman ran up to the car with his gun pointed at them and stopped them in their tracks.

Bo had previous arrests and was sent away, but this was Sandy's first, so he was put on probation and put back in custody of his parents. They were devastated and Sandy was grounded for months. If they could make more time to oversee the kids, he would not be getting into additional trouble. Eventually, the old routines and habits returned. This time Sandy was involved in stealing cassette players from autos and this time the judge sent him to "Industry".

Chapter 11

Christopher Cross was born and raised in the Catskill Mountains of New York State. He enjoyed the outdoors and loved all the snow that fell on these mountains. His home in Windham gave him easy access to both Windham and Hunter Mountain ski resorts. While he was attending Business College at Albany, NY which was fairly close to home, he would augment his expenses by giving ski instructions to some of the many tourists who flocked to the Catskills from the big city of New York. After completing school, he was employed by Empire Trucking Co., located in the Brooklyn, NY, as assistant dispatcher. He married Betty Moorage who was also employed there as secretary to the office manager.

Chris and Betty rented an apartment in Brooklyn until Sammy was born. Then they bought their first home in a nice residential section of Brooklyn. Both parents loved their jobs and their efforts were rewarded. A few years after Sammy started school, Chris was promoted to chief dispatcher and later, Betty became assistant office manager. Both were locked in to their jobs resulting in Sammy becoming evenly a latchkey kid. Many times Betty would have to call a neighbor to watch Sammy until they got home because something was always coming up to make them late. It wasn't any wonder that with the lack of proper supervision, Sammy found himself in trouble.

His first encounter with the law was when he was in his first year in High School. He became used to coming home after school, unlocking the door to the house, make a sandwich and head out to meet up with his friends . They frequented Joe's Pool Hall and became quite good at the game of pool, in fact Sammy soon found that he could pick up a few bucks hustling a game with strangers. The only problem was that he'd hustled the wrong guy one afternoon and found himself way over his head. As he tried to double up and regain his losses, he grew further behind and when he had become two hundred dollars in the hole, the player demanded his money. Sammy only had twenty dollars. The player and his big friend were about to break Sammy's arms, when the pool hall manager told them that Sammy was good for it and to give him some time to get the dough. Finally after some further talk, they agreed to give him two days if the manager would guarantee it, which he did. After they left, Sammy was reminded that he'd better get the money somehow or be ready for some bad things to happen to him. Sammy feared for his life and engaged one of his friends in helping him find a way to get the money. He knew his parents would not give him the money. Besides, his father had forbidden him to hang out at the pool hall after his Dad had caught him there once before.

Sammy knew that the manager of the convenient store not far from him always took the night deposits to the bank and put them in the outside drop shut around midnight every night. Sammy and his friend Carlos, carefully snuck out of their homes one night and were waiting around the corner of the bank when the store manager drove up to make his deposit. They had carefully wedged a sharp peg in the crack where the drop box opened, so it would take time to pry the box door open, thus giving them time to get behind the manager and take the deposit bag. This worked just like they planned it, except that they didn't realize that the manager had experienced this before and always had his revolver stuck in his waistband. Just as the boys were about to grab the money bag, the manager whirled around with the gun in his hand and froze the boys in their tracks. They were soon on their way to the Police Station. Their parents were called to make bail for them. Since it was their first time, the Judge put them on probation into the custody of their parents.

That was a wake-up call for everyone. From then on, Sammy had to call his parents at work after school every day and he was grounded from going out after school for three months. Just as everything was sort of getting back to normal, Sammy found himself in trouble again.

He had made friends with an older boy, Mike, who had a car of his own and Sammy delighted in taking rides with him after school. Mike had recently quit school and was working part-time at one of the parking garages as a runner. Mike also enjoyed drinking a little whiskey, which he tried to get Sammy to try.

Once Sammy had gotten off restriction and wasn't grounded, he began to stay out later and later. His mother was worried, but sometimes she neglected to tell Chris that Sammy was still out, on nights that he worked late knowing that Chris would be too upset, besides Sammy always was in bed by midnight. She didn't know that Sammy had been skipping school lately and trouble was knocking on the door.

This night Sammy and Mike were riding around and Mike was almost out of booze, so they drove into an all-night liquor store. Sammy stayed in the car while Mike went inside to get another bottle. Mike had taught Sammy how to drive the and this night he was letting him do the driving. Mike told him to keep it running. Mike purchased his bottle and as he was paying for it he noticed all that cash in the register and only one employee working. This was the opportunity he needed.

So Mike asked for a bottle of a rare scotch which he knew the man would have to get at the other end of the store. When the worker left the register to get the bottle, Mike reached over and snatched all the green bills out and ran to the car. He told Sammy to step on it and the car screeched out of the parking lot, unaware of what just taken place.

When the flashing lights and screeching siren caused Sammy to pull over, he realized what Mike had done. The judge wasted no time in sending Sammy away upstate to "Industry."

Chapter 12

The boys were very diligent at attending the military drills and one afternoon their instructor told them the Navy was accepting volunteers at age 17 with parental permission. This of course aroused Gar's curiosity and asked if the State would sponsor him if he was to enlist, even though he had no Guardian. The instructor said that he would find out and get back to him with the answer. This became a matter of discussion with the boys every day. Sammy and Sandy felt sure that their parents would give their permission for them to enlist. If the State approved, maybe they could all go together. This was a ray of hope that helped pass their time until six months were up.

When the Crosses and Grimes' visited again the boys waited for the right moment to tell them what they were planning and ask if they would give their permission. Their parents said that they knew sooner or later this was going to come up and they had been discussing it already. If each was very sure that they wanted to enlist that they would not stand in the way. They would be broken hearted to send them off to war, but yes, they would have their blessings. The boys were elated to hear this, and hugged and thanked their parents.

"Now we've got to get approval for Gar," they all echoed.

The news came soon, as the Administrator sent word for Gar to come to his office after classes the following day. The Administrator was very nice and told Gar that he was very sorry, but the State would not be his sponsor if he wished to enter the service from here. He said that the State would have to be sure he had a sponsor, even before he could leave Industry. This news was a set back for the group and the next few days were gloomy for them. Sandy wrote to his family and asked if they had any ideas on the matter. To his amazement, a letter came quickly back to him.

"Hey Gar, my folks want to know if you would accept them as your Guardian," yelled Sandy with enthusiasm.

"What do you mean?" asked Gar.

"Well, I wrote to them and told them that the State wouldn't let you out without a sponsor, so I guess they discussed it and have decided to be your Guardians, that is if you approve", said Sandy, with a grin a mile long.

"Oh my G-, are you kidding me? That sounds too good to be true!" exclaimed Gar.

"Hey, here's the letter. Read it for yourself. I wouldn't kid about that."

Gar anxiously takes Sandy's letter and reads it aloud for all three to hear, then lets out, "How about them apples? You write them back today and tell them that I accept their wonderful offer! I am going in to Mr.B. and ask him if he will talk to the Center and find out if the State will approve of this magnificent proposal."

The next day the center advised Gar to pick up the papers for the Grimes' to fill out. If they proved worthy of the Guardianship, the State would approve also. This was big! For the very first time, something good was going to happen in Gar's life. He said a silent prayer, "Please God, let this happen."

How could anyone in a place that kept you isolated from the world and where you couldn't breathe without permission be *happy?* Gar knew three boys that were just that! The State had given the green light for the Grimes' to be Gar's appointed legal Guardians, and all three boys were to be released at the same time next Saturday, May 5th, 1942.

Gar spent the last few days saying goodbye to the instructors and teachers that treated him kindly, making doubly sure to thank Mr. Mucci for all his efforts in teaching him not only how to be a barber, but how to operate a friendly business.

Both families arrived early in two cars. This time Sandy's sister Rose came also. She had been up to see Sandy last year when she was 14 and was just beginning to mature. Now she was approaching 15, and her beautiful blonde hair and sweet face were turning many a boy's head. For the first time Gar actually saw her, not as a child, but as a gorgeous girl.

Gar was about to ask Sandy who the cute girl was, when Rose came straight up to Gar and said, "Let me be the first to welcome my new brother into the family," and kissed him on the cheek.

Gar turned red and exclaimed, "Gee, thanks, I didn't realize how fast you had grown up! I apologize for not recognizing you at first."

By now everyone was all hugging and greeting one another with both parents telling Gar how glad they were for him. Before long everything was loaded into the cars, goodbyes were said to the Iroquois Clan and they were finally on the road to a new life.

Chapter 13

The Grimes family car with Sammy led the two car caravan started their trek back to the big City. Gar was filled with fascination in the beautiful scenery as they traveled south to pick up Route 17 which runs through the Finger Lakes area, all the way to New York City. They actually passed by Elmira and on to Binghamton where they stopped for lunch. As soon as everyone had put their order in, Mr. Cross turned to Gar and asked, "Are you enjoying the ride, Gar?"

"Oh yeah, this country is beautiful. I had never been out of Elmira before, and this trip and a new home is almost more than I can stand. I am so appreciative of the opportunity that the Cross family has given me," he said as he turned to face Mr. Cross. "Thanks again for your generosity, I promise you won't regret it," said Gar.

"Not a problem," answered Mr. Cross, "We happened to have an extra bedroom and Sammy and Sandy tell us that you are a quality kind of guy. The three of you remind me of the Three Musketeers. We are so glad all three of you are getting a second chance. Oh, by the way, Irving and I have discussed this, and it's OK to show your respect when we are in public, by calling us Mr., but when were only with each other, you can to call us Irv and Chris."

"OK," they repeated in unison.

Irving said, "We'll be crossing the George Washington Bridge and when we get to the City, we'll be branching off to go to our homes, so I suggest three guys get together now and swap phone numbers or meeting places or whatever, because we know you will want to be together soon. One more thing, Chris and I have planned a full day of sightseeing around the City this Saturday to get you all reacquainted again. It will be new for Gar, so lets plan on it!"

The closer the trip brought them to NYC, the more excited he became. All the different types of houses and tall buildings, plus so many cars and trucks caused him to burst out more than once with "wow!"

Rose was enjoying his excitement as well. Gar, Sandy and Rose sat in the back, while Irv and Mary were up front.

They soon drove into the driveway of this elegant white, two story home in upper Queens. Every window had beautiful shutters. The front porch swept across the entire front, with new brick steps and wrought iron guide rails. The side porch accommodated the driveway and the breezeway into the garage. The inside stairway made a sweeping curve to the five bedrooms above with a cherry banister that was a child's dream for sliding.

Mr. and Mrs. Grimes told Gar which bedroom was his and that he was one of the family. They said that they expect him to abide by the same house rules as Rose and Sandy do. Any problem that he had, bring it to them.

The following days were spent getting acclimated with the area getting new clothes and many conversations by phone with Sammy. On Saturday, both fathers and all three boys headed into the city for an all day tour. The

Statue of Liberty, the Empire State Building, Grand Central Station, Hudson River Harbor with the Big Ships and Central Park were about all they could cover in one day. The subway system and the tunnels to New Jersey were unbelievable to Gar.

By the middle of summer, all three boys settled into a routine and their biggest topic for discussion was which branch of the service they would enter. Both Sammy and Sandy were pushing for the Marines, while Gar felt that the Navy was more to his liking. The poster that said, "Join the Navy and See the World," got his attention. Sandy and Sammy now were 17 and were eligible to enlist with parental approval, while Gar still had a few months yet before his 17th birthday. They theorized that they most probably would not be able to stay together after they went in, so Sammy and Sandy enlisted in the marines.

Sammy was sent to the Marine Basic Training Camp at Camp LeJeune, then on to Ft. Pierce, Florida. Later he was sent to San Francisco where he waited to board a troop ship to go to the South Pacific.

Sandy was turned down for the Marines because one foot was flat, they said, but they accepted him at once for the Navy, and he was sent to Sampson Basic Training in upstate New York, then down to Camp Shelton, Virginia. There he was trained in firing and care of all types of Gunnery, and was soon placed in the US Navy's Armed Guard Division, protecting the US Merchant Marine ships. These ships were not US Navy, but were vital in transporting goods and equipment across to the united fronts. So the US Navy equipped them with artillery and placed US Sailors aboard to man the guns. It was good duty, but very dangerous since the enemy did not want these ships to cross the waters.

Chapter 14

Gar nervously waited for his 17th birthday . He had been using Sandy's bicycle to ride around on. One day he happened to pass this Barber Shop that had a sign in the window that said, "Barber Wanted." He circled around the shop a few times and finally decided to go in and find out if he qualified.

The shop had three chairs with customers in them. The owner had the first chair and when Gar walked in, the owner Joe asked, "Can I help you?"

"Yes. I was interested in the sign in your window."

"Oh, are you a Barber? You appear mighty young to me."

"Yes I am and I'd like to talk to the owner about it."

"Well, have a seat. I'll be through in a minute."

"When he finished with his customer, he took Gar to the back of the Shop to his little office and told him to have a seat.

"If you are a Barber, tell me where you learned the trade."

"Well, sir, I'm going to be absolutely honest with you. I was at an upstate school called Industry, where I was taught by a Mr. Mucci in the Barber trade. I was there because I was involved in an auto theft and had no home. I was lucky enough to have the Grimes family sponsor me here in NY I can cut hair, shave, shampoo and most all the required duties of a barber. I do not have barber tools but if you let me borrow some, I could demonstrate for you, that is, if you still want to take a chance on me."

"Well, well, that's interesting. Are you staying at the Grimes' now?"

"Yes, Sir, and I have to add that I will have to pass this on to Mr. Grimes if you do hire me. I don't do anything without his permission, OK?"

"Oh, sure, sure. By the way, how old are you and what about the service?"

"I'll be 17 soon and if I can get in, I hope to join to the Navy. I'm sorry, I should have told you that too."

"Yeah, well, that's a plus in your favor, because I think every one that can, should fight for our country. I'll tell you what. There's a customer getting in my chair. I'll tell him I have a new barber and if he doesn't complain, you can use my tools to cut his hair. If you give him a good haircut and he is a satisfied customer, you've got a job. I have an extra set of barbering tools that you can use. Your pay would be 40 percent per person."

Then he informed the man that he had a new Barber and asked if the new barber could cut his hair. If he wasn't satisfied, there would be no charge. The customer said it would be all right with him. With that, Gar proceeded to give the gentleman a good haircut and he remarked that everything was just right.

"OK, Gar you go get Mr. Grimes' OK and you've got a job. Bring a note to me from him and you can start tomorrow. We open at nine o'clock sharp, and my name's Joe Miller."

Gar couldn't wait to tell Mr. Grimes. He talked to Rose and Mrs. Grimes about it and they seemed to think that it was a good idea also. Mr. Grimes felt that it would be good to be busy while waiting to go to the Navy. He filled out a paper to give to Joe and they all celebrated with a small glass of wine before dinner.

The first pay that Gar received, he asked Rose to go to the movies with him, with her parents' permission. They caught the bus that stopped almost in front of the Rialto Theater. The name of the movie was *A Tree Grows in Brooklyn,* and it was a little sad for Rose, who softly let a tear or two roll down her cheeks. Gar saw this and put his arm around her and she didn't object at all. She even thanked Gar for a shoulder to cry on. He kept telling her that he was so sorry to bring her to such a sad movie.

"Don't be silly, Gar. Don't you know that's what girls do, cry in movies?"

He certainly didn't understand that, but she said that she loved the movie, so it must be OK.

On the bus back, she asked Gar if they could get off at Walgreens Drug Store, which was only four blocks from home, and get a sundae together. He thought that was a good idea. He had never had a date before and it was turning out to be a swell night. He had a butterscotch and she had a chocolate fudge with all the trimmings. On the way back it was nearing 10 o'clock and with the street lights on, the night was beautiful.

Even more so when she slipped her hand into his and said,"Oh Gar, thank you so much for such a lovely time. I will never forget this, and you were so worried about me when I cried."

"Shucks, it wasn't anything. I just thought maybe I'd made a mistake."

"Oh no, everything is perfect. I've had dates before with those little boys, but this is my first date with a real man."

Gar, turning red as a beet, sheepishly replied, "Thank you, Rose."

After basic training, both Sammy and Sandy managed to receive two weeks leave, at the same time, before reporting to their respective duties. Sammy proudly wore his Marine uniform, while Sandy strutted around in his Navy attire. Gar was so envious he could pop. They were always together and each had some new tales to tell. Dating was now a big thing and getting girls was no problem for these good looking guys. Both Sandy and Sammy had passed their driving tests just before enlisting and were granted the family cars for their dating game. Gar was about to do the same, just waiting for his 17th birthday.

It was a sad day for the families when the two boys had to return to Base Camp, knowing that they would be pressed into the war as soon as they were back. All three vowed to return alive and go into business together after the War.

Gar continued to work for Joe Miller and occasionally on weekends he would take a date to the movies. He suspected that Rose might be getting a little jealous, but he had to branch out a little and he was wondering if he should be dating someone in his own family.

Finally the magic day when Gar turned 17! The family celebrated with a big chocolate cake. Mr. Grimes set him up with an appointment to take his driving test and gave him the application for the Navy. The wheels were in motion!

Gar passed the driving test and the Navy accepted his application along with the Grimes' endorsement. He was soon sent to Albany for swearing-in, then off to Sampson Naval Training on the north end of Seneca Lake, NY, the same place that Sandy trained. Then he, too was granted two weeks leave before reporting to Camp Bradford, Virginia, where he would be trained in Amphibious Warfare. He would be training to go aboard a Landing Ship Tank (LST).

It was nice to have a place he could call home and be surrounded by people who care, but with Sammy and Sandy away, Gar felt somewhat awkward. His pals had gone on ahead into this war.

Chapter 15

The US was fighting the War at two fronts, Japan and Germany and every able bodied person was pressed into the services. Those that couldn't pass the required physicals, were working in the defense factories. The production of new automobiles was stopped and all the metals went to making tanks and weapons for the war effort. Factories were open 24 hours a day every day.

Because everything was being used to support the war, a shortage started hurting our citizens and the Government starting issuing rationing cards for everything, even gasoline. People without a card couldn't buy what they needed and even those making good money couldn't buy all they needed. Crooks were dealing in stolen goods and selling dishonestly causing what was referred to as the "black market."

Sammy wrote home that his address from now on was Fleet Post Office, San Francisco, California. All men serving in the South Pacific had to use that address. He wrote that from San Francisco, this platoon was put aboard a troop ship and headed west.

"I won't be able to tell you where we are, because of regulations besides every letter is now read and censored. If I slip up and write something not allowed, they simply cut it out of the letter. I am well and am surrounded by guys just like me, anxious to get those Japs. Tell Gar and

Sandy that the three musketeers, we'll be together just as soon as we win this war."

Sandy trained at Camp Shelton, VA on every type of heavy gun that was used in the Merchant Marines. They seldom used the bigger 3 or 5 inch on the cargo ships, going for less room by installing single and double 40 Millimeters, and plenty of the 20 Millimeters. He not only fired these, but had to be able to take these apart and know every part by memory.

On some weekends, he was issued 12 hour passes and he would catch a bus into Norfolk. The only problem was that every street and bar was full of other sailors also. He also wrote to his family as often as he could.

"Most of the guys that I take liberty with aren't much older than I am," he wrote, "and the bartenders won't sell to us because we aren't 18, so the older guys buy for the rest of us. The bartenders don't like that, but they do it anyway. I do not drink alot, Mom and Dad, but that's what everyone does since there aren't many other things to do. Besides, it relieves the tension and boredom. Tell Rose that I miss her hitting me in the head mornings with her pillow when I wouldn't wake up for breakfast . It's funny how those things come back to you. Guess I'm a little homesick. Tell my new Brother Gar, that I miss him and we will make up for lost time when we are home for good. Love you all, Sandy."

Shortly after that Sandy wrote he would shipping out on one of the cargo ships. He and ten other gunners would be manning the guns for it. He wrote that his only duties were to take care of the guns and to make sure that they were always ready to fire. His address from now on would be c/o Fleet Post Office, New York, NY.

Gar took extra training at Camp Bradford, VA which ironically was right next to Camp Shelton. He was trained on the 20 and 40 millimeter guns along with training as a seaman preparing for sea duty on a Landing Ship Tank (LST). These ships were used to transport personnel to battle by landing on the beaches, opening their bow doors, lowering a front ramp and letting the tanks roll off onto the land. They became the backbone of winning the war.

It was very hazardous duty because they were not fast, only 10 or 15 knots. They were easy to spot and hit by enemy planes. They were flat as a pool table on the bottom and at at rough seas, they would twist in different directions. Then if the bow raised up over a wave and that flat bottom smacked down, everything that wasn't fastened down, would bounce. The first time a new sailor had to go through one of those storms, he learned very quick about praying. It was said that an LST never had an atheist serve aboard its ship.

When Gar finished his Amphibious training, he and his crew members were put aboard a troop train for Pittsburgh, PA. His LST was nearing completion and until it was fully finished, the crew would be staying at the Carnage Institute dormitories. The crew ate at the Institute Cafeteria, and liberty was granted to them every night. A street car ran past the dormitory and it was only a half hour ride into the heart of Pittsburgh. One of the crew arranged a large bulletin board downstairs and invitations to parties that were being thrown were posted on the board, along with phone numbers and all the information needed. This had been a soldier's town until the Navy started shipping out. Some nights a sailor had a choice between 3 or 4 parties to choose from. The best part was that they would even pick the sailors up and bring them back afterward.

It wasn't long before Gar was learning just how wonderful these ladies were. With friendly advice and a lusty desire, he soon was sowing his oats. The Navy made sure that its sailors protected themselves and it was a Court Martial offense to not take all precautions.

Chapter 16

After several weeks their ship was slid down its planks adrift in the Ohio River. The crew and officers were bussed out to the pier and, after the customary navy ceremonies, went aboard their new home. They would be taking the ship down the Ohio river until it joined the mighty Mississippi. It would then continue south to New Orleans. A River Pilot would Captain the ship to New Orleans before turning over the control of the ship to the new Skipper.

The crew consisted of 110 sailors and 10 officers. Gar was Seaman 2nd class and was bunked in the after crews quarters just over the rear screws (propellers). The bunks were metal frames with canvas bottoms with a thin mattress covering. When not in use, the front side was always pushed up perpendicular to take up less room. At the rear was where the head was with the showers and in the front was the mess area where the crew ate. Directly above was the kitchen, where trays and food were picked up. Sailors would attempt to come down the ladder to the crew's quarters without losing it all down the neck of the person ahead.

Gar's sea duties at "General Quarters" were as trainer on the 40 MM gun on the aft deck. The pointer on the left side tracked the target horizontally and the trainer tracked the target perpendicular from the right side of the big gun. The 40 MM shells were in shell cases, which were situated all around the inside of the circular gun turret. As needed, the shells were handed four at a clip to the loader who stood on a platform that rotated with the gun movements. He pushed the shells down into the gun as quickly as they were fired. The loaders wore thick gloves because after the shell was fired and discharged to the floor of the turret, it would have to be shoved down a hole in the deck and the shells were red hot.

When the ship was not at "G.Q." and at normal sea conditions, Gar's duties were 4 hours on the helm, where he learned to steer the ship and read the compass. He would receive orders for his course from the conning tower which were relayed down through a large metal tube that looked like a megaphone at the end. He would have to repeat every message that was given and report up to the Captain or O.D. as each order was executed. He had 12 hours off to sleep, then reported to the Boatswain for more seaman duties, such as cleaning the deck, securing all lines, making sure all life rafts were properly maintained, chipping and painting the decks and anything that the Boatswain ordered. When the ship was at "beaching condition," Gar's duties were at the forward bow doors control on the starboard side. When the ship was about to hit the beach, the Captain would order, "open bow doors," and Gar had to be sure they came open. Then as the order was given, he had to lower the forward ramp, so the tanks and Army personnel could roll off the ship.

The ship had to go through a "shake down" cruise from New Orleans out into the Gulf of Mexico before it was loaded for the trip over seas to find out if it was built seaworthy, or would it sink and to get all the bugs worked out before action. Then Gar's LST, #347, was brought back to New Orleans and loaded with supplies of food and ammunition. The crew was granted liberty while in New Orleans and Gar and his buddies visited and enjoyed everything that it had to offer. The trolley cars ran day and night throughout the City and dating was not a problem.

Gar and his pals had chipped in together to enjoy a bottle of liquor and they all decided to each get a tattoo. Some were reluctant to try it, but the rest declared that you really weren't a true Navy Bucko if you didn't have a tattoo, so everyone had to get one. Gar decided on just a Navy anchor and the letters USN on his left upper arm. They thought liquor would take away the needle bites, but they were surprised to find that it stung like a bee, but they were proud to show off their trophies to their shipmates.

The day before they were to start their journey overseas, they were not allowed shore leave. To insure that everyone would be sailing together they all had to be aboard 12 hours before sailing.

The ship joined a few other LST's as they went through the Gulf on the way to the Panama Canal, stopping at Guantanamo Bay, Cuba along the way.

Passing through the Panama Canal was a very educational and an exciting event. Just before starting through the Canal, the ship took on additional fuel and supplies to sustain the 40 days that was expected to take to cross the South Pacific. The port was at Coco-Solo, Panama, on the eastern shore. The next day the ships went through by rotation and they would enter a series of locks where the locks were raised or lowered to accommodate the level of water that the ship would travel as it left each lock.

When all were across they were joined by Destroyers, Destroyer Escorts and a Cruiser which would act as an escort and protector for the big convoy. It appeared to Gar that there were at least 40 ships. Rumor had it that it would take over a month to cross over, mostly because LST's could not travel more than 10 or 12 knots per hour. They had a "scared speed" of about 17 knots, but that was only a short burst, to try to run out from harms way. Rumor also had it that if any ship broke down, the Convoy would not stop and wait for repairs. It would put the safety of every ship in danger if they lingered in these submarine infested waters.

Chapter 17

Sammy was ordered aboard the USS Rocky Mount, along with 400 other Marines, which sailed out of San Francisco headed for Pearl Harbor. Their convoy was joined also by Destroyers and Cruisers to try to protect them from the Jap Subs.

The entire crew of the Rocky Mount took delight in held initiations for the first time crossers of the Equator and the International Date Line. The Navy had a traditional ceremonial ritual every time they crossed the Equator , that imaginary circle around the earth, midway between the North Pole and the South Pole. The ceremony was an initiation for everyone aboard into the realm of Davy Jones and King Neptune. Those being initiated were blindfolded, painted with heavy grease, rotten eggs and garbage, and whacked on their backsides while trying to crawl through a tunnel, while a large fire hose was hitting them with 80 lb. of pressure head on. They would be issued a certificate afterwards that declared them now as trusty "Shellbacks." Naturally, those that resisted the most received the roughest treatment.

Sammy was quartered in C deck, two levels down. The ship had no air conditioning , but air was forced through the ventilators. At times it was like being in an oven. When the seas became rough, the poor guys became very sick, and the stench from all the vomit was unbearable.

At chow time he had to stand in line as every one else did and take what they offered. In fact, every place he went he had to fight a long line.

They played Craps and Poker most all the time, anything to fight the boredom. Travel on the troop ships was rough duty for all the soldiers, and they were eager to get to their destination, even if it meant hand to hand combat. Some lost 10 or 15 pounds from being seasick.

Sammy's ship arrived in Pearl Harbor, Hawaii. Everyone was allowed to leave the ship on a rotating schedule, because the ship was only expected to be in port for 48 hours, but the Generals wanted the soldiers to be completely healthy when they sailed again.

Sammy and his Marine buddies were allowed off on a 4 hour pass and they visited the PX station and then found a bar where a glass of beer tasted like heaven. Being on shore never felt so good and they made the most of it. The Ladies of the Night were very busy that 48 hours. Those who participated made a stop at the VD station on the way back to the ship. Every Marine was warned not to come back aboard inebriated because they might become sick, but a hangover was welcome, compared to that terrible seasickness. Everyone was accounted for and the ship set sail for the final destination with these fighting men.

Sandy's ship was leaving from New York, passing through the upper bay past the Statue of Liberty, heading south under the Verrazano bridge and into the Atlantic Ocean. From there, it would begin it's voyage across the submarine infested waters of the North Atlantic. Their destination was reported to be England. Its cargo was ammunitions of all kinds to help resupply the fighting forces. These ships could handle the foul weather and rough seas better than the LST's, but crossing the Atlantic Ocean is much worse than the Pacific and the crossings were always treacherous.

The convoy was made up of ten Cargo ships, a Destroyer and two Destroyer Escorts. Every one aboard had been issued heavy, foul weather gear and gloves. At General Quarters, Sandy was trainer on the forward 40 millimeter gun. His mates were on the aft 40 mm gun. There were smaller 20 mm guns on each side of the top deck that were manned by members of ships crew of merchant seamen. These men were trained by Sandy and his gunners to help out on these guns at GQ.

If they never had an air raid or had to go to GQ, it would be nice duty for the Navy gunners, but that was never going to happen. They not only had to worry about the enemy, but fighting the nasty weather also. Being on the Atlantic in winter time was a nightmare in itself. Most of the time they had to keep the guns covered with a heavy canvas because the spray from those big swells would soon turn the weapons into ice. They relied on the life rails while on deck, otherwise they would be swept overboard and no one could survive in those freezing waters for more than a few minutes. In spite of this, the Chief Gunner's Mate sounded General Quarters for the Navy personnel so many times and all hours of the night that everyone wanted to string him up on the yard arm. He kept saying, "Some day you'll all thank me for these drills and making you efficient gunners. The closer we get to the coast of Europe, the more you'll see those German planes. Those Nazis play for keeps, so I'm going to make sure you guys are able to take 'em down."

Six days out of New York General Quarters woke the crew at 4 AM. The PA system was blaring GQ's now. An enemy submarine had been detected by the Navy Destroyers and they alerted the convoy, while trying to track it down. Sandy was still half asleep as he and his crew made ready the gun. Waiting was as bad as fighting, it seemed. He was mighty glad for the heavy clothes as he sat at the gun, his teeth chattering.

"I'd give anything for a hot cu..." Suddenly there was an ear shattering explosion, followed by fire erupting on the far starboard side. The German U-boat had been able to penetrate the convoy's perimeter, sending a torpedo into the side of one of the cargo ships. The ship was entirely engulfed in flames and Sandy sat there frozen in time as the horrifying tragedy unfolded. The ship was on the outer fringes of the convoy, but the fire and smoke made it appear to be closer than it was. The torpedo had not only torn a hole in the ships side but the explosion had set off the munitions that were stored in the hold, causing a chain reaction of more explosions. There was no hope and in a matter of minutes the ship completely disappeared beneath the icy water. It would be a miracle if anyone survived.

The commander issued direct orders to all ships that the convoy would not stop and that the Destroyer Escort would be looking for survivors. Then the Destroyer could be heard laying a pattern of depth charges in the area where the Sub was last reported to be. The depth charges were set to explode at various degrees below the surface and as each one detonated, a silent prayer from each ship's crew was asking that this one would destroy the enemy U-boat. The Convoy stayed at full alert for the next 8 hours before securing from G.Q. The Commander relayed a message from the Destroyer that they had recovered 18 bodies, but all were dead.

Chapter 18

Several days had passed since the large LST convoy left the west coast and beards were getting larger and hair much longer, so Gar began picking up spare change by cutting hair for 25 cents each. There was a nice space under the aft gunnery tub, where the rear anchor was located. It was naturally shaded and a cool breeze flowed through there most of the time. Crossing the Equator was one more bit of excitement for all of the crew. However, one sailor tried to escape this ordeal by hiding in the laundry compartment, but the laundry attendant reported him to the captain.

The boy apologized to the Skipper for hiding, but the Skipper told him, "Son, you don't owe me an apology, you owe the whole crew an apology. Everyone on board has taken their traditional initiation except for you. I can't order you to take it, but unless you want this crew to make your life a living hell while you're on this ship, you'd better go see the Boatswain's mate and take whatever the crew hands you!"

The crew accepted his apology, and he was ordered to kiss the crew! Everyone on deck dropped their pants and shorts, and the sailor had to kiss everyone's buttocks! From then on, he was an accepted crew member.

Part of the convoy had stopped at Pearl Harbor, while the rest continued on to New Caledonia. Gar's ship, the 374, was among them. It was a sad sight to see the USS Oklahoma still laying on its side and the USS Arizona sunk to its grave. They became resting places for so many dead heroes. The devastation that Japan brought to this place would always be etched in the brain of every American.

While anchored at Pearl Harbor, the Captain allowed the crew to open the bow doors, lower the forward ramp to the water's edge and swim off it for exercise. Everyone was ordered to swallow a little white pill daily. It was "atabrine," an extremely bitter pill taken for prevention against malaria. The Pharmacist mate would issue it at the water fountain and stay to see that they swallowed it

Gar's ship and it's convoy was at Pearl Harbor a short while, headed for their first invasion at New Guinea. General Mac Arthur wanted to establish a stronghold at the Admiralty Islands and New Guinea before making his move on the Philippines. The Japanese were using the straits between these two important bodies of land as regular shipping lanes. The General was using the Cruiser USS Salt Lake City as his flag ship. This was the beginning of the US Seventh Fleet and of the Seventh Amphibious Force. Later, the Navy was quite put out at General Mac Arthur calling it "his" navy.

The first assault was the landing on the Huon Gulf at Lae, New Guinea. Gar's ship, along with several other LST's, some with Australian soldiers troops from Buna, were first to hit the beaches. The Japanese shelled the beaches with everything that they had.

The new recruits were put to the test. Cruisers had shelled the area before the troops went in, but it wasn't enough to crush the Japs. The B-24 liberators had bombed the Jap hills and caves before daylight. The Japanese were sending their high flying bombers at the invasion party, along with some very accurate 5 inch shells from the entrenched cannons in the hills. Gar's gun was credited with hitting the tail section of a bomber, sending it spiraling into the sea. Before one of the Cruisers found the range and obliterated the cave where a big cannon was firing from, it had landed a direct hit on the LST next to Gar's and practically blew apart, killing half the crew.

In the air, the Jap Zeroes and US flyers were engaged in an intense dog fight, while every gun on each ship was blasting away at kamikaze dive bombers. At the beach, Marine and Army soldiers were taking a shellacking from the Jap concentration situated at the hillside. It was late in the afternoon before they were able to move the Japs past the hill and put them on the run. First aid stations were established at the beach and the wounded were attended to. All of the LST's were unloaded by 4 AM the next day and were ordered to retract off the beaches at daybreak. Gar's ship was ordered to go back to New Caledonia with a convoy for reinforcements and supplies.

Chapter 19

As the 347 was trying to retract, it was discovered that it was stuck on the beach. The tide had gone out just enough that there wasn't enough water for her engines to reverse thrust. It was soon apparent that some of the other LST's were also stuck on the shore. The flag ship Commander devised a magnificent plan that was unheard of until now. That plan was to send 3 of the biggest ships, 2 cruisers and a Destroyer directly at the beach and suddenly do a hard right turn, causing a gigantic wave to wash onto the beach while the LST's would reverse their props and pull themselves off the shore. This amazing feat was executed perfectly and if there weren't so many men dying everywhere, it would have been cause for a rousing cheer!

Mac Arthur's seventh fleet was now making landings at the Admiralty Islands, and up and down the coast of New Guinea, Morobe, Finschaffen. The Japanese were losing many of their ships and our fighting men were victorious on land, but not without a price. Our casualties were enormous and Japan was not about to just quit and run. They had been taught to fight 'till death and defeat was worse than death.

Gar's flotilla of LST's participated in the initial invasions and were also used to ferry supplies between Islands and to replenish troops and tanks to the various strong points won in recent months. One of the worst battles that these ships were engaged in was just 400 miles south of the very large Japanese base at Rabble, Cape Glouster, New Britain. At the time they were landing at the beaches, Japanese dive bombers arrived in swarms, attacking our B-25's as they were bombing the forward beach areas, shooting down several. Then, turning their fury upon our fleet. One of our Destroyers sunk as a Jap dove into the ship, hitting a vulnerable spot, setting off several internal explosions. Several ships were damaged before the Japs returned to base.

Mac Arthur was ready to make his notorious return to the Philippines and he had chosen Leyte as one of his biggest invasions. He had been licking his wounds and chafing at the bit ever since he'd surrendered the Philippines and other islands and flee to Australia. The Japanese had captured, killed, tortured and forced death marches upon our surrendered forces earlier in the war and when Mac Arthur left, he broadcast to the Philippines, "I shall return." Many Sailors and Soldiers had taken umbrage to this, feeling that he should have said, "*We* shall return." However, now it was pay-back time for the good guys.

While Gar's ship was taking on supplies, tanks, and troops at Hollandia , he was making some spare change on the fantail, cutting hair. It was close to dinner time, so he finished up and was strolling towards the chow line, passing soldiers along the way, when one of them deliberately stuck his foot out, tripping Gar and he went falling to the deck. There was immediate laughter and Gar became enraged and yelled, "Who the hell did that?" both fists clenched for battle.

"I did," he said "Do you want to make something of it?" The sun was at his back so Gar couldn't see him clearly.

"Yeah, I'll make something of it, I'll knock your damn block off," said Gar and as he was about to swing, his tormentor said, "What about a game of mumblety-peg?"

"What the hell you mean?" replied Gar as he shaded his eyes for a better look.

"Oh my God, *It's Sammy*!" screamed Gar and they both grabbed each other in a bear hug and went around in circles hugging and patting each other on the back.

"How did you get here?"

"How did you know I was here? Why are you here?"

A million more questions flew back and forth before they settled down to recall everything that had happened to each other over the past year or so.

When the Captain heard of the reunion, he told Gar he was excused from duties the rest of the day so he could spend time with his best friend.

Chapter 20

Sandy and his shipmates were still in shock after witnessing the horrible sight of the sinking ship completely disappearing, leaving no trace of evidence that it ever existed. The terrifying thought that it could just as easily have been his ship was an additional fear for each of these sailors.

The convoy commander sent information that the Cruisers had not killed the U-boat and from certain blurbs on its radar, felt there might be a nest of these lurking in the area. They requested additional Destroyers for assistance, with air reconnaissance to help in their survey. The next few days were spent closely monitoring the radar, while the watch crew were ordered to stand 4 hours on and 4 hours off. It was two more days at full alert before they went back to 4 on and 8 off. Sandy and his gun crew made sure all guns were cared for and ready for any sudden attacks by the enemy. The ship had been keeping her proper position in the convoy while crashing through treacherous waves that at times were 7 feet high.

One morning, just as dawn was breaking, General Quarters sounded, sending sleepy warriors rushing to their respective positions. A large pack of German fighter planes had been picked up on the radar and the whole convoy would be under attack. A dispatch had been sent off to the Aircraft Carriers with hopes that they might intercept before the convoy lost too many ships. It wasn't long before the spitfires were spotted and as they started their run at different ships, the order for "commence firing!" rang out.

Sandy's forward gun was trained dead-on at the first menacing craft and it was coming straight towards him. With its cannon blazing, a 40 mm shell caught it square center, causing it to explode and plunge into the waters just beside the ship sending pieces flying as it fell. Before Sandy's crew had a chance to celebrate, another spitfire made it's run from the starboard side, made it all the way through the flack and just before it pulled up, it released one of his bombs that just missed the ship, exploding starboard, sending a fountain of water cascading over its side. The sky was filled with planes and the black remnants of exploding 40 mm shells. The noise of the big guns sounded, "pom, pom, pom!" The convoy was under fierce attack, but the excellent marksmanship of the gun crews were also taking their tolls. So far, no ship had been lost or sunk, but several had been crippled.

Now the fight was changing, as Navy planes from the carrier came onto the scene and the enemy planes did not want to stay and engage in a dogfight. They started to leave with the Navy fliers right on their tails.

Before the battle was over, one of the Spitfires that had some damage was leaving a trail of smoke. Since the pilot couldn't get out of his plane, he was going to take a ship with him to the bottom of the ocean. As luck would have it, he headed for Sandy's ship. The aircraft crashed forward of mid-ship, taking all the life boats and small 20 mm. guns off of that side and skidded into Sandy's 40 mm gun tub, then exploded into a fiery ball of flames, killing everyone in it's path. The explosion threw gas and metal parts everywhere. The gun tub had become twisted from the extreme heat and some of the metal was melting like lava. Because Sandy was at the trainer position on the right side of his gun, he didn't take the blunt of the hit as much as the left side did. All of his gun crew were dead except Sandy and the loader. The loader, Joe, was pinned under this hot metal, screaming for help to get him out. As Sandy was coming out of his semiconsciousness, surveying what had happened, he heard Joe's screams. Without hesitation he started grabbing metal with his bare hands and attempted to get him loose. His legs were somehow trapped around the gun-tub rail and in a frenzy of brute strength, Sandy pulled and tugged enough to finally get them free. As Joe was released he passed out and he carried him all the way to the sickbay where the ship's Doctor took over.

As Sandy was laid Joe on the gurney, the Doctor exclaimed, "My God, boy! What happened to your hands?"

His hands were raw meat and the skin was hanging off like strings of fishing lines. There was a trail of blood after every step that Sandy had taken. He had saved this boy's life out of sheer guts as he was in a state of shock. Now he was coming out of it and as he stood, staring at the Doctor, he collapsed in a heap. The doctor and a helper managed to get him onto a bunk and start morphine running into one of his veins, while they cleaned what they could of his hands. They also found pieces of shrapnel in both legs. Joe had fractures on both legs and multiple bruises over his body, but he was alive and his wounds would heal in time. The doctor was more worried about Sandy's hands, afraid of infection and the possibility of losing them. He was very busy, as well, caring for other wounded sailors and preparing the dead.

The enormous Convoy continued on in a zigzag pattern across the Atlantic and as they sailed closer to the European shores, half went to Africa and other harbors, while Sandy's ship joined the others continuing on to Southhampton, England. All of the deceased boys were buried at sea, with scriptures being read over them.

Because of the severity of the burns on Sandy's hands, a helicopter was sent to Sandy's ship and they winched him up into the craft to quickly transport him to a burn hospital in England. If they waited to fly him back to the States, he may not survive the trip. Wounds of this kind took more lives than they wanted to report. Sandy was kept sedated and the pain that he had to go through was unbearable. After a specialist had examined him, it was determined that they could hopefully save his hands, but it would demand many skin grafts and more therapy. He would have to stay in England until most of this procedure was completed. Thank God he was alive, but for this brave, noble, American Hero, his war was over. Now he had other battles to conquer.

Chapter 21

Gar and Sammy enjoyed each others company while the ship was getting ready for the big push and the return of Mac Arthur to the Philippines. Leyte was to be the next objective.

Meanwhile, the US Paymaster caught up with the LST fleet and came aboard to pay each sailor five months back pay. The Marines had received theirs just prior to boarding and now everyone had lots of cold hard cash. Ordinarily, gambling is not allowed aboard ship, but these were not ordinary times, and the officers deliberately made themselves scarce. The long mess tables were covered with olive colored blankets and crap games were in full swing. Poker games were set up all over the top deck and there were lots of ready and able participants.

Gar took Sammy to the crap game. This was one game that he certainly was knowledgeable in and Sammy agreed to follow his lead. The first class Boatswain Mate, Scotty, had been in the regular Navy over ten years and knew all the ways to win at craps. No doubt he had taken many new sailors' pay without blinking an eye.

Scotty had the dice and it was obvious that he was winning, because he was holding several bills in his left hand and getting the dice in his right. He yelled out the number he needed and slowly rolled the dice on the blanket. Gar knew that the dice were supposed to be tossed hard enough to hit the back wall and bounce back. What Scotty was doing was cheating the new sailors that didn't understand the game. Gar and Sammy wedged themselves into the game by finding a spot opposite of where the shooter was.

As Scotty won and raked in more cash, he yelled, "OK, I am betting $100, anyone want part or all of it, put your money on the table, and fade me."

Gar and Sammy each placed $20 on the table and others took the rest.

Scotty yelled, "OK, I see I'm covered. I'm coming out, for a number or a seven or eleven," and he cleverly, slowly rolled the dice partway towards the back wall coming to rest with seven on top.

"Seven! A winner!" he yelled, and scooped up the cash again.

"Hey," yelled Gar, "you are supposed to hit the back wall with the dice, for a legal roll. That didn't count."

"Who the hell you talking to boy? You trying to say I'm cheating?"

"No Boats, I'm saying I know how craps is played, and you have to hit the backboard for the roll to be correct."

One of the other sailors said, "Hey that's right, now I remember. No wonder we keep losing our money, he's not tossing into the backboard!"

Scotty's face reddened as he bellowed, "You're all wrong and I'm playing the game right and if you're in, just put your money down!"

He put another $100 down, "OK, who wants to fade that?"

The sailors didn't want to the Boats mad at them, so they reluctantly faded his bet.

"OK, I'm faded, so here we come-out again," and he rolled the same slow way.

Just as they stopped rolling (a long way before the backboard), Gar reached down and snatched both dice and yelled, "No roll! The dice didn't hit the backboard."

"What the?? Hey, put the damn dice down now and get away from the table or else I'm gonna smack your Wop head!"

Gar dove for him, knocking him flat on the deck and with his forearm against his throat and his fist in his face.

"Don't you ever call me that again, you freaking salt bag. You may have more service years on me but at least I don't cheat my shipmates. I'm not going to let you up until you apologize to these guys for cheating."

"No way and I'm gonna—," cried out Boats. Gar tightened the hold on his windpipe. He coughed, gurgled, sputtered, coughed, and his eyes started to bug out.

"Let him up, Gar, before you kill him!" said Sammy.

"I'll let him up when he agrees to apologize to all of us." He slightly released his grip.

Boats whispered, "OK, I apologize, damn you." and both started to stood up and brushed off their clothes.

"Scotty, I harbor no bad feelings towards you, but only my friends can call me a wop, and I can't stand a cheat. We'll forget all that and get back to the game, if you are willing to play game right, what say?" and he stuck his right hand out for him to shake.

Boats looked at Gar, then at the other players, then back at Gar. Finally, he took Gar's hand and said, "OK." Then the game continued and all the players started talking and making bets as if nothing happened. Before the night was over, both Sammy and Gar had each won over $1000 and in the morning, they had the mail clerk send a money order for that amount back home for safekeeping.

Sammy and Gar talked of home and the good ol' USA for most of the night. Each was searching for an answer to what they would do when the war was over and they returned home.

Sammy said, "The only skills we have are what we learned at Industry and what the Navy has taught us. I just don't have a clue as to what I would like to do when we get out."

"Oh, you know , we could steal cars or be pool sharks," joked Gar, laughingly messing up Sammy's hair.

"Yeah, sure and we wouldn't need to look for work either, because we would be in the slammer, wise guy!"

"I wonder where Sandy is right now and if he's OK. I sure do miss him and his Irish wit. Ya know that North Atlantic is a bad area for subs."

"I know, but he's a tough nut and he'll be all right. The three of us will do something together, God willing, when we get out. Maybe you could own a barbershop and we could shine shoes, ha ha!"

"Yeah, we could do that all right," quipped Gar, "But seriously, let me run an idea by you. When we get out, and before we even think about starting a family, and we will surely have a nice nest egg. When we get discharged, all three of us could go out to Las Vegas and have a good time. We might even try their craps tables, too. What do you think about that my friend?"

"Hey that sounds great, buddy, but there is a little matter of a war that we gotta take care of first. So we'll just not think on that till we get back home, old pal."

Gar's ship had been fully loaded and winched itself off the beach, and joined with the very large convoy that headed for the invasion of Leyte. Several Destroyers and Cruisers were already heading towards Leyte, along with Admiral Nimitz's fighting fleet. Early the next morning the huge convoy started out. It had been reported that a huge naval battle was raging near Leyte with the Japanese thinking that they had Admiral Nimitz's fleet boxed in, but the US fleet managed to make midway another victory for "the good guys." Mac Arthur was aboard the USS Rocky Mount transport, directing this war like a true General. The Japanese had to be aware that the momentum was on our side, but they would rather die before accepting defeat. Many US soldiers would die also.

The huge Cruisers had been shelling the beach area for hours and B-25's had been running their bombing patterns, but the Japanese mortars and cannon shells were creating mass destruction with their accuracy. Before the LST's were sent to the beachheads with the tanks and heavy equipment, the LCVP's (smaller boats) were lowered from every LST. Marines and Army soldiers were ordered over the sides, climbing down the cargo nets and into the VP's, Landing Craft Vehicle Personnel. The VP's would circle in a pattern until all of them were loaded, then a command was ordered for them to hit the beaches. Some took direct hits and when they exploded, at least 35 sailors and soldiers died. As they approached the beach at nearly full speed the bow ramp was dropped and the soldiers had to run or crawl up the beach to find shelter to fire from. At the same time, the Coxswain on the VP kept the boat in forward gear to keep it from turning sideways or broach, raised the ramp, reversed throttle and hoped they could pull back off the beach before a shell would hit them. Then it would return for more soldiers, until every soldier or marine was put ashore. The VP's consisted of a crew of 3: the Coxswain, an engine man and a bow hook man. They usually carried 35 assault troops, or a jeep and 10 or 12 troops.

The next larger landing craft was the LCM (Landing Craft Machinery) that could carry troops or a tank or both. Living conditions were hard and grueling for boat crews. They often spent up to 6 days and nights in their boats during an amphibious landing operation, sleeping very little, running around the clock. Sometimes food was lowered to them from the ship they were attached to, but more often they ate field rations mooched off the Marines or Army guys. They were not adverse to begging, borrowing or stealing whenever necessary. They were unimpressed by critical sailors from the cruisers, battleships, aircraft carriers and any other so called "fighting ships." They were extremely proud of what they did and were very loyal to one another. In port, or on liberty, they wore the insignia of the amphibious force on the shoulder of their dress uniforms as though they considered it a military decoration. It was a badge of honor to them. They were a rough and tumble lot, many of them noted for their beer drinking and fighting talents when on liberty.

The LCS's were larger and had more firepower. They had 20 mm, 50 caliber, and three twin 40 mm anti-air craft guns and carried a crew of 65 enlisted with 6 officers. They were very important for getting in and out of strategic areas. These were ships, not boats, and the crew were very proud of this and it came down hard on anyone who didn't make this distinction. Another type of ship was the LCI's, Landing Craft Infantry and they delivered the troops right to the beach without needing a small boat. All of the crafts were very important to the war effort.

Chapter 22

Sammy was in the first wave ashore. The enemy mortar and rifle shells were reaching their mark and his company took alot of causalities. It wasn't until radio contact with the Cruiser that they were able to pinpoint where the enemy were firing from, and finally it found the target.

The Marine recon men were able to establish that the enemy firepower was being directed from a church steeple high on the hill and communicated this information to the others. After the steeple was demolished, the marines advanced through the hills and, after several hours, secured the beach area. Another problem facing these troops was a Japanese pill box directly in front of Sammy's unit. Its chattering machine gun had already killed several heroes attempting to get close enough to toss a grenade in it.

Sammy heard his Lieutenant say, "We need a volunteer up front to try getting close enough to silence the machine gun nest in that Pill Box, or we will all be slaughtered."

Without fear for his life, Sammy yelled, "Cover me!" and he sprang from his hole and dove two feet closer into a mortar shell hole.

Checking his grenades, he started a zigzag running pattern towards the Pill Box, as the Japs machine guns came within inches of taking his life. He was able to close the gap within 20 feet before a bullet hit him in the right thigh, causing him to hit the sand hard and roll to a stop beside the trunk of a fallen palm tree. Taking him for dead, they trained their guns on the rest of his unit. With blood gushing from his wound, Sam carefully tied his kerchief tightly around his leg, then with every ounce of strength left in him, pulled the pins on three of his grenades, and lobbed them as hard as he could through the opening of the Japs' Pill Box. He hit the sand again and rolled over and over, trying to be a moving target, just as the grenades went off, killing every Jap in the box. The unit was able to reach the crest of the hill and try to secure the beach area.

The medic that attended to Sammy's leg, found that the bullet had gone straight through without hitting any bone.

"We have to get you up to the top of this hill where that other medic that went on up ahead. He has some blood plasma."

He had Sammy lean on him as they crawled together to the crest of the hill, where both medics bandaged his wounds Once they had started administering the plasma, the second medic left to catch up with the advance Marine team.

Suddenly, three Japanese soldiers came out from under cover and attacked their position. The first Jap fired his rifle, hitting the medic in the back and he practically fell on Sammy. He immediately pulled out the plasma needle, rolled to his own rifle and fired almost point blank into the first two Japanese soldiers, killing them at once. A third Jap fired at him and a bullet just grazed his forehead, going through his helmet, almost causing him to blackout. He somehow managed to get off another shot, hitting the third Jap fully in the chest.

Sammy started to pass out, but hearing the medic's moaning, he quickly came to his senses. He saw the wound in his back and that he would need plasma. The medic was awake enough to guide Sammy, administering what was left of the plasma into his own vein. Their roles had reversed and Sammy had to care for him, even as the blood was pouring out of his own his head. He was holding the plasma up high, so it would easily flow into the wounded medic when another Japanese soldier came charging toward him and shot, hitting him in the left shoulder. As he staggered, still holding the plasma, he managed to grab his own rifle. With the butt resting on his stomach, pulled the trigger with his free hand, but the gun only went "snap!" He was out of ammunition. The Jap had come close enough for Sammy to hear the metal click and a big smile broadened across his face and he took aim at Sammy's head. Just before he squeezed the trigger, a bullet passed between his eyes. He was dead before he hit the ground. The Marine rear had guard caught up with Sammy and saw this one man battle with the Japs. They shot just as the Jap was about to finish him off.

Sammy was a fallen hero. The Medics took good care of Sammy and attended to his wounds, in fear of losing his leg. He was taken to a field MASH facility and, later on, to a Hospital at Manus. He was later flown to a hospital in Seattle, Washington. This brave, noble, American Hero had served his country well, and for him the war was over, but he was alive, and there would be other battles for him to conquer.

Chapter 23

Gar knew it would probably be many months before he would see Sammy again, and he prayed for his safety. He had no way of knowing what had just taken place.

The command came for all LST's to hit the beaches. The beach soon became a beehive of activity as the tanks and heavy equipment rolled off and entered into the battle. The Navy Construction Battalion, known as the C.B.s, whose main purpose was to unload supplies and build roads and airstrips, fought along side combat troops. The enemy shelling was becoming lighter as the troops followed the retreating Japs further inland. The Navy had taken a pounding before they finally sent the Jap planes back for more fuel. Six enemy planes had been destroyed, but three Navy ships had sunk and there were many casualties. Some soldiers were loaded on the beached LST's to be taken back to the nearest Hospital ship.

The morning the beach was secured, General Mac Arthur made his famous return by stepping off into shallow water from an Amphibious small boat and as the cameras were rolling, he declared he had returned. The momentum of this war had shifted to the United States and it's Allies, but the Japanese were not going to just give up. They would have to be driven from every Island in the Asiatic Pacific. The Japanese Fliers became

Kamikaze pilots, vowing to dive their planes into our ships, even killing themselves, before they would ever be defeated. Their families had a funeral for each pilot before he took off, knowing that he had sworn to go down with his plane in suicide dives on American Ships. One pilot was found to have a copy of his funeral stuck inside of his flight suit, describing the event and all the attending relatives.

Martyrdom of this magnitude made for a very formidable foe. The word "kamikaze" (divine wind) struck terror in every one as they watched with a hypnotic fascination plane after plane, dive at ships, scoring hit after hit. They just could not understand what evil force could make a pilot so determined to die.

Gar's ship, the LST 347, joined a convoy of the Navy's finest and left Leyte with a load of casualties. They headed for the Admiralty Islands at Manus, where they took on more supplies and tanks for another invasion. The crew was given permission to have a beach party at a spot the Navy had designated the area for such occasions. Each man was allotted 4 beers and those who didn't drink, found themselves in a nice position of auctioning off their 4 beers to the highest bidders. The VP's were lowered and the beer loaded in along with enough food for the picnic, also softballs and bats were lowered into the boats. Just where they found them was a mystery to all. The crew started in on the beer, then to the ball game and back for more beer.

The hot sun baked them as they played, and as the beer began to change these fun loving shipmates from swabbies to landlubbers, it wasn't any surprise to see friends transformed into drunken enemies. The Officers that had been along for the party had all they could do to keep this from getting way out of hand. Before it was over, nearly every sailor there was said to be on report. The Officers had to threaten Captain's mess on many before they had them under control. On the trip back to the ship, most had vomited in and over the boat and on each other, making for one huge mess for the coxswain and his crew to clean up . Of course, after deliberation, the officers decided not to press the issue of placing the guys on report. After all they were just letting off a little steam and tension.

This scene was repeated by every ship in the Navy. This had always been so and would always be. Otherwise, the sailors would perhaps become nut cases with much worse resulting consequences. The LST 347 was home for many young and frightened boys who matured so very fast, some becoming old before their time.

Chapter 24

As the war magnified more manpower was required, which meant more food, medical supplies, ammunition, and heavy equipment was badly needed. This was the responsibility of the US Navy. Cargo ships could cross the ocean faster but the LST's could move more of everything from island to island, much easier and had more firepower for protection. Gar's ship continued with combat landings at Wadke-Biak, Morotai, Noemfoor, New Guinea,The Philippines, Leyte, Cebu, Balikpapan, Lingayen, Mindora , Mindinao and Borneo. At Tarakan, Borneo, the 347 and seven other LST's were high and dry for several days on the beach because the tide went way out. The Japanese planes and mortar shells had a picnic with these ships. Not one ship escaped some sort of damages or casualties before they were able to retract from the beach. It was 13 days before the 347 was finally back off that drastic beach and back into a convoy for the Philippines.

They were about one day away from reaching Mindoro when the engine room reported that there was a problem with one of the engines and had to completely shut down one engine. The Captain wanted to know how much time was needed to repair the engine and could they make it to the Philippines with only one engine. The Engineering officer surveyed the problem and reported that they needed 24 hours and that both engines had to be at stop in order to make this repair. The word was passed over to the Convoy Commander, who instructed one Destroyer Escort to stay with the 347 for 12 hours only and that the Convoy had to continue on. He could not risk the lives of hundreds and several ships, due to one crippled ship, plus they were only one day from port. The Convoy continued on it's way.

At 7 Pm , the DE radioed the 347, that their Sonar had detected activity west of the area and Jap Submarines were suspected. It ordered General Quarters and for the 347 to stay at G.Q. the rest of the night. It also advised the ship that even though the Machinists and engine crew had to work all night, they must take all precaution in not making loud noises while doing repairs, as the enemy will pick up on this and know that you are immobilized and it will be like a shark going after a wounded fish. The repair crew wondered just how they could make these repairs in silence, but they tried their best anyway.

The 347 crew were at G.Q. and Gar was in his Trainer position on his 40 MM gun, when he witnessed a tremendous explosion and this huge fireball off his port side, followed by more explosions. The Japanese sub had put a torpedo into the Destroyer Escort and it had caused a series of explosions from it's ammunition holds. In a matter of minutes it was completely destroyed and it was as if it was never there. The DE could not have had time to send out a "Mayday" radio signal. The Captain of Gar's ship told his radio man to send a mayday request for help *now*, and kept sending until he got a reply. Every man on board was praying that survivors would be found from the DE, and that they would not be the next one to go down. The Captain ordered the LCVP's be lowered to look for survivors, but before that was accomplished, the inevitable happened. A torpedo struck the 347 at mid-ship, almost cutting the ship in two. The workers below had no chance at surviving. So many of these torpedoes had gone underneath the ship because the LST is flat and doesn't sit far in the water like an ordinary ship, which indicated this Sub may have come partially to the surface before firing. The 347 was filling rapidly with sea water and she was going down fast.

It was pitch dark and although the burning ship gave off some light it was total chaos for those topside scrambling for their lives. The Captain was yelling orders for everyone not to panic and for anyone close to a life-raft, cut it loose now! The screaming of dying men below was terrifying. The LST has water tight compartment doors and at G.Q. the last man through each compartment had to dog these doors tight. Under certain circumstances a shell going through one of these compartments, wouldn't mean that it would sink, but this torpedo passed through the port side and into the large tank deck, allowing all that sea water to rush in and pull the ship below the surface.

Gar was able to find his way to the life boat just as the ship went out from under him. As the men splashed and tread water they located the life boats and proceeded to get into them. They weren't real life boats but were rafts that would support a few men, and contained a small keg of water, k-rations and emergency supplies. The forward half of the ship survivors had managed to get one loose, and there was one also available for the rear survivors.

When it seemed as though everyone was in the rafts, the captain yelled for everyone to paddle close to each other so they could tie the rafts together and take a body count to see how many survivors we had. There were 24 all together, 4 officers and only 20 enlisted men. The Captain, the executive officer, the Navigation Officer, and the Gunnery officer. Of the 20 sailors, 8 had wounds from shrapnel and other flying debris. The highest petty officer was Gar's crap shooting buddy, First Class Boatswain's Mate, Scotty.

"We need for everyone to stay calm," the Captain said. "I want two of the officers in each boat they will be in charge. Make sure each boat has some water and rations. Those in need of medical attention must be cared for now. I don't know if Brown, the radio man, ever reached anyone with his 'mayday,' and since he's not with us, we can only pray that help will be coming. If we stay calm and listen to orders, we will be all right. It's now midnight and when it gets light, we will see if there is anything on the surface that we can salvage. May God bless and care for all our shipmates that went down with our ship."

Chapter 25

On the rafts, inventory was being taken and someone was bandaging the wounded with some gauze that was found in the kit. Someone found a flashlight and was using it to help find the repair kits.

"Captain," said Gar, "I may be hearing things, but I thought I heard something over yonder. It sounded like a metal door or something metal."

The Captain exclaimed, "Everyone be quiet, let's listen!"

In the quiet, the waves were splashing against the raft, but no one heard anything else.

"We can't be sure, but that Sub could be near and it's entirely possible that it might surface to see if there are survivors. I hope not, because we are helpless in our present condition."

"I hear some voices and splashing," said one of the officers, "If they have a spotlight they'll have us in no time. Our only chance is that they do not hear or see us."

"Sir," whispered Gar, "I see something bobbing in the water, about 15 feet from my raft, I would like permission to ease into the water and bring it to the raft. It may be food or something from our ship."

"OK, Gar, but be very quiet about it."

He silently slipped over the side of the raft and softly paddled over to the bobbing object. It was a canvas bag about a foot square. He grabbed it and pulled it over to the Skipper's raft.

"Sir, if we could shade the flashlight on the further side, away from the enemy Sub, we could see what's in it."

"OK, bring that light over to this side."

As they slowly opened the canvas bag, they saw explosives, grenades and fuses.

"Where in the world did this come from?" exclaimed the Captain. "It's not from our LST."

"Hey, I know that bag," said the boat Coxswain, "That's one of the bags that those CB's had when I took in the first wave at Borneo. They had several of those. This one must have been left behind in all that assault at the beach."

"Well it won't do us any good out here now, but we'll keep it stored in the raft. Can't tell. Maybe we can kill some fish with it."

"What was that I just heard?" someone said, "Sounds like metal clashing." Then they saw flashes from the submerged Sub as it fired a burst from their 20 mm guns, hitting the water far from the rafts. Then every few feet they would fire again. They continued this as they started a circle from the Sub.

"They have seen our light or heard us," said the Captain. "When they find us, it will be all over for us. Apparently they do not know exactly where we are yet."

"Sir," said Scotty, the Boatswain, "I suggest that we all get into the water and hang on at the opposite from the Sub. That way their bullets will hit the raft instead of us, if they ever figure out where we are."

"That's a smart idea, Boats. Everyone quietly ease into the water and hang on the furthest from the Sub. Any wounded who can't do this, try getting as low as you can inside the raft."

The enemy shells came closer as they were making a sweep towards them. The next burst hit the first raft with a loud, slapping sound, which was followed by much loud chatter aboard the Sub. They must have realized that they had succeeded in hitting the survivors or a life boat. More shelling in that area brought more destruction to the raft and the wounded were unmercifully slaughtered. Their screams brought loud cheers of joy from the Sub. Both rafts were shattered, but the men stayed afloat on the pieces. It would only be a matter of time before the sharks would detect the blood in the water and they would go into a feeding frenzy.

Chapter 26

Gar reached out onto the raft and brought the canvas bag to him. As he felt into the bottom of the bag, he found this flare gun. It had only one flare. He thought of a plan and slid over to the Captain.

"Skipper, I know how to use these explosives. It's going to be daylight in another hour and when those Japs are able to see us, you know we won't stand a prayer of a chance. They've already indicated that they want no prisoners, so we are dead men. I am, as you know, a certified life saver and am an excellent swimmer. I'm taking these explosives and flare gun with me and try swimming around to the far side of that Submarine and if God allows me to, I will set a charge on their conning tower that will blow it so they cannot submerge and just before it blows, I plan to pull the pins on these grenades, and drop them down the hatch. I'm hoping that this flare gun will save me against those on topside. This is our only chance."

"Gar, that's an impossible task and I can't ask you to throw your life away on something so bazaar as that."

"Sorry Cap, but I'm going on my own. There aren't any choices left."

"In that case, Gar, you have my blessings and may God be with you. We will all be praying for your success."

With some string from the bag, Gar tied it to his leg and set out towing it as he went far above the Sub and came in from the far side. He heard Japanese chatter from the other side as they were concentrating on raking the rafts to shreds. He had a problem getting a foothold at the side of the Sub. He saw a small hook part way up, but it was too far to reach. Besides, he couldn't take a chance trying to jump up on the side. It might cause too much noise. He took off his belt . If he could toss the buckle over that hook, he just might be able to pull himself up. He waited until the Japs fired another burst and started tossing the buckle at the hook.

After several failed attempts, the buckle finally bounced over the hook. Gar slid up to get a hand on something solid and crawled up to the tower. He frantically set the charge and the fuse to give him just enough time to dive back into the water. As he lit the match, he was spotted by a Japanese lookout, who shot at him with his rifle. He quickly fumbled in his bag and pulled out his flare gun. All of the topside Japs ran towards Gar, yelling and firing their rifles. Lucky for Gar, they weren't good marksmen, however one bullet ricocheted off the steel Sub and tore through Gar's left shoulder. If he hadn't been braced against the tower, he would have gone overboard. He almost dropped the flare gun, but held on tightly. The hole in his shoulder hurt like blazes, but his determination was stronger. It seemed the Japs knew they had him. He pointed the flare gun at the crowd and fires. The flare sped out enough to burn every Jap and blow them off the Sub. He lit the fuse and as it was starting to burn, he pulled the pins on three grenades, keeping the fourth for a safety net. Tossing them down the hatch and into the Sub, he ran to the side, dove into the ocean and swam as fast as he could.

The first blasts tore a large hole in the Sub's port side and the last tore the top off the tower, splitting it down the seams. It wasn't long before the sea water pulled the ship beneath it's salty waves, taking everyone inside down with it.

Gar felt the shock waves and kept on swimming. He felt like his body was on fire. Then he stopped and watched as the Sub sank. The pain was bad but the turn of events pumped new energy into his veins. He headed back to his crew and wanted to be with them very badly, but he was losing control. He knew he couldn't go much further and the loss of blood must now be draining away his life, sending him into a dark abyss.

So this is it, he thought. This is where I finish my life. This is how it feels to die. Have I made a difference in the world? Will God allow me to enter his kingdom? I'm going!

Chapter 27

The Captain and crew waited and hoped and prayed that Gar would be able to pull this off. They knew it would take a miracle for him to succeed.

The Sub guns let off another burst into the raft area. They were shooting blindly at the raft and with each sound that signified a hit, they let out a chorus of cheers. They were enjoying the fun, like shooting fish in a bowl. They were waiting for daylight to finish off the survivors. The men inside the raft were dead and riddled with those terrible Submarine shells. They, too, died a heroes death. The Captain grieved for those poor shipmates, but here was absolutely nothing he could do for them. When he saw and heard those explosions, he and the remaining crew let out a loud cheer. Then, as they witnessed the Sub slowly sink into the ocean, they yelled with extreme joy.

"Boats, take a couple good swimmers and go see if you can find Gar and see if he needs assistance. He just pulled off the miracle of the Century."

Scotty called a couple sailors and they started swimming in that direction. They heard Gar floundering and splashing in the water. Just before he went under for the last time, Scotty grabbed his head while the others kept him afloat. They shuttled him back to the raft and placed his body on far enough to care for his wounds. Someone took off his shirt and wrapped it around his shoulder after they stuffed other clothing in his wounds. He was out for nearly two more hours and each took turns caring for him and keeping him from rolling off the raft .

It was daybreak and they could see debris all over the water, including the dead.

Suddenly a sailor screamed, "Oh, my God, they are coming again. See over that horizon. Their submarine is just coming into view."

"No, no, that's a ship! Now I see the shape and it's a ship. I think it's one of our Destroyers!"

"Praise God, it is!" others were yelling.

Gar came around and as he woke completely, he asked, "Am I in heaven?"

Then he saw Boats.

"Scotty, you sure look good to me."

"Not as good as you look to me, pal, and the same for all of us. You sure did a hell of a job on that Sub, saving all your shipmates."

The Destroyer lowered their small boats, rescued all of the survivors along and recovered the dead heroes and cleaned up any debris that was salvageable.

Gar was attended to by the ship's Doctor and kept in sick bay quarters until they reached the Philippines. Every day, members of his crew kept him company until the Doctor had to chase them away so he could get some rest. One of his mates who seemed always there was Scotty, the Boatswain mate. Gar and Scotty had become great friends and had many laughs over their encounter at the craps table.

"What were you doing when the war broke out, Scotty?"

"Well I had been in the regular Navy before the war and had been discharged about a year before the war started. I have a friend that became Vice President at one of the hotels in Las Vegas, Nevada and he offered me a job as a dealer at their craps pit. I took the job and was being considered for a promotion when the Japs attacked Pearl Harbor. The Navy said they needed me and offered to reinstate my time and gave me Second Class, with a promise of first class in six months. How about you?"

Gar related his time in Industry and didn't skip a thing, "Bet you didn't know you were friends with a gangster, did you?"

"Hell you aren't a gangster. You just got a bad break , Gar. I bet you don't even realize that you are a hero and you can get any job you want when you get out of this Navy, unless you plan on making it your career."

"Oh, no. I'm getting out when they say I can go, and I'm going to take plenty of time resting up before I think about work. Shucks, I might even go back for more schooling, when I'm discharged. Heck, I might just become a professional gambler," he jokingly said.

"Hey, that brings up another thing that I want to talk to you about. I know you were kidding about the gangster thing, but let me run this by you. When I get out, I'm going back to Las Vegas and my old friends. If you get serious about craps as a business, or need anything else, I want you to call or look me up. OK? I will be at the Flamingo Casino Hotel. It's under construction and will open early next year. You can remember that, right?"

"Oh sure, Scotty, I won't forget, and thanks for the kind offer, but I just don't know what's going to happen with my body. Only time will tell."

"You're right Gar, but I just wanted to lay that on you before we get separated once we get docked and they transfer you off to their hospital. One more thing. If you ever need anything, please contact me any time and, just in case you forgot, my last name is McAllen. Everyone gets so used to calling me Boats or Scotty, that my last name is forgotten."

"OK, Scotty McAllen, I have you written across my memory, and again, thanks."

Chapter 28

When the Destroyer docked at Manila, the Navy was ready to receive it's wounded and survivors. Gar was flown directly to a hospital in Hawaii. After 6 days there, he was taken to the Navy Hospital in Seattle, Washington. His wounds were healing slowly and the doctors still hadn't decided if they needed to surgically repair his internal parts at the shoulder or wait to see if the body would heal itself. They did declare him lucky that the bullet passed through his body, barely missing the lung. They wanted to wait before operating. Gar was becoming impatient and lying in a hospital bed was worse to him than fighting the Japs. Finally after another week the Navy Board of Doctors met with Gar and told him that he had healed well enough to travel home. He would be going to Washington soon and be receiving the Congressional Medal of Honor and because he was in the Navy Reserve, he was offered the choice of of either staying in the Regular Navy or taking a medical Honorable Discharge. Of course, he would be able to receive free medical help through the VA any time he needed it. Gar told the board that he preferred to take the discharge since he felt that the war would be over soon, and he was looking forward to employment and civilian life. The Board told him his decision would be finalized after the trip to Washington DC.

"In the mean time, starting tomorrow you will be on leave and you can return home to New York. We will contact you when it's time to go to Washington."

Gar was very pleased with both decisions. The Paymaster met with him later that day and paid him his past salary and he had plenty of cash to spend on leave.

Almost every day he had been talking with the Grimes'. They informed him of the terrible burns that Sandy had received. He was at the Presbyterian Hospital's Burn Center in New York City going through the painful series of skin grafts, but they were very hopeful of him being able to regain full use of his hands sometime in the future.

They also informed him that Sammy Cross had been wounded. After time spent in a California hospital, he received a Medical Discharge and returned home. He was still mending, but in time he should be OK. The Grimes' were so glad all three boys were not killed and that they would all be home soon. They ere thrilled that the three boys would each receive the Congressional Medal of Honor and the Purple Heart. They reminded Gar that they were all heroes and that the papers were full of what the three had accomplished for their country. He told them that he should be arriving at Laguardia Airport the next day at 3 pm and he was very anxious to see every one.

After he hung up, he dialed Sammy's home and the two were excited about seeing each other again. Sammy said that he wouldn't meet his plane, but when his visit with the Grimes had calmed down a little, he wanted Gar to come over. Gar asked about Sandy and he told him that it wouldn't be a good idea to try calling Sandy, because his hands were still a handicap to using the phone. They agreed to both go over to the hospital after Gar got home.

Gar was now going back to a home where he was wanted and his two best friends were. He could hardly contain himself.

"What will I do?" he thought to himself, "Will I be able to live up to being a Hero? Will all this publicity give me a big head? I think I'd rather be left alone, maybe."

Chapter 29

The personal items that Gar wanted to keep were sent by rail to the Grimes' address and Gar took a small travel bag with him on the plane. This was his first flight on an airplane and he was experiencing some angst as he boarded. He had to change planes in Chicago, but by then he was very relaxed. His only thoughts were about seeing the Grimes family again. Mrs. Grimes had made it clear to him that this was to be his home and that they were his family now and forever. She had said that because she had picked up on Gar's mixed emotions about coming home. She could tell that he was a little unsure of how his homecoming would be accepted . After all, he knew that the Grimes' took him in so that he could be released from Industry and they were instrumental in helping him enlist in the Navy. For her to put him at ease was very special for him.

Coming from the plane at Laguardia into the waiting area and seeing both Mr. and Mrs. Grimes, along with Rose, was too much and Gar was overcome with joy and he wept uncontrollably. They showered him with their love and tears were like falling rain as they embraced each other. Gar had never experienced such affection and love from anyone before. After a few moments the homecoming banter, Mr. Grimes said, "let's all walk over to the baggage area and get Gar's luggage. We need to get this Sailor home."

"That's right," they all chorused.

"Say, how about we stop by on the way home and see Sandy?" Gar asked.

They all looked at each other awkwardly and Mr. Grimes said, "Uh, well, if it's OK with you, we thought we would all go over tomorrow together and see him. We talked with him this morning and he is expecting us then. Besides, we need to get you home and rested up."

"OK, you're right, I was just anxious to see both my buddies, but I guess I'll have plenty of time now that we are all back home."

The ride home was bringing back so many memories to Gar and after being gone for so long, it was heartwarming. Things were starting to happen quickly. The family was trying to help him forget the war and to think of the future. Gar told Rose how beautiful she had become and wanted to know how many hearts had she broken so far. She was slowly becoming a young woman. Her 17th birthday had just passed and she was a Senior in high school. Mrs. Grimes was still doing volunteer work at her favorite hospital and Mr. Grimes was prospering in his building trade.

They let Gar roam around the house and walk around the street and neighborhood before having a late dinner. Cocktails were in order before dinner and they toasted Gar and the other boys over and over. Mrs. Grimes had remembered how Gar loved Italian food and prepared a large beef lasagna just for this occasion. After dinner, Mr. Grimes asked Gar if he wanted a cigar, but Gar declined and said that he had never tried smoking.

While the ladies were washing up the dishes, Mr. Grimes said, "Gar, now that you're home (and we are so glad to have you here), I need to have a serious talk with you about Sandy. I know how much you want to see him, and rightly so, but I need to prepare you before we go. You see, his world has changed for him, both physically and mentally. Physically, both of his hands are unable to function as before. The burning of the skin went deep into all the meaty and tendon area of both hands. He cannot get the use from them that a normal person can and never will. The doctors have suggested amputating them, with the hope that someday soon modern science medicine would invent a way to replace them. All they can offer now is a claw made out of metal. Sandy has refused this route.

Mentally, he has nearly given up all hope of a meaningful life. We have had both a Priest and a Minister try counseling with him and he listens, but refuses to enter into meaningful discussions. He says that his life is not worth living, in fact he has no desire to even come home. He hasn't threatened suicide yet, but his family is worried sick about him."

Gar was shocked to hear how bad it had gotten for everyone. He had experienced similar feelings when waiting for his wounds to heal, as all Vets have gone impatiently through their healing process, but not to the extent that Sandy was going through.

"I had no idea that he was so bad. Poor Sandy! I do know that having seen extreme cases when I too was recovering, many went from boys to men much before they should have and many need help from psychiatry and modern medicine. I'm hoping that maybe seeing

Sammy and I together again will help him or it might have a reverse effect, seeing that we have our hands. Have you discussed this with his Doctor?"

"Yes, Gar we did. He doesn't feel that will be a problem, since he sees us and hasn't given any indication about our hands. Let's hope he perks up when he sees you. He'll be expecting us tomorrow afternoon around 2 and Sammy said he'd come with us. Maybe you could go see Sammy in the morning and bring him over here then so the three of us could drive in to the city together. Mary and Rose will be staying here this time since they know this is so important to Sandy's health. We felt that too many people might complicate things. Oh, by the way, you can take my car when you go see Sammy."

"Thanks a lot Mr. Grimes."

"Hey, no more Mr. Grimes. I want you to call me Irv or Irving from now on, OK ?"

"OK, sure. It's a little strange, but I like it."

"Since the girls are still putting away dishes, let me ask, have you given any thought as to what you might like to do with your life in the way of employment or schooling?"

"No, I haven't. I just want to take it easy until the Navy discharges me after I go down to Washington. Then maybe I will decide what to do."

"Well, there certainly isn't any hurry and when you need help or want to talk about it, I'm here for you."

"Thank you, I appreciate that."

Chapter 30

The next morning Gar was up early. After breakfast, he went for a stroll around the neighborhood. It was so good to just walk around smell the street, the grasses, the fumes and just life and nature in its rawest form.

He kept repeating to himself, "I'm Home."

Before he realized it, he was standing across the street from a barber shop and outside in big letters was "JOE MILLER'S BARBER SHOP." Gar suddenly discovered that this was where he used to work. He opened the door and saw Joe sweeping the floor.

"Hi Joe!"

Joe turned and said, "who?? Oh my God in heaven, it's Gar Savino! How are you?"

He threw his broom away and gave Gar a big bear hug." I've read all about you and I tell all my patrons that you used to work for me. Are you home for good now?"

Gar had a real nice chat with Joe and promised to be back when he needed a haircut.

He continued to walk around for a while, then drove Irv's car to Sammy's home.

Sammy was in the kitchen and when they came together, they gave each other a warm hug and began telling each other what had happened from the moment that they had parted back at the invasion at Leyte. Sammy was healing well and had only a slight limp in his leg. He looked great to Gar. Gar asked about his parents and was told that they were both at work at the Empire trucking company.

"They both are anxious to see you again. I think both families are planning some sort of coming home party for us this weekend. I told them to wait until Sandy gets out of the hospital but they said we'll have another when he does, so I don't know what we should do. I'm very concerned about Sandy."

"Yeah, me too. I just hope that seeing us today might give him some new spirit or hope to fight for himself. It's just not like Sandy to give up, but I know it must be ungodly tough to not be able to use your hands for anything.

Chapter 31

Sammy, Gar and Irving entered the hospital and proceeded to the 4th floor. The floor nurse directed them to Sandy's room where he was waiting in his chair, looking out his window. When she announced that he had visitors he turned to see his father and his best friends.

"Sorry, guys, that I can't shake your hands but maybe a little hug will do."

Everyone gave Sandy a hug and started some small talk, saying how good he looked.

Finally Sandy said, "Let's cut out the bull crap. We all know I don't have hands anymore and I'm as useless as tits on a boar hog."

"That's not true Sandy," said Irving. "There will be lots of things that you can do. It just will take time to adjust. The Navy is doing everything in its power to help you."

"Yeah, Dad, like cutting my hands off and putting steel claws on me!" he yelled Gar tried to calm him.

"Sandy, we know you have gone through alot and there is still more to do, but we are here and we will always be here to help you."

"Oh, and I suppose you guys will be here to blow my nose for me, and wipe my eyes, and dress and undress me every day of my life. Hell Gar, I can't even wipe my own ass!"

He sobbed uncontrollably and they all gathered around him with their soothing support. His Dad helped wipe his nose and face with kleenex.

"I'm sorry guys. I shouldn't have said that."

Gar knelt down in front of him.

"You need never have to say you're sorry again to anyone. You've had a bad time and we know it's rough, but Sandy, you are a tough SOB, and you are going to lick this. You are not the first guy to lose his hands, nor will you be the last, but we are going to beat this damn thing together. YOU WILL!! But we need you to put on a positive attitude now and let us and your doctors help you. OK. pal?"

Sandy threw his arms around Gar and cried.

After a while he said, "Thanks guys, I needed that, and I need you. I won't let you down. My family has been so good to me, but seeing you two is just so wonderful. Gar, you always could see my weakness and kept me straight many times up at Industry."

"You do not have any weaknesses Sandy, and everything is positive, right you old swabby?"

Their mood became happier and some fun and jokes started to take away the bitterness that had been tearing Sandy apart. Once, the nurse ran in to see if everything was all right because of all the commotion in his room. By the time visiting hours were over Sandy was almost back to being his old self. When they said their goodbyes, he promised to fight this problem and they all would win. The boys said they would be back tomorrow.

On the way home, Irving told them that this was the best day that Sandy had had, and he was sure that Sandy would beat this thing. He was so grateful for what the boys had done for Sandy.

Chapter 32

The next day, and over the next few months the boys faithfully visited Sandy at the hospital. He had consented to amputation of both hands at the wrist. The Surgery had gone well and the Prosthesis devices were the next step in this ongoing procedure. Sandy was doing very well, drawing his strength from his pals and his family. The minister from the Baptist Church was also helping him gather strength from the knowledge of God and of His Son, Jesus Christ. Sandy seemed to grow stronger with every passing day, to the point that he hardly ever complained any more of his loss, only of the future. Everyone was so pleased.

Shortly after Sammy and Gar had made their original visit to the hospital and were able to help Sandy back onto life's path, they received a call from Washington. It was the Secretary of the Navy, Mr. James Forestall. He told them the Navy had been following the progress that was being made by America's three heroes, and were waiting until Sandy could travel well enough for all three of them to come to Washington to receive the Congressional Medal of Honor. He reminded them that they were still in the Navy and right after they received their Medals, they would have their medical discharges. They would always receive an allotment from the Government and be able to receive medical treatment through the Veterans Administration. He advised them they should be getting travel instructions in the near future. This was one more bit of information that the three shared at their weekly visitations.

Soon Sammy and Gar enrolled in a local Veterans School to study for their high school diplomas. By special permission, they had enrolled Sandy also and they tutored him each time they visited. They were eager to learn and the school was able to obtain tests from New York State for an Equivalency Diploma. They studied very hard and all three passed with flying colors. Sandy took the test with the aid of his nurse, who wrote his spoken answers in front of an appointed witness. This diploma stated that the recipient was a high school graduate. This cut through years of studying with the same results. They were as proud of these diplomas as their medals.

Sandy's remarkable improvement with his therapy, made it possible for him to return home and continue as an outpatient with his doctors. The artificial hands were very difficult to master, but his determination was something to behold. He seemed to take such pride in showing his friends and family everything that he now could do with his new hands. It was possible that maybe sometimes they wished he wouldn't call so many times to come see if there was anything he could do."

But that was to be expected and he was the center of everyone's life at this moment.

Chapter 33

The war in Europe had been over for a while and the bad guys had been defeated. The Allies had stormed ashore at Normandy and just kept on sweeping across every town and city until Hitler and his band of evil was destroyed.

Now all efforts were directed towards eliminating Tojo and his kind. United States and its Allies had the Japanese on the run and it would only be a matter of time before they would have to surrender. However, these Japanese had sworn to die before they would give up. It looked like we would have to sweep every island before it was over and that would take another year or so and many lives.

On April 23,1945, America and the world lost a remarkable man. Our President Franklin D. Roosevelt, died. He was replaced by the Vice President, Harry Truman.

President Truman took over just when America had finished testing her new bomb and he decided that it was time to finish that awful war. He ordered the Atom Bomb to be dropped on Hiroshima, Japan. It was a devastating bomb, killing people by the thousands but still no surrender, so he dropped another, and this time the Japanese smartened up and surrendered unconditionally. On August12,,1945 the war was over. Our boys could return to their homes and get on with the task of raising their families and worshiping their religion together.

It was later that same year that the three heroes from New York, were invited to the White House, to receive their medals from the president of the United States. Both the Grimes family and the Cross family were in attendance. They were proud of these men. Yesterday they were boys, now they were men indeed.

Sandy continued his weekly visits to the hospital's rehab and physical therapy department. His progress had been going well, but his Doctor had warned him that he will reach a point where it would seem that nothing is going well and he will get depressed, dispirited, and despondent . He told him that it happens in every type of healing. The mind expects fast improvements, while the body says we're going too fast. Sandy had reached that period and he was fussy and feeling depressed. The nurse that had been his therapist for a few weeks accidentally pinched the tendon in his wrist socket while reapplying his prothesis and he lost his temper. She was a pretty red haired Irish girl and she lashed right back at him.

After some heated words from each, she dropped everything and said he could go to blazes, and stormed from the room. The Doctor came over to Sandy and took care of the problem.

"How are you doing Sandy?"

"Terrible , These things are hard to manipulate , and these stupid nurses hurt me more every day I come in."

"Nonsense! You are doing remarkably well. You know it takes time for these but you have shown that you can do it, and we know you can. As far as the nurses go, nurse Sally Malone is one of our best I'll just tell her to come back in and you can tell her you're sorry, OK?"

"Hell no. I want someone else. She thinks she's too smart."

"OK, but you 've got to have more patience with our nurses."

Chapter 34

When Sandy left the hospital, he started to realize that he might have come down too hard on the nurse and he should not have had that little tantrum. He realized that his doctor was right on both accounts.

His doctor had said, "You see, the healing process is exactly like trying to lose weight. You'll lose pounds in the beginning fairly easy, then you may go for days that seem like you aren't doing very good. If you stay with it, you start losing again. The body is simply making the adjustments for you, making sure that you really do want to lose the pounds."

The next visit to the hospital Sandy was assigned to a new nurse therapist , and he asked why. The supervisor told him that nurse Malone was off his case because he had told the Doctor that he disliked her.

"That's silly, he said, "I was only kidding. Would you send her to me? I know that I need to apologize to her."

When she came Sandy immediately stood up and said, "Miss Malone, I want to apologize for my bad behavior. I would like to ask you to continue having me as your patient. I can assure you it will never happen again."

She looked hard into Sandy's eyes and after she made him wait further said, "Well suppose we could try it one more time, if you are sure I'm not too smart."

Sandy got the message and smiled, "I think I had that coming. Either way, I answer that and I'm in trouble, so let's shake hands and start over ".

She offered her pretty hand and Sandy awkwardly put his claw in hers. Sandy saw that this red haired lass was a real beauty and she wasn't skittish about touching his claws. They proceeded to the therapy room where they continued to work together. Sandy would open up to her and they began a friendship that grew more every week. She found that she was attracted to him also. The amazing thing that Sandy found out she also lived in Queens. After getting to know each other better, she consented to dating Sandy. Sally had her own car and on most dates she picked him up. They rode the subway together or occasionally took a bus ride. They both enjoyed a broadway play and dinner afterwards.

Sandy was becoming more and more proficient with his metal hands and his father had promised to buy him a car just as soon as he could demonstrate that he was able to pass a driving test. Both Gar and Sammy had purchased used cars and Sandy was so tired of having to ask someone to drive him here and there. He was so nervous on the day that he took the test, he didn't think he could ever do it, but Sally had given him her pep talk and now it was time to do it. The only problem he had was parallel parking and his right rear tire bumped the curbing and he was sure he had failed.

When it was over, the inspector gave him his slip and said," Congratulations, you passed!"

Sandy was so overjoyed that he could hardly wait to call Sally and tell her. He had become able to be independent and from here on his life was going forward with great strides.

Sandy couldn't decide what he wanted to do, knowing that he was limited to something that didn't involve extensive hand or finger work such as baseball or typing. He decided that he would have to use his brain and his mouth to be successful. He enrolled in a class in public speaking with the Dale Carnegie course. He had not been told what the requirements were and when he was asked to stand up and give a 5 minute speech right off the bat, it took him back somewhat and then everything he said, the class would critique. This made him angry until he was applauded for his spirit. When he was asked to do it again later, he rattled off another story without the least bit of anxiety.

He passed his course with honors. He later received a letter from The New York Life Insurance Company, asking him to come to their NY office for an interview for employment. It seemed that the Carnegie people had made it public that Sandy was available and that he was a talker and would be an asset to any sales oriented company.

The interview went well and the company was so impressed with Sandy that they offered him an immediate position as sales manager in one of their sales divisions. They were captivated by his motivation and his high spirit. Because he was able to overcome any setback that he had proved to them that this company needed a man like him to inspire and motivate its sales force. They made Sandy feel wanted and the artificial hands would not deter his ability to be their rising star. Sandy accepted and after spending four weeks attending their training schools, took on the job of training new recruits. He was a natural and in a matter of six months was offered a position as Vice President in the sales department.

Chapter 35

Sammy and Gar had spent most of the fall either visiting Sandy or taking him somewhere and now that he was employed, they began looking towards finding employment. They hadn't gotten very serious about it before and whenever they discussed it, they ran into the same problem.

"I just do not know what kind of work I want to do."

Mr. Cross offered to try getting them on at the Empire Trucking Company, but so far neither had asked him to do it.

He had also told them that the old Cross homestead in Windham that his parents willed to him was available to them. All they had to do was open the place, clean it and get a supply of wood and food. The water and electricity would have to be turned on, but other than that they could go up there and spend the winter. They could ski and perhaps find a job at he ski lift .He said it would be nice if someone were there to see that the house was cared for. This sounded like something that they could do, so when the first snow flake hit New York, Gar and Sammy headed for Windham. It was in the Catskill mountains, directly south of Albany about 75 miles. It was famous for it's Ski-Windham facility resort and directly below it, about 15 miles was Hunter Mountain and its ski resort also.

Tourists would flock there all winter long. On weekends one or the other resort had music, like a German "oom-pa-pa" band or Beerfest and Craft Show, while the hills were alive with skiers and lift rides.

The Cross house was in good shape and after supplies were brought in and the utilities turned on, the boys had the place looking like a palace. They found that the basement was huge and water free. They set to work, cleaning this out and felt that this would be an excellent place for a few beer parties.

One day when they were cleaning the house, they were surprised to answer the door and see this big guy, the Sheriff standing there wanting to know who they were. He knew that the Cross Mansion was vacant and wanted to be sure no one had broken in or was trespassing. His name was John Gillis. Gar put him at ease and soon they were friends. He invited him in for a beer and yelled down to the basement for Sammy to come up and meet the law . Sammy came bounding up the stairs and Gar quickly introduced him to John. They eyed each other closely and after a few seconds Gar could see that the Sheriff was looking suspiciously at Sammy.

"Sheriff, is there something about Sammy that you don't like?"

"What? Oh. excuse my staring. I thought for a minute that I knew your friend."

"Well, I did just get out of jail, Sheriff." Sammy jokingly said

The Sheriff kept looking Sammy over and finally asked, "Were you ever in the Marines or in the Philippines?"

Now it was Sammy's turn to stare,"Yeah, I was. Now let me ask you the same question."

They stared at each other again and the Sheriff said, "were you at the invasion of Leyte?"

"Yeah, I was. Were you there also?"

"Hell, now I got it. You were the one that blew up that pillbox and also saved that medic, aren't you?" he said with a big grin on his face. "I don't suppose you remember someone putting a bullet in that Jap that was about to take you down?"

Sammy yelled ," Was that you?"

"Yes it was, Sammy." he declared. They grabbed each other for a shake and hug. They spent the next hour getting to know each other and sharing old times together. Gar, John and Sammy all enjoyed each other's company and agreed to get together again soon. John told them that if there was anything that they needed, do not hesitate to ask him.

The next few days the boys visited the ski lodges and attended all the beer parties. It wasn't long before everyone in the area knew who they were and welcomed them into all the community affairs. The Sheriff might have had a hand in spreading the word.

Chapter 36

One of the many parties they attended was held at the Mayor's home and all the important people were there. The drinks were flowing freely and the dinner was roasted pig. The Mayor toasted our two heroes and included the sheriff in his PLAUDITS.

Later there was dancing in the living room with the local country band. Nearly everyone wanted to shake our heroes' hand and tell them how proud they were to know them and to have them in the area. One of their well wishers was a chunky, dark, complicated fellow that introduced himself as Toni Frantelli. He told them he owned the local restaurant/tavern known as the "Beef and Bottle."

"I would deem it an honor if you boys would stop in for a drink on me sometime. I can also lead you in the right direction anytime you get bored and would like a little action."

"What sort of action do you mean? Girls or gambling?"

"Well, Jim, the Sheriff, told me you guys could be trusted, so here's the scoop. I run a little game in the rear at my place and we like to have people that enjoy playing a little poker or whatever. Why don't you stop in sometime and I'll show you around? I'll be there all day if you like. Just be sure you keep it to yourself."

"Thanks, Toni. We just might do that."

After Toni left, Gar turned to Sammy and said, "What do you think?"

Sammy said," A little diversion wouldn't hurt, as long as we are discreet about it. Apparently, the town knows about it, from what he said about our friend, the Sheriff."

"Yeah, makes you wonder doesn't it ? We know this goes on in every city in the nation. People want to gamble, but they haven't made it legal, except in Nevada."

The next day the boys dropped in to the "Beef and Bottle." The bar was on the left with bar stools the length the bar and a few small tables in the rear. At the rear next to the ladies and men's room was an office with a sign stating "Authorized Personnel Only".

There was a big guy at a table in front of the door that left the distinct impression that If anyone wanted in to this office, they had to ask him first.

To the right was the dining room, where each table had white linen tablecloths and beautiful shaded lamps. The room certainly delightfully charming.

The bartender wore black with a white apron and asked for their order. They both ordered a beer and asked to see Toni. The bartender asked for their names and went to the big guy at the back. He returned and told them that Toni would see them shortly.

Halfway through their beer, Tom appeared from his office and exclaimed, "Hey, there they are!"

He shook their hands telling everyone at the bar that they were war heroes. He instructed Joe, the bartender, not to take their money for the drinks. He then ushered them to the back and through the office door.

As they passed the doorman, Toni told his gorilla, "Remember these two faces. They are to be admitted any time they like." Then after traveling down a short hallway with another big guy at the next door, they entered into a large room that had several poker tables, a few blackjack tables and a craps table. There was a door at the rear that was guarded by another large fellow. Toni was surrounded by large men who left no doubt that if they disliked you, they wouldn't hesitate to break your face. They were very polite to their guests and made every effort to put them at ease. At the far corner was another bar and to its right were "his and hers" toilets. The room was without customers and Toni advised them that they receive guests only after 7 pm, except on weekends when they are open at noon time, closing at 2 am every night.

"I know this is a silly question," said Sammy ,"But is this legal?"

"I'm going to pretend I didn't hear that. Look, you're mature men now, you know the score. People want to gamble and we provide them that opportunity. Of course it's not legal, but provided certain palms are greased and we keep a clean house with strict guidelines, making sure we do not draw attention to ourselves. The law turns a blind eye towards us. We make sure that no one enters without a referral from one of our members. You two were referred by the Sheriff, Jim Gillis, who said he trusts you with his life, and he did so once. He told us you guys played alot of craps aboard ship and how Gar was a stickler for an honest game.

"Well, we only have honest games here. A cheater would never survive our rules."

After another beer, thanking Toni for the tour and telling him that they would be back, the boys left for home.

Chapter 37

Another snowstorm was blanketing the high elevations and the ski resorts were bracing for another rush of weekend revelers from the big cities. Sammy was waxing his skis and looking forward to more practice runs down the mountain. Gar was not that avid a skier and enjoyed just riding up the lift to see the valley from the mountaintop and returning by the lift. He knew Sammy would make several trips and with the new lights, the lodge had installed the slopes were lit up like a wonderland.

After a few rides on the lift, Gar waited at the bar until they left for the house, when he noticed the cocktail waitress. He'd been coming there enough now that she could welcome him by name. By now, he had found out that she was divorced and renting an apartment in town. She told him her name was Debbie Morton and let him know that she was attracted to him.

"Everybody in Windham knows you are a hero," she said, "I've never danced with a hero and I'm getting off at eight, if you care to stay for a dance."

"Sure, Debbie, but you have to promise me that you'll forget about calling me a hero. That is old stuff now and I'm sure people are sick of hearing about it, including me."

"OK, if you want it that way. May I call you Gar?"

"Sure thing. You can call me anything. As a matter of fact, I was trying to find a way to ask you for a date, 'cause I'm so shy," said Gar with a big grin on his face

"I also asked the bartender if you were married a long time ago. So you see, I've had my eye on you for a while."

When Debbie finished her shift, she came over to Gar and they found a table in the corner. They were so involved talking with each other and comparing notes, they completely forgot about dancing and neither saw Sammy approaching until he was standing at their table.

"Oh, hi," said Gar, and stood up and introduced Sammy to Debbie.

After the usual greeting, Sammy said, "So nice meeting you Debbie, and I don't want to intrude, but if you two don't mind, I think I'll head over to the house and turn in. I'm a little bushed after all those runs down the slopes, so I'll see you guys later."

"All right, Sammy , I'll be in later. Get a good night's sleep buddy."

With that, Sammy left and the two continued their chat.

When a break came in the conversation, Gar exclaimed, "Hey, we never did get to do any dancing, Debbie."

"Well, the band's about to go home anyway, but I've got an idea. Why don't we go to my apartment? I've got all kinds of music on my stereo and I even have your Scotch, if you want a drink. What do you say, or do you think I'm too forward?"

"Shucks no, Debbie. I was going to ask you the same, but I'm a little rusty getting started."

"Gar we are going to fix that rusty problem right away."

They both got in their cars and Gar followed her over to her apartment. It was a cute one bedroom apartment over the owners garage with her own private entrance in the rear. She had fixed it up with nice lace curtains, and wall to wall carpeting. She immediately put on Glen Miller and proceeded to fix the drinks. He remarked that this was a real nice place. She kept the lights low and soft and brought the drinks into the front room. After placing them on the coffee table, she swayed slowly with the music and kept her eyes on Gar. She wanted to dance with Gar and she just knew he would be a good dancer. He had the body for it. She also knew instinctively that he would be good in bed once she got his motor running.

"Hey, penny for your thoughts," said Gar.

She shook her head and smiled at him, "Oh, nothing," and reached for him, pulling him up to dance with her. He was smooth as silk. He held her in his strong arms, as they glided across the room. He danced well, just like she knew he would. He held her close and without realizing it, she rested her head on his shoulder and sighed gently . She felt a touch on the top of her head and knew he had just kissed her.

The hand around her waist pulled him ever so slightly and she pressed her thighs against his. She could feel him, hard, wanting her and she pulled away, but his strong hand was insistent and she allowed it to pull her back into his enfolding arms. As they danced, she moved her hips from side to side, rubbing against him and feeling him grow harder and bigger. She thought how different she felt from when her ex-husband would touch her.

He wanted only to go to bed with her, to get it on. Then it was over. She was raging like a mountain on fire and he hadn't even kissed her lips yet. He stopped and softly cupped her chin in one hand and holding her back side with the other, softly pressed his mouth to her lips. She felt her nipples harden as he gently slid his hand from her chin down across her breasts. There was a sigh of passion as he increased the slight pressure. She wanted him to know she wanted him, that she was wet between her legs. He kissed her softly, over and over, until she thought she would explode. She wanted to drop her hand, to slip it between his legs and feel him. She wanted to rub and feel him grow, but she didn't want to lead him. She was afraid if she led him, he might feel that she was too controlling and a man such as he needed to always be in control. This was a man of substance.

She was about to explode when she heard him say, "Debbie?"

With her mind spinning, she said, "Yes?"

"Debbie, why don't you show me the rest of the house?"

She was trembling as she said, "Oh yes, Gar," and she could hardly walk.

She felt him put his arms around her and, in one motion, picked her up as she put her arms around his neck. He carried her into her bedroom and gently placed her on the edge of the bed. She reached over and turned the night light on. As the soft light came on, they both looked at the front of him. His hardness was pressing through his trousers.

"Oh Gar," was all she could say.

She slipped out of her clothes as he took off his pants and under shorts. When they quickly disrobed, they stood up to each other and kissed with violent passion. She ran her tongue all around the inside of his mouth. As it invaded him, she was making all sorts of grunting noises. She ran her hand slowly down his skin till she felt his hardness, grasping him so hard he gasped. He slowly eased her onto the bed and she spread her legs in anticipation of his entry.

It was everything she had expected. She kept saying over and over, "Yes, yes, yes!"

Gar was gentle with her and stayed with her until she fell asleep. Then he quietly dressed and left. He drove back to his house and went directly to his bedroom.

Chapter 38

The next morning, Gar and Sammy slept late and when ten o'clock came around, Gar awoke to the smell of bacon frying. He drugs himself out to the kitchen.

"What's happening, Girine?" (a slur word used by marines).

"Well, there's the lover! Looks like you did some good last night, swabby."

"Yeah, Debbie is one sweet girl. I stopped over to her apartment for a nightcap and we danced some."

"What else did you do? Oh hell, forget I said that. It's none of my business."

Gar turned to Sammy, "Hey, anytime we can't share our lives will be when we're dead. I had a good time at Debbie's last night and I think I may go back, but I'm never going to get too serious over anyone until I'm ready to get married and that's a long way off."

Sammy put some eggs and bacon on Gar's plate and sat down to eat his also.

"I was thinking maybe we could mosey over to the "Beef and Bottle" tonight, if you care to . I'm thinking about a little blackjack . What about you?"

"Sounds right for me. I've got to call Debbie later. She fell asleep last night and I didn't want to wake her to say goodbye. I wouldn't want her to think I'm the kind that kisses and runs," Gar said as he smiled at Sammy .

That evening Gar and Sammy went to the "Beef and Bottle" for dinner. They were pleasantly surprised at the delicious food. Gar enjoyed lasagna and Sammy delighted in a New York strip steak. Afterwards, they went to the bouncer gorilla, who recognized them and ushered them into the game room. It was a little early, but there were plenty of players in attendance. Sammy took a seat at one of the blackjack dealers table She was a cute red head and gave Sammy a big smile and a nice hello. He thought to himself, this may be all right.

Gar went over to the craps table and found a spot on the end of the table. He bought in for two hundred, and was told the minimum bet was five dollars and double odds. He hadn't heard about odds, so he asked what they were. The dealer told him that when he makes a pass-line bet, like five dollars, he is allowed to make an odds bet of double the pass-line or ten dollars behind the pass-line bet. If it wins, he gets even money for the pass-line bet, but on the odds, depending what the shooter's point is, it pays a lot more.

"For instance, odds on the four or ten is two to one. Odds on the five and nine are three to two and on a six or eight, they're six to five. So, if the shooter has a ten for his pass line number and you had five at the line with ten behind it for odds, you would get paid five for the pass-line, plus twenty for the odds, since it's two to one, or you'd get paid a total of twenty five for your fifteen investment. Got It?"

Gar said he understood, and joined the game. He found craps an enjoyment because he could yell for his point just like letting off steam at a ball game and he found he made great friends while everyone was mostly against the house. They all had the same goal: beat the house!

Gar noticed that just as the stickman pushed the dice to the shooter, he would shout, "The dice are out." He asked why he said that. He was told that this was to alert the other players that the shooter had the dice and that they needed to keep their hands off the table and no more betting.

By midnight, Gar had lost his buy in and decided that he had had enough. He moved over to the blackjack tables and saw that Sammy had a nice stack of chips in front of him and the same lady dealer was conversing with him. Gar watched for a while, then stepped up beside Sammy and told him he was going home. Sammy said he was on a roll and would be along later.

On his way out, Gar ran into Toni Frantelli, who asked him if he had enjoyed himself.

"Yes I did, Toni. You have a real nice place here and I'll be back. Sammy is over there and he's having a good time also. Thanks for the invitation."

Gar waved to the doormen, went out to his car and drove back to his house.

Chapter 39

Gar had almost fallen asleep when he heard Sammy come in the back door. He guessed that he had not scored with the new girl. He had called Debbie earlier and the two planned dinner for tomorrow night. He liked her alot, but needed to go slow. It would be so easy to get heavily involved with her, and he definitely was not ready for that.

He had been giving some serious thoughts lately about what kind of employment he should get into. He still had funds that he had saved plus the VA was now sending monthly compensations, but he needed to think about his career, whatever that might be. He would always have a limp in his walk, but he was almost 90% ready for physical labor. He and Sammy discussed this often, but neither had come up with any sort of solution. They had decided to finish out the winter there, and in the spring try for big employment.

The next few weeks went by rather fast and to both of their surprise, Ski-Windham lodge offered Sammy employment as ski instructor. This paid very well with full time benefits including insurance. After the two talked about it, Sammy accepted the position and Gar encouraged him to go for it. He found it to be very exciting and he was meeting lots of pretty girls, besides nice pay.

Gar of course was seeing less of Sammy and spending more time at Toni's back room. He was becoming fairly lucky at his craps game but felt the odds were not in his favor. He also could hold his own at the blackjack table. One night after it seemed that he could do no wrong, he fell into lady luck's trap and started to bet heavy at the crap table. Before the night was over, he had lost a huge portion of his savings. He was devastated and left the table in complete disgust with himself. He went over to the bar and tried to wash his bad luck away with double Scotches. One of the gamblers that he'd seen there most every weekend came over to the bar and introduced himself. He said his name was Bob, but was known most everywhere as Bucko. He proceeded to engage Gar in conversation about craps. He told Gar that he liked his enthusiasm for the game, but to be a winner he would need to learn how to roll the dice. Gar stopped drinking and asked how that could be accomplished. After the two talked for a long time, Gar asked him to come by his house for a night cap and to talk further about how to beat the game.

Bucko told Gar all about rhythm rolling and how he needed to practice setting the dice in a certain way to attain specific numbers. He told him that he had a friend in Nevada that teaches this system and that he has several books out about casino gambling. If Gar was serious about gambling, he would put him in touch with his friend, Jerry Patterson.

Gar was very much interested and after a phone call to Jerry Patterson, Gar bought a craps system that included a manual with art drawings, four sets of dice, a portable dice table with actual casino felt padding, and a talking record that explained every detail that he needed to know. It came with a six month guarantee that if he wasn't completely satisfied, he could return everything and get his money back. Jerry told him that the Flamingo Casino opened this year and that he intended to start having clinics on how to play casino craps as soon as more casinos are built. When that time came, he would invite him to come out and attend a class for free. He also told him that Bucko was a true friend of his and could be trusted.

Chapter 40

Gar couldn't wait to receive his merchandise and begin his practice. He had made a place in the basement to put the table. When it arrived, everything was just as Jerry had described. The dice were casino size and four different colors so that in practice he could see how each die traveled in the air. He measured off the correct distance to throw from and used a small table to set the die on. Everything had to be exactly as it would be in a casino. Sammy helped him get it all set up and was his best fan. Of course, Sammy was learning to toss the dice too. Sammy was not as interested in gambling as Gar. He did enjoy things that Gar liked. He would much rather teach skiing than gambling.

After several weeks of devoted practice and a few phone calls to Bucko , to clarify why the dice weren't reacting right , he was ready to try his luck at the Beef and Bottle."

Bucko told Gar he would drive up that weekend and he wanted Gar to wait before going to play for real, so he could critique his throws.

When Bucko arrived, the two went directly to the basement where Gar proceed to demonstrate what he had learned from his latest practice. Bucko could see that Gar was doing very well, but he also could see that more disciplined practice was needed before heavy betting would be allowed.

"You still have alot more practicing to do before you try for casino money, plus you'll need to experience some losses to know that you will not always win. You will be able to accurately throw the dice, but there is always an element of the unknown that you need to be aware of. For instance, when shooting for the far back wall, you will see where the player at end has put a stack of his chips right where your dice land. You can't tell him to move them. You need to avoid them. Also as you are doing well, maybe the stick man will lower his stick into your line of vision. He may do this on purpose to distract you. If you are taking too long to set the dice, the boss might yell at you to hurry up. There are several ways for us to handle these situations discreetly, so as not to take you out of your rhythm or zone. I am here to teach you that today. You need to go out to Las Vegas and attend one of Jerry's clinics, but in the meantime, I will try to teach you enough to get you started in the right direction. I also want you to practice with chips and get used to a betting series. Have yourself a real game here in your basement, with play chips and keep track of every roll. Document all your tosses and see what numbers come up more frequently. This way you will recognize a trend, and you will establish a ratio of so many rolls before the seven shows. That's called your SRR, or sevens to roll ratio. I suspect your SRR is about five or six. Mine is about ten, but at one time I had it up to about twelve to one. We will go over to Toni's back room and I want you to shoot, but I only want you to bet on your pass line point. Do not make any other place bets. This way I can see how you play under pressure, but we won't lose much. Then when I have the dice and I appear to be on, we can bet on all the numbers, thereby we should make back that bankroll that you lost a few weeks ago, OK?"

"Sounds good to me, Bucko, and I sure do appreciate everything you have done for me. I only hope I can make it up to you someday."

"You will, Gar. If I didn't recognize your desire, I wouldn't bother, but you have everything that's needed to be a successful player. Later you'll need to learn how to read the blackjack tables and card counting for diversification. I'll help you there also."

After some more practicing, they drove through town to the "Beef and Bottle" and went directly into the back room. It was Saturday night and the place was busy with those who had driven in from the big city. Gar was able to find a spot at SR2 or two positions right from the stickman. Bucko was able to move in right next to the stickman, or SR. When the dice came to Gar, he put a ten dollar chip on the pass line. Then he set for a seven. He tossed and hit the 4-3 seven.

"Winner!" yelled the stickman.

Next, he rolled a new come-out number of 5. He set the dice for 3-2 on top and rolled a 9 then 3, then the 5.

"Winner!" yelled the stick man.

"Hey we got us a shooter here. Get your bets down. Dice are out and he's coming out again."

This time he rolled a 9. Then he rolled a 12, 3, 12 and a 7.

"Seven out," yelled the stick man, "New shooter coming out."

Bucko took the dice and put ten on the line.

"Ten on the world bet also."

He then set the 6-5 on top and rolled the 6-5 or eleven, getting paid for both the world bet and the pass-line. He made the same bet and rolled a 12, thereby losing the pass-line, but was paid $52 for the world bet.

Gar whispered to Bucko, "What's a world bet?"

"It's one bet on each the 2, 3, 11, 12, and the 7. If anyone hits, you get paid. I'll tell you more about it later, just follow my lead and bet the same. I feel like I'm getting zoned in. Do not talk to me anymore while I have the dice."

Bucko's next number was a 9, for his point. He then told the dealer that he wanted $25 each on the 4, 5,10 and $30 each on the 6 and 8. Gar followed with the same bet. Then Bucko rolled a 4, collecting $50. Then a 6 for $35, then a 5 for $35, then he rolled his point of 9, collecting $10 for the pass-line and $30 more for his double odds bet. Gar was right with him all the way.

Bucko was back to $10 pass-line, and another $10 world bet. Next he set for a world number and hit the11 again, collecting on both. He told the dealer to raise up his world bet to $20. He hit a 12, losing the pass-line but collecting $104 for the world.

He said, "Parlay the world bet."

This meant putting all the win back on the world bet. He hit the 12 once more, losing the pass-line but collecting $720 and down or off the world bet. Gar could hardly contain himself and the table came alive with excitement.

Bucko set just for a number and got a 10 for his P/L (pass-line) number. He still had his place number bets up but he told the dealer to move the money on the 10 to the. He then put $20 behind his P/L bet for double odds. He proceeded to rolled a 6 and told the dealer to press the 6. Then the dealer doubled the bet from $30 to $60. He then hit the 8 and pressed that amount also. Then he came right back for an 8 and collected $70. He hit the 5 and pressed that also. He then hit his point 10 and collected another $50. He now put $25 on the line and got a point of 5, and put $50 behind, for odds. Then he moved his place bet of #10 over on the #5. He hit #4 and pressed it up to $50, then hit the 8 and pressed it up to $120. He next hit the10 and collected $100. He then hits the 9 and pressed it to $50. Next he hit the 8 again for $140. Next the 6 and pressed it to $120. He then hit the his p/l # 5 collecting another $100. He then puts $100 on the P/L and hit a 5 again and put $200 behind for odds. He then hit the10 and pressed it up to $100, then hit the 8 for $140. Next came the 6 and he pressed up to $240, next the 9 and pressed up to $100, then hit the 6 for $280. The place was wall to wall with everyone cheering and yelling for the shooter. Bucko winked at Gar every time he hit a number and other than that, they did not speak. Bucko made bets for the dealers and they were all pulling for him. They made sure no one tried to squeeze in beside him or to jostle him when he shot the dice. Gar was amazed how Bucko had complete control of the table by making bets for the dealers. When they were paying out the bets, Bucko would simply look down at the table, avoiding eye contact with anyone and not engaging in conversation. He was staying focussed on making the next roll and to keep his rhythm rolling.

When he finally sevened out, everyone in the place gave him a nice round of applause, even the dealers.

Bucko and Gar cashed out and went into the restaurant for a late dinner. Gar had cashed in nearly $1500 and knew that Bucko's was more, but it wasn't proper to ask him. Gar told Bucko that he certainly did learn how to make money this night. No amount of practicing could ever teach him of what he just saw.

Bucko told Gar, "It's important, when you are the shooter, to keep your thoughts on making good throws. Try not to talk to anybody, except to make bets, or you might lose your rhythm or focus. We call it being "in the zone". Many of the professional players think of a happy place as they pick up the dice. This will automatically send you into your zone. My happy place is a waterfall. When I'm trying to stay focused, I think of a large waterfall, like the Niagara Falls, or sometimes I can just say the words and I go into a zone. As you start to set the dice you take a deep breath and exhale. Then as you start, you throw you inhale and just before you let them go, you exhale and hold your breath. It's a four step process that you need to work on. It helps for a perfect toss. This will become second nature as your skill improves. When I come back in two weeks, I want us to try the team play that I use with good players."

They talked about this for another hour before they left for Gar's house and Bucko returned to the hotel where he had rented a room for the weekend. Gar waited for Sammy to come in from work and they talked about what had just happened with Bucko. Gar was so hyper that he doubted he could ever get to sleep. Sammy was more interested in telling Gar about the cute blond that he met today and she agreed to have dinner with him tomorrow after work.

Chapter 41

The winter was passing too fast and Christmas was only a week away. They promised the Cross family and the Grimes' they would drive back down two days before Christmas and stay till after New Years Eve. The boys shopped in the city of Catskill which was only twenty miles from Windham and were all ready for the trip over in the morning. Gar had been seeing Debbie often and had left her gift at her house. He had dated several other girls, but no one in particular.

Early in the morning, they left together in Sammy's car His Ford was newer than Gar's Chevy and there wasn't a need for two cars. Besides, Mr. Grimes always insisted that Gar use his new Lincoln. They wondered how Sandy was getting along at his new job and if he was still going out with that rehab nurse. Sammy reiterated that his mother told him on the phone that Sandy was doing very good and it would not be a surprise if he married that pretty nurse. She took very good care of him and his disability was not an issue with her.

Sammy went into the Grimes' home with Gar and said hello to everyone there, wishing them a Merry Christmas. The two families planned to get together for dinner after Christmas for a family reunion at a place not yet agreed on. Sandy was asked to bring his pretty nurse over for that party also. He had an apartment close to his office and promised to be home the day before Christmas to be with his family and to see his pals.

Everyone was glad to see the boys. Mrs. Grimes asked Sammy to stay for lunch, but he declined, wanting to get over to his home where the Cross's were expecting him. Irv made a point in telling Sammy to wish them a Merry Christmas from the Grimes family and that they were looking forward to dinner with them. Sammy continued on to his home, where his parents, Chris and Betty were anxiously waiting for his return. They closed the truck terminal early and advised their dispatcher not to call them unless an emergency came up.

The Empire Trucking Company was getting bigger each year. Chris had become the manager of the Eastern division, while Betty was the office manager. The war had curtailed them from buying any new tractors, but now the competition was replacing all their old Rios, Whites, and Brockways with new Macs with sleeper cabs. To a truck driver they were beautiful machines.

After dinner, Chris had a long, serious talk with Sammy about his future. He wanted him to come to work for Empire Trucking. The Company would start him as an apprentice driver, only making short local runs, then train him in the big tractors that made long distance runs. If it worked out good for everyone, he would be brought in to the offices starting as assistant dispatcher and from there, anything was possible. The offer was a good one and Sammy was very interested. He asked his Dad if he could start in the spring. That way he and Gar could close the home in Windham and to also finish the term out as ski instructor.

Chris said that this was a sound idea and when he was ready in the spring, the trucking career would be ready for him, also. The more Sammy thought about it, the more excited he became. This was a great opportunity for him.

Each celebrated Christmas at home and two days later they all agreed to meet at Sandy's Manhattan apartment. He insisted that they all come to his place so he could show them how well he was doing. His friend, Sally Malone helped him arrange for a caterer to serve the meal. She brought in several flower arrangements and together they decorated a medium sized tree. Before dinner, Sandy opened champagne and when everyone had been served, he tapped on the side of his glass with his metal hand for their attention.

"I have an announcement to make to you lovely people. Actually, we have an announcement. Sally and I have become engaged to be married!"

Everyone in the room congratulated them with hugs and a toast.

"In my wildest dreams I could never imagine finding an angel like Sally, let alone her wanting to marry a guy like me! We haven't set a date yet, but we will give you plenty of notice when we do."

He had made tremendous strides with the Life Insurance company. He was a natural as a motivator and once he'd gotten passed feeling handicapped, he became a real go-getter. He knew New York Life would exploit him and his Navy past, but that is what big companies do, so why not capitalize on it? His therapist and psychologist used phrases like, "make hay while the sun shines," or "he who hesitates is lost" and, "It's a poor dog that can't bark for himself."

He took their advice and ran with it. It was amazing how dexterous he had become with his metal hands. He didn't smoke, but in one of his seminars he laid a pouch of tobacco with a few sheets of tobacco paper near it and proceeded to roll his own cigarette, even to pull the drawstrings tight, closing the bag tight afterwards. His motto was, "Nothing is impossible if you want it bad enough."

This was not a motto that he thought of by himself. He and Sally had found God through their many talks and were attending church with regularity and when the Pastor had said, "Nothing is impossible with God," Sandy took him at his word and put those words to the test.

He soon found it to be true and he wanted very much to incorporate his faith into his work, but he was smart enough to know that in selling, you must be aware that not everyone has the same beliefs and his turn-on might be a turnoff to others. So he felt this motto would work and if the opportunity was there, he would make sure God got the credit.

Gar enjoyed Christmas with the Grimes family and the love that they gave him was really something. He felt that he was so lucky to be part of this wonderful family. Rose had grown into a beautiful lady and was now preparing for college. Irv was very successful and was getting much credit for some of his modern designs and helping to promote those new tall buildings that were reaching for the sky in NYC. Mary was busy with her volunteer work at the hospital, plus taking care of the needs of her family and home. Sandy was no longer dependent upon his family and was well on his way to a successful future.

Gar was cogitating about his future. He knew it was time to get serious about a profession or a trade. Sammy told him about his decision to start with his Dad in the spring and had asked Gar if he might want to try it also. Gar had told him that at this time he wasn't interested in trucking, but acknowledged that it was a terrific opportunity for Sammy. Gar had talked with Irving about his problem, but they hadn't resolved anything yet. Irv had offered to help him get into a college, but Gar just couldn't bring himself to going that way. He resigned himself to finish the winter at Windham with Sammy and to settle on something in the spring after they closed the house.

Chapter 42

Sammy and Gar returned to Ski-Windham where Sammy continued to give instruction to fee paying customers on the art of skiing and Gar went back to practicing his hobby of winning at dice. The "Beef and Bottle" was becoming his hangout and he caught the attention of some of the heavy betters who frequented the place on weekends. One of these was an elderly man named Albert Lucia who also enjoyed playing craps. Gar had taken a break from the tables and was making small talk with the bar tender when Lucia made himself known to Gar.

"Excuse me for interrupting, but my name is Albert Lucia and I couldn't help but notice how well you manipulated those dice when it came your turn to shoot. May I ask where you learned to play with such skill?" asked Lucia as he held out his hand.

Gar accepted his hand and shook it in friendship. "Glad to meet you. I have also watched you play, but you play too rich for my blood. I've been in awe at some of those four and five hundred bets that you place. My name is Gar Savino."

"Thanks for the compliment, Mr. Savino, but I'm still curious as to how you are able to control the dice when it really counts."

"Please, call me Gar. Well, I learned from playing with my Navy friends and there isn't a better place to learn than from those tough Navy guys. Well, maybe I should include the Army guys also. We sure did have some big games whenever the paymaster caught up with us. Are you retired Mr. Lucia?"

"Call me Al, Gar. Yes, I guess you could say I'm semiretired. I own a business in Hoboken, New Jersey. I have reliable employees, so I do not have to worry about it. Toni, the owner here is a friend of mine and I come up now and then. When he comes over to the big City , we usually play together at one of the private clubs. Has anyone mentioned to you about playing there?"

"I have heard there are game clubs there but I haven't actually been invited to one yet. I'm small potatoes, Al. I do not have the resources to play with the big boys at this time."

"Well, you may not have a large bankroll, but you sure know how to control those dice, I've seen many shooters and I can spot a winner when I see one, and you have the best delivery of all them. If you have the desire, you could make a living playing this game for big money. If you'll allow me to be personal, are you employed at this time?"

"Actually, I'm not," said Gar, "My best friend is working at the ski lodge and we share his family cottage together for the winter. We will be leaving in the spring. He has a job waiting for him and I will be looking for employment then. Are you looking for someone for your business?"

"I'm always looking for good help, Gar, but I doubt that you would want to work at my shop."

"Why not? Oh, maybe I'd need a college degree."

"No, No. Excuse my manners, Gar, I didn't mean it to sound that way. I was referring to the fact that my business is in garbage. I own a waste management operation. We only handle garbage and trash. It would not be a job for someone with your good looks or your talent. No, I had something else in mind, but I need to know you better before I'm ready to discuss it with you. I don't want this to sound mysterious, Gar, but this is something I've just now thought about and I need a little more time. I probably am jumping the gun, as they say, and should not have said anything to you until the time was right. Will you let me get back to you on this?"

"Sure thing Al, I've got all the time in the world. In the meantime Let's go back to the tables for another session."

"I think I will be heading back, Gar. I have reached my stop loss for tonight, besides I really wanted to meet and talk with you, and I've done that. I will be back up here on Friday night. Could we have dinner in the dining room, say seven PM?"

"That would be fine with me, Al."

They shook hands and Al started for the door. Gar saw him nod towards two big bruisers as he left and they immediately followed him out. Gar thought that was strange but he got involved in the crap game and dismissed the thought for more important things.

Chapter 43

Gar kept up his practice with the materials Jerry had sent him and when Bucko came again, he was now proficient enough to set for hardy numbers and the come out seven-eleven. Bucko also taught him how to bet and set for the come-out "world" numbers.

"By golly you sure are a quick learner, Gar. You are about ready to make some real money. Which leads me to talk to you about winning big. Let's sit down a minute and let me fill you in on a few things."

They both drew up a chair at the table and Bucko started to tell the rookie the ins and outs of big time gambling. He told him there was both a right and wrong time for winning. He made him aware that there were times when winning too much at these small operation back rooms would cause problems. It was possible that the owners would cause bodily harm to winners after they were away from the gaming rooms.

"They employ professional people to do those sort of things ," he explained, "You either have to have muscle behind you or you need to play where you are certain that you wouldn't get whacked if you won. Even here in this little town of Windham. If you take a large win out of here, you are certain to meet up with some sort of accident sooner or later. If you see a gambler who wins, you can be sure he has someone watching his back."

"Hey, stop right there," said Gar," Just the other night, a nice guy introduced himself and he really liked playing craps with me. We had a nice chat, and he asked how I learned to play craps so well. I told him from the Navy and I got the idea that he was about to ask me to work for him in some sort of gambling deal, but he said he wanted to know me better before he could tell me more. I said OK. Then, when he left, I noticed these two big gorillas follow him out after he gave them the nod. Do you think they were his, what you call, muscle?"

"Oh yeah," said Bucko, "You might have just been contacted by one of the big guys. Do you remember his name?"

"Yeah, it was Al, uh, Albert Lucia. He said he had a waste management company in Hoboken, New Jersey."

"Yep, he's a heavy hitter. I've heard of him. I even saw him play once. He's sort of bald and about sixty years old, right ?"

"Yeah, that's him. What should I do if he comes back with some kind of deal about playing craps. Is he bad news or what?"

"I don't think he's bad news for you Gar, I was only talking to you about how these money guys usually have someone with them for some type of protection. Don't be confused with the bad guys that bust your head if you welch on paying a debt. Which brings me to advise you not to make bets, borrow money, or get involved with anyone in this gambling world that you do not know. Even if you do know them it's best not to borrow or bet without having the bankroll to back it up."

Gar looked at Bucko with a question on his mind, "Say, Bucko, do you think I need an agent or a partner, if

I get good enough to play as a business or become professional?"

"You are almost good enough to become a professional now, but you need more exposure time at the tables. You need to be more aware of the little things and the jargon that transpires as the game progresses. This can only be acquired by experience. You might want someone like your best friend Sammy ."

"No. Sammy has already told me he doesn't have the desire to gamble all the time. He has a good job offer with his Dad this spring. I do know someone that I like who would make a nice partner, though," said Gar.

"Well, that's great. Does he or she have the desire for this sort of thing?"

Gar turned and looked directly into Bucko's face and said, "Gee, I don't know, do you?"

"What? You mean me? You don't want me. I'm too old for you. I would slow you up. I've made my mark. I'm only playing for the love of the game and the fun at the tables."

"Hey, you're not too old and you are not slow. Besides, you have a world of knowledge stored in that noggin of yours and if you let me team up with you, I would be so honored. We could make one hell of a team."

"You really think so? Tell you what. Let me think on that for a while. I'll let you know my decision when I come back next week, OK? In the meantime go slow with Al Lucia until we meet later on."

"Right you are, Bucko!"

Chapter 44

Later that night Gar and Bucko played at the "Beef and Bottle" and were able to take a nice profit for their efforts. They were careful not to hit the place too hard and mess up the nice playground. Gar usually would drive over to the lodge and see Debbie before going home, unless it was too late, then he would stop by her apartment for a night cap of scotch. She would have very much liked to have Gar more attentive to her, but he had made it clear that he was crazy about her as a friend and a serious relationship was not something he wanted. She didn't want to hear this but had reluctantly accepted the situation if she wanted to continue seeing him.

Gar was by far the best looking guy that Windham had ever seen. His six foot body was all man and his black wavy hair accommodated his Clark Gable face. Debbie was happy just to have him touch her. He could turn her into jelly with that beautiful smile. What was amazing to her was that Gar didn't know that everywhere he went the girls broke their necks, getting another look at him. His gentle manner and soft voice made it so easy for people to instantly like him. The Mayor had invited him and Sammy over for a get together some months ago and ever since then, they seemed to be at every party that the important citizens held. It was as if the town had embraced the Heroes and made them their favorite people.

Gar and Sammy both agreed that it would be tough leaving this wonderful community and its fun loving people and they would need to thank them and promise to return next winter.

The next Friday at five minutes to seven, Gar strolled into the dining room of the "Beef and Bottle" restaurant. He was surprised to see Al was already waiting for him at the corner table, waving a friendly hand to get his attention.

Gar started towards his table and deliberately scanned the rest of the room to see if Al's big boys were near. Sure enough, on the opposite side of the room sat the same two guys that Gar saw follow Al when he left last week.

Al stood up when Gar approached, extending his hand.

"Good evening Gar. Nice to see you again."

They shook hands and Gar said,"Thank you, it's nice to see you also."

"Care to join me for a cocktail before dinner?" asked Al as he motioned for the waiter.

"Yes, I'll have a scotch and water."

Al told the waiter their order and then engaged Gar in small talk of the weather, traffic, and skiing.

When the drinks were before them he raised his glass and said, "To us, and future winnings!" and they touched glasses in friendship.

"To us," repeated Gar.

"Well now, I know I must have sounded mysterious at our last talk and I apologize for that, but I needed more time to form my ideas. I think I let my mouth get ahead of my brain. Anyway, I'll not keep you in suspense any longer. Gar, Here's what I have in mind. I would like to form a partnership with you. By that I want to make money, big money, and I want to do it by playing craps. I am not skilled at having any control over the dice. You do! On the other hand, you don't have a large bankroll. I do! So I'm suggesting we team up as partners. I supply the cash for the bankroll , and you supply your knowledge and play to win. You do not have to bring any money into the deal. I pay everything. We stay at the best hotels and eat at the best restaurants. Everything we need, we take from the expense account. The split is this. It's a three-way split. One third for you, one third for me and one third for expenses. Profit is an easy way to figure. We simply subtract the amount that we buy -in from the amount we cash in at. If we have a bad night, I will take the loss the first night. If we have a loss two nights in succession, you will have to pay one third of the loss from the next profit night. Is there any questions?"

"Only one, Al, I know you are taking a chance on a new player like me, but after I become seasoned and more proficient will you increase my percent? In other words, will you provide an incentive for me to improve or is this the ironclad deal?"

"I hadn't thought that far yet Gar, but that's an important point and I will think on it and get back to you on that. Anything else?"

"Yes. If either one of us decides that we need to end our partnership, will there be any problem? I couldn't help but see that you always have two bodyguards with you everywhere you go. This doesn't bother me, but I would need to know every detail before I become partners with anyone."

"Oh those boys have been employed by me for years. They will not harm you. I still have a numbers game in operation and these boys run errands for me. You have my word that if you ever want out, all you have to do is say so and we part friends. On the percentage, I think maybe it's negotiable. This is the first time I've ever attempted to try this with craps, so we'd need to be able to talk to one another and see how it goes. No matter what you and I will always be honest to each other."

"That sounds fair enough, Al, but something this big needs alot of thought. How soon will you need an answer?"

"Let's say you give me your answer next Friday night. I'll be here the same time. We can have dinner again and maybe play later, OK?"

"OK, next week will be just fine."

They left the restaurant and went into the rear gaming room. They played craps for a while, then Gar said his goodbyes and drove back to his house where he put a call in to Bucko. They agreed to see each other the next day.

When Bucko arrived the next day around one o'clock, Gar had the coffee hot and was eager to talk with his friend. He had been wrestling all night with his conversation with Al. He had already talked with Sammy about what Al had said. This was a huge undertaking, and he certainly didn't want to make a mistake. Bucko wanted to hear every word. Then they discussed the pluses and minuses about the deal.

"Well," said Bucko, "like I've said before, alot of money can be made that way, if the partnership is built on trust. You are young at this game and it's a tough grind. Unless you are experienced or know how to handle the small crises that come up , you could get eaten alive. The places that you would be playing at most are illegal joints, just like the one here. The best place for you would be at the casinos, but there are none here in the east. In New Orleans, there are gambling rooms or houses as well as in Chicago. Las Vegas, Nevada opened their first casino this year. It's called the Flamingo. I'm told by insiders that three other casinos called the Sahara, The Sands, and The Desert Inn will be built in the near future. That, of course, is in the future. If you really want my opinion, I would suggest you put a hold on your professional gambling debut until there are more casinos built. Our friend, Jerry Patterson has told me it's only a matter of a few short years before we will see casinos built in every major city. I know this is probably not what you wanted to hear, but you are a young man with tremendous talent and you can continue to keep up your practice or play at your convenience until the time is right. In the meantime, try finding a career that you can always fall back on that will give you an income while you are waiting."

Gar listened intently and carefully digested every word. He was not surprised by Bucko's wise advise for he, too, was just a little uncomfortable with hooking up with someone like Al until he knew him better or had more experience at the game.

"You make a lot of sense, Bucko. Sammy sort of indicated the same when we talked last night. So I think I'm going to take your advice and sort of cool it for a while. I might try looking for a job when Sammy and I close this place for the summer in April."

"I think that makes alot of sense," agreed Bucko.

That next Friday, Gar had dinner again with Al Lucia and very tactfully told him he had decided not to form any partnership for a while and if he was willing, maybe sometime in the future they would become partners. To his surprise, Al was very receptive of his answer and didn't try to change his mind. He wished Gar luck in locating other employment and gave him his card and asked him to call any time he was ready to talk about the deal again.

The winter went fast. Just as the snow was disappearing and the spring rains were bringing out those beautiful flowers, our heroes were closing up the house until next winter. They had been making the rounds thanking every one for their friendship, hoping to see them again next season. Debbie cried when Gar finally said that he was leaving in the morning. She knew he was leaving and had tried for a more lasting relationship, but it just didn't happen.

Chapter 45

Sandy and Sally were married that spring and the June bride was beautiful. Her gorgeous white gown with that splendid 10 feet of train was a sight to behold. Sandy had decided on tuxedos for the men. There was much conversation when he announced he would not settle for anything less than both Sammy and Gar would be his best men. The Pastor had said that no one has two men as their best man, but Sandy was so adamant about it that he finally just shook his head and said OK, and The First Baptist Church of Queens became the first to accept two best men in a wedding.

The church was packed with friends of both families plus those that wanted to see how the ring ceremony would be handled, especially since that famous columnist Walter Winchell had put in the paper about the wedding of one of America's Heroes, and how he had lost his hands in the war. But this was not a problem for Sandy, for he had become so dexterous from showing how he could roll cigarettes in his training classes, that this was a piece of cake for him. Afterward a grand reception was held at the Grimes home, with all the trimmings.

Sandy had become one of the icons of his insurance company and his vice-presidential position was bringing him a very nice salary. Sally continued as a nurse and they agreed that she would stop working when they decided to have children.

Sammy decided to take employment with the Empire Trucking Co. where his father had now become a partner in the ownership and his mother was office manager. The company was located in Brooklyn and their big trucks with sleeper cabs traveled nationwide. Sammy had tried to get Gar to come to work there, but Gar had declined, stating that he just didn't have the desire for trucking at this time. He appreciated the offer from Mr. Cross and told him that it wouldn't be fair to the company unless he could give 100 percent to the job.

Sammy rode with the local drivers for a few months, then after learning how to find the right gears, maneuver through traffic and how to jockey or back-up those big rigs up to the loading docks, he finally was given a truck of his own and all the responsibilities that went with it. His father had long discussions with him about his future and had laid out a path for him to follow. Driving the trucks and knowing the routes was the first step to completely learning everything from the ground up. He enjoyed the challenge, and the pay was great. The best part was that Sammy really liked the work and he made friends fast. He was dating but he hadn't become serious with anyone yet. He was living at home and was starting a little nest-egg for future expenses.

Gar took his time trying to find some type of employment that would satisfy his desire of excitement or his need for the unknown that would fill that deep down passion for something. Just what was it?

He spent countless hours by himself trying to understand what it was that seemed to be gnawing at his soul. He thought maybe he should become a craps gambler, but he knew Bucko was right, when he advised Gar to hold off on this until he had more experience. He understood that until he was on top of his game, there would be many peaks and valleys that he would have to pass through. Probably more valleys than peaks. So he ruled that out or at least shove this to the back of his priorities for the time being.

He had many discussions with Sandy's dad, Irving about his employment, and Irving wanted to pay for Gar to go to college until he could decide what he wanted most to do. But Gar wasn't leaning in that direction either. He felt he needed more physical exertion to get rid of that magnetic pull that was driving him nuts.

Chapter 46

After weeks of talking they both agreed to a compromise. Gar was to accept any employment that he cared to for up to two years. Then if he hadn't fully decided on a career, he would attend college and get a professional degree. This satisfied them both and Irving would still pay for his tuition, a wonderful solution to his dilemma.

Gar saw an ad in the local newspaper for a salesman at the Queens Sears Roebuck store and the next day he hired on as a salesman in their kitchen planning department.

After a week of learning the ropes, he would put time in on the floor selling sinks and cabinets and picking up leads to go out to homes and measure for built- in cabinets that were needed for the kitchen. He was learning how to sell, how to measure, how to special order plastic counter tops, and how to use his brains. He found that he liked dealing with the public. Was this going to satisfy his long desire to be on the move, or wanderlust ? No! He still felt that certain unexplainable force.

In one of his discussions he described it to Irving like this, "It's like that story of Buck in Jack London's book, 'Call of the Wild' where a big lovable dog, Buck ,a big St. Bernard, had at one time fallen in love with this beautiful she-wolf, and she wanted Buck to stay with her, but Buck knew he had to stay with his master, the trapper, that also loved him. So every time Buck would hear the wolves at night, he was tormented with this pull, this desire to run away to the hills, while at the same time he knew he could not abandon his master."

"That's a good metaphor," said Irving, explaining the word to Gar.

"Yeah, I guess that would be one. My, I sure am getting smart in my old age." said Gar with a large grin across his face.

He quickly apologized to Irving, who waved him off by having a good laugh with him.

Gar happened to be looking in the want ads one day and came across this ad by Socony Vacuum Oil Company, where they were looking for healthy, energetic men for the Eastern Pipeline Division. They would start as laborers and those with ambition and desire, could advance to machinery operators after serving as journeymen or trainees. Some travel would be necessary.

This struck a nerve with Gar, who answered the ad at once. He was granted an interview and after understanding the requirements, wages, etc. He was hired. He gave notice to Sears and later reported to the pipeline office at Rochester, New York.

Chapter 47

Gar had rented a room by the week in Rochester and a refrigerator and range came with the room. Also if he cared to, he was allowed to fix his own meals. He had been told previously he could either bring a lunch or if not, he could share the cost of having a runner bring sandwiches and sodas to the job-site, which this week was near Batavia ,NY. He chose not to bother taking a lunch with him.

The home-base for the pipeline was a large warehouse on the south part of the city. Here they kept barrels of a tar-creosote type of solid material that was used for coating the pipe. Also stacks of 6 inch pipe, and all kinds of equipment . All of the workers would arrive in time to clock in at 7 A.M. From here they were transported out to the job site by truck. One of the flat bed trucks had a large covered building fastened to the bed that resembled a miniature house, or a oversized doghouse so in this dog house that had bench seats, the workers sat while they were carried out to the job.

The Eastern pipeline division for Socony Vacuum Oil company mainly started from Paulsboro, New Jersey, where the crude oil was received by tankers, then it was transformed into many products at this huge plant, known as "The Refinery". The process that changes crude is often referred to as the Cracking unit in the refinery. From this Crude oil comes regular and high test gasoline, kerosene, diesel, naphtha, motor oils , waxes, and many other useful products. The gasoline, kerosene and diesel liquids are stored in those huge tanks until they are pumped out as orders come in. The different products all have different flash-points, smell, and weights.

The various products are pumped from the Refinery Plants through the many pipe lines along the way into various bulk plants that were stretched all the way to Buffalo, NY. To help push the product, there were Booster pump stations built along the way that kept the pressure constant. To separate one type of product like gasoline from kerosene, the pumpers would send a batch of Naphtha, or another type of separator between products. A "Gauger" would be alerted at the receiving point, taking samples when a change of product was expected to arrive. It was his responsibility to switch these products to another tank by opening and shutting valves.

The company was experiencing an enormous amount of leaks lately and from their testing and research it was determined that as the product traveled through this steel pipe, it was developing a electromagnetic phenomenon. The pipe was pitting and becoming old before its time. To replace the entire line would be a disaster. So they found that if they recoated the worst sections and at various areas along the line, build a run-off for the electrolysis, by way of electrolysis beds, they could save the pipe and the unbearable cost of total replacement.

After the engineers had decided which areas to repair or replace, and they mapped it out for the superintendent, the big back-hoe digger would be dispatched by way of a large lowboy flatbed trailer to that area. The operator and his Swamper would always be a day or two ahead of the repair crew. A Swamper was someone who was an operator's helper. He would help the operator in anything that the operator needed, such as hooking cables watching for power lines, removing fences and making sure that the ditch diggings were in a straight line. He also had to clean the tractor treads at quitting time and make sure the machine was fueled and change it's oil.

Next, one of the big Boom-Cats (a Caterpillar tractor with a long side boom) would raise the pipe from the ditch while crew members had to place skids across the ditch under the pipe. Then the pipe was lowered onto the skids. This way the pipe would be high enough to work on. The skids were 4 by 6 inch wooden planks and each weighed about a hundred pounds .It took a real man to toss these around. This was where Gar began his duties with the crew. After the first day, he was wondering if maybe he had made a mistake, because every bone and muscle in his body was asking him to quit. But after a few tough days he was starting to get used to the tough work and all his fat was becoming muscle.

Chapter 48

After the pipe was lain out in sections, which some might be a half mile or more, the cleaning machine was lifted onto the pipe and the operator would start cleaning debris. This machine had large metal brushes that rotated the pipe and when it passed over it left the pipe so clean that all pits and bad places were easy to find. If the section was not to be replaced, then the welder and his swamper would weld the bad pitted spots, making sure not to burn a hole into the pipe. The cleaning machine would only clean enough pipe the crew could dope that day, because if it was not all doped that day the clean pipe that had lots of scratches on it would rust overnight.

At the time of doping, the dope wagon that held all this hot stuff, would be pulled, which was on wide runners that looked like skis, to the area alongside the pipe. This dope wagon had kerosene burners under the dope pot and this way it was always very hot.

Each time the cleaning machine would come close to the skids, the big side-boom Cat would raise the pipe slightly and a crewman would remove the skid and after it passed over, the pipe was again lowered onto the skids. The crews had to repair the bad sections, clean the pipe, weld the bad pits and even replace sections that were too far gone. Then they recoated the pipe with a tar-based type of creosote which was heated to 375 degrees, and had to be delicately poured by hand from buckets making sure it totally surrounded the pipe. Then, a wrapper came along and would wrap the pipe with a coating that looked like a roll of tarpaper. All this was done as quickly as possible while the tar was still hot. It was at this time that alot of accidents occurred. At coating time, there were men carrying buckets of hot tar to the pipe, which was up on skids, a man on each side of the ditch or pipe holding some tar paper as sort of a sling to catch the tar as it hit the pipe in order for the undersides be coated as well. The men were permitted to apply a coating of salve or cream to their faces to help ward off the burn that came as the steam or vapor was constantly in their face. They wore long sleeve shirts, buttoned at the neck, and gloves with gauntlets, but still the vapor burnt their faces. It reminded Gar of the times when he was in the Navy and as a new recruit, they were ordered to remove their gas masks, then put them back on, just to feel how the tear gas made the skin smart and burn. The tar substance came to be called "dope",and it was always poured in the last part in the afternoon, so the crew could clean up before going home. Most headed for the first bar room after returning to base, in order to get some relief from that burning sting.

One day as the crew was applying the "dope", the pourer's foot slipped and he accidentally splashed alot of the dope into the gauntlet part of one of the worker's gloves, allowing it to run down inside of his glove. He gave out an earth shattering scream and when they removed his glove, the skin came off as well. They immediately rushed him to a local hospital, but the poor man went through horrible pain before he got there.

Chapter 49

Gar was very fascinated by these big Caterpillar tractors and thought that to be an operator on one of these Cats, would really be something. One day, the swamper of one of the side-booms, didn't show up for work and Gar had expressed his desire to be a swamper, so the superintendent told Gar to take over. The operator's name was Ansil and he taught Gar what he was supposed to do. Gar worked hard and his work did not go unnoticed. Ansil's original swamper didn't show up the second day, so Gar, again, was told to take over his duties. Because the helper hadn't asked for the time off, he was fired the next day. This was a break for Gar. He worked hard and asked lots of questions. He was determined to learn how to operate the Cat-Boom.

As the crew gradually worked closer to the base camp, he asked the foreman if it was OK for him to drive to work with his own car. He volunteered to help the dope man chop dope in the mornings. The dope was in large steel barrels and it was in solid form, so it would be chopped into chunks and then placed into the dope kettle where it could be heated into liquid form. Gar was glad to help chop up the dope, but his real reason for coming to work early was to learn how to run the Cat Boom while no one was around. Before long, he could start the machine and manipulate all the pulleys and gears. He had sworn the other guy to secrecy and if ever a chance came his way, he would be ready.

After the pipe was repaired and doped, the skids were removed and the Cat-Boom would lower it back into the trench. After it was lowered into the ditch, a bulldozer would push the dirt back over the hole and smooth out the landings. Some of the time all of the pipe would not go back into the ground. That was because steel pipe will expand or stretch when pulled from the ground, especially in warm weather. When that happened, a section was left open overnight and during the night the pipe would shrink back some and cause it to take its place in the ground. If it didn't go back down by itself, skids were lain on it and the bulldozer would drive upon it and its weight would be enough to push it down.

At 11:30 each day, one of the truck drivers would go to the local convenient stores and buy 2 or 3 loaves of bread, sliced cheese, sliced ham & baloney, potato chips, and soda. Then at noon everyone stopped for a half hour lunch and would sit under the closest shade tree. One of the men always brought his own lunch and every day he would remove a hard boiled egg from his sack. He made sure everyone was watching and with a sly grin on his face, he would hit himself on the head with this egg. Then with the eggshell cracked, he would peel the shell and eat the egg. One day, when no one was looking, one of the crew replaced the egg with a fresh one and as they were all seated under the shade tree, the man reached in and took out the egg and after removing his hat, he hit the egg on the side of his head. Immediately raw egg ran down across his ear and neck. He sat there in disbelief, staring at the mess, while the rest of the crew were laughing hard.

He finally realized what happened and he began laughing also. He was able to take the joke in stride. The crew was always pulling small pranks on each other.

Chapter 50

One morning when Gar had gotten to work early and was moving the Cat around, the foreman arrived at the job site before Gar was able to return the Cat to its original spot. After he shut the machine off, the foreman wanted to know why Gar was running the Cat. He had to confess how he had learned to run the big Cat and it was his desire to one day become an operator. The foreman chewed him out real good, then later he told Gar if an opportunity came up, he would give him a chance to try out on the Cat.

The season for pipe cleaning was closing and fall weather was about over. The pipeline crew was being transferred into a winter maintenance program. Many of the laborers were laid off until spring. Gar was one of the lucky ones that the company wanted to keep. The company was installing new pumping stations at Waterloo and Flemingsville, in New York and one in Lehighton, Pennsylvania. The buildings were partially installed, but the piping, pumps, and many valves would have to be installed by the maintenance crew.

Gar saved his money and bought a new Hudson Hornet. It was a beautiful maroon speedster. He enjoyed the feel of speed and would, on occasion, open it up on those long straight stretches when he traveled back into the Big City on weekends to see Sammy, Sandy and the families. On one weekend, he traveled back to Windham and spent some time with Debbie Morton. She was delighted to see him and convinced him to stay at her apartment all weekend. She told him she had not dated anyone since he'd last seen her and thought about him all the time. He told her he had feelings for her but wasn't ready for a full commitment.

She said she would wait for him and that she loved him very much. Gar tried to persuade her to date and not wait for him, because he didn't want her to get hurt. Besides, he knew that there were many things that he wanted to do and places that he wanted to go, and being tied down was not in the cards. Debbie told him she understood and was willing to wait .She reminded him that if he didn't love her, he wouldn't have come back to see her this time, and from the things he had been through during the war, he just needed a little more time. She agreed not to push him for a commitment.

"I am never going to give up on you. You are my man."

"OK, Deb, I just hope you know what you're doing."

One of Gar's problems was he could never find anyone that knew anything about his family. The Orphanage had always told him that he had no relatives, that there wasn't any one left in his family after his parents died. They said they had even tried to trace his mother, whose name was previously Landry, but hadn't gotten anywhere. Gar still wanted to go back to where he spent his first few years and perhaps try one more time to talk to the orphanage people. There was something that kept pulling on his heart and he knew he had to go back or else he would be tormented the rest of his life until he satisfied that unknown desire.

On a Friday afternoon, he checked into the Langwell Hotel. Things sure were different. Elmira put its trolly cars in moth balls and had a very nice Bus transportation in its place. The Hotel was slated to be torn down soon to make way for a Clemens's Parkway through the center of town but business was good and Gar was delighted that next door, Schannakers' Diner was still open for business. He remembered back a few years to the day he had run away from The Hickory Home for Children. He could still feel the strap that came across his buttox so many times before he ran. But he would have to put it all in the past and once more make a visit there to try to find a link to his ethnic background.

After a nice early dinner at Schannakers' Diner, he strolled down State Street to Water Street and noticed that the Ideal Hot Dog restaurant was still there. He noticed that the Rathbun Hotel had been torn down, though. He then strolled west on Water, past Kobackers Furniture, Rosenbaum's, the five and dime stores, Gorton Coy's Department Store, Ray Jewelers on Main Street and Izard's Department Store next to the Mark Twain Hotel at the corner of Main and Gray Streets. It was nostalgia, big time. The next day he visited The Hickory Home Orphanage only to find that it was being readied for demolition as well. He felt dejected, but maybe if this was the last closed door to his past, he might finally be able to shake that longing for answers that had been tugging at his heart strings.

"I don't need to know. I will begin my heritage from this day forward", he shouted to himself. "As God is my witness, from here to eternity, the world will know of me and my family. I will never let my name be forgotten."

With that, the tears rolled down his face as he stared into the Heavenly sky.

Chapter 51

Before going back to the Hotel for his clothes and leaving, he decided to visit a place where he had gone for a picnic years ago, while at the Orphanage. It was called Harris Hill, known for the setting for glider meets every year. In fact, Elmira had been recognized as "The Glider Capital of America." He drove to the top of Harris Hill on the northwest side of the city. At the very top, it was flat and here was where the tow planes would pull the gliders across the top to that sudden drop-off, putting them into the air quickly. It was such a sudden rush; first an airfield underneath , then in an instant, up thousands of feet into the sky, sailing out over the Chemung River and that beautiful landscape below. It was Springtime now, no Gliders, but the beauty was here.

Gar parked on the north end of the hill overlooking the town of Big Flats and could see the stretch of the Chemung River as it wound its way down from Corning. Off to his right was the Chemung County Airport. This was a magnificent thing of beauty. It wasn't any wonder the Indians fought so hard to keep this land.

After a long pause to take all of this in, Gar traveled back by going off the hill on the southwest side, following the Chemung River as it ran right through the center of Elmira, splitting the south side from the north side. He knew now why Elmira was called a beautiful city.

When he took the elevator up to his room, he noticed the elderly black man who ran the elevator was very friendly, so he engaged him in conversation and asked him if he liked Elmira. The black gentleman related how during the Civil War Elmira was known for two very historic things.

One: Elmira was a military center of vast importance to the Union cause. From the Elmira Military Depot were twenty four organizations of infantry, four Artillery Companies with 975 officers and men, six Calvary Units with 1,650 officers and men, all enrolled, equipped, trained and forwarded to the battlefields from the Elmira military point.

Two: Elmira was selected by the Union Army for it's Civil War prisoners. In 1864, barracks were set up along the Chemung River on West Water Street extending North to Huffman Street. This tract of 30 acres was enclosed by a 12 foot plank fence along the top of which was a walk and boxes for sentries. Sanitary conditions were terrible, as were all prison camps, because of the crowded conditions. Medicines were in short supply. In 1865, Smallpox broke out and in March that year, the Chemung River overflowed, flooding the entire prison camp. The Elmira Prison Camp was later renamed by many as "Hellmira."

Records showed that the Elmira Camp housed 11,916 prisoners of whom 2,994 died. Of these men, 2,973 were buried in what is now known as the National Cemetery. The burials were reverently performed by a man named John Jones. Years ago, this wonderful black man, a slave from the South, wandered into town in rags. He found friends that taught him to read and write and gave him work. Here he lived out his days. But the real significance of God's workings was how this man, John Jones, kept a careful record of every man who died at the camp, his company, regiment and state, and the location of the grave. In later years the wooden headboards which first marked the graves, were replaced by uniformed stones. Later, the families of these dead men came to have their loved ones' remains moved to their southern homes, but after finding what humane and precise care had been extended to these that had died, they decide to leave them as they were.

Gar thanked the man for all this information and told him Elmira should be proud to have him as an Ambassador. The gentleman told Gar he was related to John Jones and had volunteered much of his time to helping the Chemung County Historical Society.

Chapter 52

Gar and his crew from upper NY were helping the crew from PA finish the completion of the pumping station at Lehighton, when word from the Plainfield dispatchers came that they had an emergency.

"The pig has gotten stuck somewhere near Tuscarora, PA."

Gar at once asked how a pig had gotten in to the pipeline. He was told that a living pig hadn't got into the line. "Pig" was the name of the small device the dispatcher periodically sent through the lines to self-clean any sludge or particles that might be building up inside the lines. It consisted of alot of fine brushes that rotated as it was sent under pressure through the pipeline. It was not very long and it seemed that for the first time it had gotten hung up. They knew approximately where it was, but not exactly. The emergency was that they would not be able to pump any product from either direction, until the pig was freed-up or removed. Worst of all, they had to locate it's position first. Every man available was at once sent to Tuscarora Mountain, which was west of Harrisburg, Pennsylvania.

At Tuscarora Mountain, the men were dispatched to certain locations. They were equipped with what looked like a metal detector, but it really was a "pig" detector. They each had so many miles to walk over the entire stretch of pipeline, until the "pig" was located. The terrain wasn't flat. It started from the town of Tuscarora, then going north over Tuscarora Mountain. Everyone hoped it wasn't stuck up on that mountain, because getting heavy equipment up there wouldn't be easy. Other crew men were dispatched on the north side of the mountain and would walk south, hoping to find the "pig" before they met the team coming north.

The Line Superintendent ordered the Back-hoe digger, Side Boom Cat, Bulldozer, and Ranch Wagons be sent to Tuscarora immediately so that when the Pig was located, the machinery would be close by. The Ranch Wagon, sometimes referred to as a War Wagon or Welding Wagon, was a heavy duty, short flat bed truck with 4 wheel drive. It had a winch on the front and one in the back. It had a gas driven Welding machine mounted in back of the cab, plus both oxygen and acetylene tanks for gas welding. Welding supply boxes were mounted on either side and two heavy duty steel pipes were also on each side that could be raised to form a tripod and raise something heavy with the rear winch. There was not any place it could not go, plus it could easily travel the speed limit on the highway.

Gar's team worked its way to the bottom of Tuscarora mountain. They hoped to locate the Pig before going up that steep incline. The worst place possible would be on the side of the mountain, for the machinery. As luck would have it, that was exactly where the alarm went off on their detectors. The Scope and the metal device was telling them the Pig was jammed solid at this point. A section of pipe would have to be cut out , removed and be replaced with a new section. They informed the Super and all equipment was ordered to the mountain location. Everyone knew that from this moment on, they would be on emergency status, and no one could leave or sleep until the problem was completed. The pipeline had been shut down and if it wasn't repaired quickly, many homes and factories would have to shut down for lack of fuel.

Gar and the crew cut some trees, brush and shrub to make a way into the area for the heavy equipment. The Digger had to dig a trench on both sides of one or two thousand feet long in order to be able to raise the pipe enough to work on it . Then Gar and the other Swampers returned to the bottom of the mountain to help the operators bring up their heavy equipment.

The pump stations on both ends were able to back off the pressure to enable the workers to cut out a section of pipe above and below the Pig. The tools they used were of a special material that wouldn't allow for a spark to happen. There wasn't a problem removing the bad section of pipe with the Pig. The real problem would come when they had to weld the new section in place.

By the time they removed the old pipe and were preparing to lower in the new section before welding, 30 hours had slipped by. Every man was dead-tired. Gar was seeing men so tired that at times some one would fall into the trench as fatigue took over their body. Everyone was ordered to watch out for each other. Coffee and sandwiches were consumed as fast as a runner could fetch them. No one was allowed to be alone, even when he had to relieve himself, for fear of falling asleep and hurting himself.

After the bad section of pipe was removed and an engineer used an apparatus to suck all the fumes out , the new section was lowered into place with the Side-Boom. Welding both ends in place would complete the job. As the welders and their Swampers were placing their cables and equipment at the trench, the Cat operator, mistakenly, instead of grabbing the lever for the cable gears, he grabbed the brake and released it. The pipe and the long boom fell sideways, pinning two workers underneath. At the same time, the Cat pitched sharply to one side, throwing the operator completely out into the trench breaking his left leg and knocking him out. The men trapped under the Boom were screaming for help and the Super was yelling for someone to climb up onto the Cat and try raising the Boom. The foreman said the other operator was not here. He was bringing up the Bulldozer. By this time Gar could see that no one was there who knew how to operate the Cat, so he jumped up in it, put the cable in gear, and raised the Boom up and off the trapped workers. Lucky for them as the Boom fell, the end of the Boom landed on a pile of branches and small trees. They had sprains and bruises but no-one was killed or had broken limbs. The operator was rushed to a hospital after he was removed from the mountain. The Super gave alot of praise to Gar and told him that from this day forward that Cat was his to run if he wanted the job. Gar of course wanted the opportunity and because he taught himself last summer, he was ready and able to take over the job. The operator's pay was very good also.

When the emergency ended and the pipe was back into the ground and the bulldozer had finished covering it, a total of 36 hours had gone by. These men were ordered to a rooming house in Tuscarora, where they ate and slept before they were allowed to return to their routine jobs .

Gar was an operator and drew operators pay . Some of the workers tried to call him a Hero, but Gar wasn't having any of that. Saying that he just happened to be at the right place at the right time.

Chapter 53

Gar was getting itchy to move again. He had saved his money and made some wise investments. He created a nice nest egg for his next venture. The portable Craps table he purchased from Jerry Patterson, was used by him when time permitted. He was able to keep the muscle memory in his arm fine tuned. He learned to shoot from the left side as well. He kept in touch with his friend Bucko Bob, but he had not gone to a Casino or betting room in a long while. His investment portfolio included several shares in Socony Vacuum Oil Co, General Motors, AT&T, and Sandy convinced him to take stock in NY. Life Insurance Company.

Sammy was doing great in the Trucking business with his Dad and had recently married a nice girl from his neighborhood. There again, Sandy and Gar were the best men.

Sandy was very successful with his Insurance work and life was becoming a wonderful routine. They all appeared to have found happiness. But for Gar, he was still not satisfied. He couldn't shake that certain feeling that wanted him to keep moving. It was like a restless force that gripped his achievements and said to his inner peace, "Why are we stopping here? We still have a ways to go."

He had thought that by staying those 5 years with the Oil Co., he might have conquered his wanderlust. "Not so," came that soundless voice from within him.

He visited Debbie several times at Windham and she realized she couldn't push Gar, but she knew he cared for her. Their were times when this big handsome tough guy, this Hero from the war, would bury his head in her lap and just let the tears flow. It was always after they had enjoyed a drink or two and something might be said about starting a family.

Debbie knew his background and she found that when he broke down like this, she could see and feel his inhibitions and confining restraints leave his body. She knew that he was still suffering from the early loss of his parents and for having a fun childhood snatched away from him.

He was very much aware of how Debbie was becoming his sound board. He also was very much aware of how she kept him sane. She was the glue that held his fabric together and the last time he was with her, he made a strong commitment to her. He told her he needed his independence and a little time to do a few more things.

"If you are willing to wait, I pledge my love to you, will be forever faithful to you and we will get married."

He stressed that he didn't want her to get hurt. If she didn't feel like waiting, or if it seemed the agreement was too lopsided in his favor, she could terminate the deal.

"Gar, If this is really from your heart, I am willing to accept the conditions.

Then for the very first time Gar told her he loved her with every fiber in his body.

"Wherever I am or whatever I'm doing, I will call you every week and I will be here whenever I can, and if it's possible, I'll send for you to be with me. Anytime you need money, just ask me. From now on you are my responsibility."

She was elated, to say the least.

Gar called Bucko and asked, "Are you ready for a trip to Las Vegas?"

"I was ready a long time ago, just waiting on you. Are you still working for Socony?"

"They have granted me a leave of absence, and I can come back any time I want."

He told him he was giving his new car to Debbie and would be ready to fly out of Laguardia Airport next Friday. He also told him he made reservations for two at the Flamingo Casino-Hotel. Bucko told him that he was packing today and he would meet him at the airport.

"Lets go."

Chapter 54

Their flight left on time and after a stop in Chicago, they flew nonstop into Las Vegas. They took the shuttle to the Flamingo Hotel-Casino. After they checked in, Gar picked up the phone and asked to speak to the Hotel Manager.

"This is Mr. McClain. May I help you?"

"Yes, you can. Mr. McClain, my partner and I just checked in and we are interested in playing some craps. I was wondering if you could settle a question for us. My partner tells me that in your casino, the dice do not have to hit the back wall when they are thrown. Is that correct?"

"Of course not. Your partner is in for a surprise if he thinks that. Anyone who shoots Craps knows that the dice always have to hit the back wall for a legal roll."

Gar was trying to keep from laughing.

"I once knew a Boatswain mate who used to shoot that way. He also won alot of money that way. What do you think of someone who would do that?"

"Well, I'm sure those playing with him would straighten him out. Is there anything else I can do for you?"

"Mr. McClain, your voice sounds awfully familiar. Did you ever serve aboard an LST?"

Scotty was trying to recognize the voice on the other end of the line, "Yes, I did,I... say who is this anyway? Do I know you? Were you on my ship?"

"yeah, Scotty. I can't keep from laughing myself crazy. This is your old pal Gar Savino."

"Gar! Is that really you? Oh my God, don't move, I'll be right up."

When Gar opened the door for Scotty, the two let out a roar and held each other in a big bear-hug. They pounded each other and kept saying how glad they were to see each other. After greeting each other and introducing Bucko, they sat down and tried to bring each other up to date with their lives.

After about an hour Scotty said, "This calls for one big celebration. You guys are my guest for dinner tonight."

He went to the phone and told his secretary, "Arrange for a gourmet dinner in their steakhouse for him and his two guests, including the best champagne that they had. We have a Congressional Medal of Honor Hero in our Hotel and he's my best friend."

Scotty made sure everything went great with the meal and the service. He couldn't do enough for Gar. He was so glad to see him. When he found out he was unemployed, he offered him a job with the Hotel, but Gar quickly told him that he and Bucko were there to see the sights and do some gambling. Scotty told him that would be OK, but he didn't want him to lose his shirt. He told him gambling is for losers. He told Gar that the Hotel pays him to attract players, but most of them lose in the long run, and he just didn't want him to be amongst the losers.

After Scotty was through trying to be Gar's protector, he told him he knew the risks and was prepared for any turn of events.

"I need to know something Scotty, and I want you to be completely honest with your answer. Will you be in any sort of trouble with the Casino owners if Bucko and I happen to get lucky at the crap table?"

Scotty looked somewhat perplexed, "No , Gar, we are in the gambling business. We even encourage people to try winning. Many do, but we know we will win it back in the long run. We accept all bets and we will give "High Rollers" free food and room as incentive to stay and play with us, providing they are honest with us and the game. Cheaters have no place in our city and I know for a fact that there were some that had a few fingers cut off before being run out of town. Now, Gar, I know we haven't seen each other in years, so I don't know what you're planning, but if it's not legal and honest , we have a problem. Which is it?"

Gar took some time before he answered.

"Scotty, you and I have gone through fire together and I love you like a brother, so I guess you have a right to ask me that . My answer is that we do not cheat and we will never have a plan to defraud or a scheme to harm other players or a Casino. Having said that, I have been shooting dice for years and I believe I am good enough to make a living at it. The reason I asked you my question was that we didn't want to jeopardize your hospitality and you're friendship, OK?"

"OK, Pal. No harm done and I'm going to move you two guys up into one of the Luxury Suites. Then if you're as good as you say, just sign all meals and drinks and everything else you need to your room and it will be on us."

"Thanks Scotty. Bucko and I will be going down to take a look after a while".

Chapter 55

Around 8 PM, Bucko and Gar scouted out the crap tables. Their were six crap tables , several blackjack tables, 4 roulette tables, several poker games, and lots of one arm bandits. They found most of the crap tables were 14 feet long and the bounce seemed good.

There was two openings at one table at stick right, so Bucko and Gar moved into those slots. They bought in for $1,000 each. The dice was at the far hook to the right of Gar, meaning 3 more shooters would have their turn before Gar could shoot. The table was a $5.00 minimum and $500 max. While they were waiting on the dice to come to them, Gar went conservative and only bet on the 6&8 for $12 each. The shooter hit the 6 then 7nd out. The next two shooters didn't make a point, quickly 7nd out. The shooter next to Gar passed the dice, so he put a green chip on the pass-line, picked up the dice and set for the 7's and rolled the 4-3 win. He set them again and got the 5 for his point. He tossed out 4 green and 2 red and told the dealer, "one ten on the inside, including the point."

The dealer then placed $25 each on the 5&9 and $30 each on the 6&8. Gar set the dice and rolled the 6, collecting $35. He then rolled another 6, and said, "press the 6," now the 6 had $60 on it. He then rolled the 5, collecting $35 more. He then hit the hardway 6 (two threes), collecting $70 more and said, "betting the hard 6 and hard 8 for $25 each"

The dealers took his two green chips and put them on the hardway layout in the middle of the table. Gar hit his point 5. Collecting both pass line and the odds ($100). Gar caught Bucko's eye. He had been betting right with him, and they gave each other a wink.

Things were looking good . Gar increased his bets $50 pass line and after the point, put $100 each across the board, and after every other hit-collect, he pressed them up. He now also has $100 each on all the hardways (4, 6, 8,10). Gar pounded the 6 and 8's and got the place bets up to $500 each. He saw that he was really "ON" the hardways, so he put $300 on each and when they hit he collected $2700 each time and another $600 each off the place bet.

By now the craps table was packed and spectators were six deep, all trying to see this great shooter play. Every time he won, a huge cheer went up from the crowd. Gar was tipping the dealers with $5 chips on all the numbers, so they collected also every time that Gar did. The pit bosses in suits were watching very close to see if he was cheating and every other toss, they would change his dice. Gar didn't care, because he wasn't cheating. At one point, Bucko laughingly said, "I guess I'll not be shooting tonight."

Gar continued to shoot for another half hour, before hitting a chip at the far end and 7-out. He received a round of applause from both the dealers and the crowd. He told the dealer to "color him up" and they took all his chips and changed them to higher value chips, that was easier for him to carry over to the cashier. His total was

$17,260.00. Not bad for the first night. Bucko was right with him and he also carried over $10,000 in chips to the cashier. They were cashing in when Scotty appeared behind them, with his hand out to congratulate Gar on his big win. All three went to the lounge to celebrate.

"Well Gar, I guess you have been practicing some since I last saw you. That was quite an exhibition. Is this what we can expect every night ?" asked Scotty.

"I would like to think so, Scotty, but I'm not so naive. I know that tomorrow I might lose it all back to you, so for now, I'm just gonna enjoy the moment."

"We were lucky tonight, Scotty. Everything went our way. We want to thank you and your fine hotel for your fine room, food, and wonderful hospitality."

"You guys are welcome. We welcome your play and as long as it's honest, we will be happy to have you here. You may be interested to know that I asked the pit boss and the supervisor if they were able to spot any cheating from you guys, and they both reported you 'clean', which made me very happy, especially since they know I am the one who is comping your stay."

"Hey Scotty, you have my word there will never be any slight-of-hand trickery from either of us," said Gar. "As a matter of fact, if we spot anything that's not looking right, we will tell you or the pit boss, OK?"

"That's great, guys. Now, I've got to catch up on some work, so enjoy and I look forward to seeing you tomorrow. Oh, By the way, if it's OK by you two, I'll try to set up some time in the next day or so and we can do some sight-seeing and I will be your guide. See ya later."

Gar and Bucko shook his hand and said their farewells. Then they had another round of Scotch and compared notes . They agreed that they may have hit the Casino too hard the first night, realizing that it could put Scotty in a bad light with his boss or owners.

"Tomorrow we should probably lose some back, not alot but at least not be a winner," declared Bucko.

"I agree with that, Bucko, and I also want to see you shoot, so you can keep your arm limbered up. But I'll plan on losing some back, maybe around a grand or so."

Chapter 56

The suite on the top floor had a fully stocked wet bar, a gorgeous living room full of overstuffed furniture, a beautiful view overlooking the valley, three bedrooms all with full bathrooms, a kitchenette fully stocked, along with a refrigerator full of food.

They did not plan on cooking, because Scotty had told them that whenever they wanted to eat, just call the room service or go to any of the fine restaurants. They do not need reservations. Anything in the hotel was theirs just for the asking. Scotty told them that no one would bother them and housekeeping would never wake them in the mornings, and that when they wanted their rooms made-up or cleaned, please call the housekeeper. After a good night's sleep and ordering up breakfast, Bucko and Gar decided to wander around and see everything the casino and hotel had to offer.

As they emerged from the elevator they were struck by all the different sounds that came from the casino. The slot machines were the noisiest with the constant banging as the silver dollars were dropping into the metal buckets whenever it made a payout. They also made alot of different noises as a jackpot was hit. It was like being at a carnival with all the big pretty lights and all the crowd noises. The casino wanted all the attention drawn to any payout that happened to hit to encourage and excite the players to continue playing. The song "Baubles, Bangles and Bright Shiny Beads" must have had a casino in mind. It must be working because it was midday and there were lots of people spending lots of money. The blackjack tables were not crowded, nor were the other table games. Only one craps table was open. Most of the money players came out after dinner or after the first show. The casino had more than one showroom and they usually had a well known headliner like Sinatra, Crosby, or Hope for their drawing card. At the present time, Jimmy Durante was appearing nightly in the main showroom.

The lounge had free entertainment, and as long as customers bought drinks, they could sit in their soft chairs and be entertained by an unknown trying to be noticed.

The players at the tables and at the machines, were offered free cocktails or any beverage that they desired from one of the cocktail hostesses who were constantly asking if they could bring a player something. She gladly accepted a tip for the service.

At one end of the casino was Keno. This game provided nice chairs to sit in while players watched the big board on the wall light up as each number was called. There were 80 Ping-Pong balls in a wire see-through basket and for each game only 20 were pulled. All the player had to do was guess which numbers would be called. This was nearly impossible to do, but some did win. A player could bet on one to fifteen at a time. This game also had Keno runners, who would go into the restaurants and sell tickets to each game and return after each game with either your winnings or to sell the next game. An easy game to play and an easier way to lose, many couples found the Keno lounge an excellent place to meet, have a drink and play some while slowing down the pace.

"I think there are a couple things that we need to do, Gar."

"Oh, yeah, what?"

"One: I think that we should go downtown and start an account with one of the local banks. We both are carrying much more cash than than we should, and I don't think that we should let the Casino hold it for us. They shouldn't know all our business. We just might want to play at a different casino occasionally and we need to be smart with how we handle our money, assuming we win again. Two: I think I'll call Jerry Patterson and ask him to join us for some serious craps playing. He may want to see you and of course he has a great system on how to beat the casinos at blackjack. I talked to him last month before I knew we were coming out here and he told me he is trying to put together a few good players who could teach others how to beat the casinos with his new system on craps."

Gar was staring out into the desert and turned back to Bucko.

"I think you are right on both ideas, but getting our own banking accounts may be a very good one for us to do right away. I've been using a money belt under my shirt and this trouser belt with the zipper inside for a long time and it's too full, already. As far as the idea on Jerry, I'm willing, if you think we should. I've never met him and this would be a good time to do so."

Chapter 57

They took a taxi from the Flamingo, heading for downtown. Along the way they saw the Desert Inn Casino, the Sahara, the El Rancho, and a few others. Las Vegas was developing more casinos every month. They had the driver drop them off at the First National Bank on Freemont Street, where they both opened an account separately.

After leaving the bank, they decided to walk to Binions Horseshoe Casino. It was in the afternoon and not as crowded, so upon seeing a table with their positions open, they decided to play some.

"I'm going to be sure you get the dice today, Bucko, so I'll stand on your left, that way you will get the dice before me."

Bucko grinned and said, "OK by me , partner ".

The dice came around to Bucko, who put $5.00 on the pass/line and tossed out a green chip, saying, "a quarter on the world." Then he set his famous world set and tossed the boxcars that paid him 30 to 1 ($150) but lost his pass/line bet. He told the stick man, "parlay the world," which put all the win back on the world bet. He set and rolled snake-eyes (two aces) that now paid him $900. A good amount for only two rolls of the ivories . He next rolled a 6 and after putting odds behind his pass/line bet told the dealer $132 across. He had all numbers covered with green chips. He proceeded to roll several numbers until he 7nd-out. Gar hit some numbers and after his 7-out, they retired to the cashier to change their chips back to cash.

They decided that it would be a short roll, mainly because they were still a little tired from the big day yesterday. They were also trying to get used to the 3 hour time difference from the East Coast. They took another taxi back to the Flamingo and as they headed for the elevators, they were hailed by Scotty.

"Hi guys, I just wanted to check with both of you about tomorrow. I have a limo and driver standing by for 10:00 A.M. to drive us out to Hoover Dam and any other place you care to see. Does that meet with your schedules?"

"That would be nice, Scotty," Gar answered, "We'll be here in the lobby at 10:00 sharp."

"Okay. I'll see you then. Oh, by the way, do you fellows object if I invite a couple of the show girls along? They like to sight-see also."

Bucko looked at Gar and they both smiled, "Sure Scotty, we don't mind."

Chapter 58

After dinner at the Steak House, Gar and Bucko walked to the crap tables and found one that wasn't full, but the only positions that were open were at the very end of the table.

"You can do the shooting," Gar said, "because I'm out of position at the end, and I know you can shoot from any place. I'll bet, but I'll just pass the dice when it's our turn ".

Gar usually stood to Bucko's right, so when the dice came to him, he just passed the dice to Bucko. Bucko, set for the world and after a couple crap numbers, got the 9 for his point. He then said $440 inside, including the point. He then rolled a 6 then the 5. He noticed that the dice were bouncing more than he liked, so after the two good hits which he received $140 on each, he told the dealer to take his place bets down to table minimum. On the very next roll, he sevened-out. They both agreed to change tables.

"That table was just too bouncy and the dice didn't want to respond to our type of shooting, so we are better off going to a different table.'

"You're right, Bucko. I'm glad you picked up on that. Why don't we check out all the other tables without playing. We might as well know now which are the bad ones."

At 10:00 AM, when Bucko and Gar arrived at the lobby, Scotty was waiting for them along with a lovely looking blonde and a gorgeous brunette.

Scotty waived them over.

"Good morning. Let me introduce our other guests, Bucko and Gar. This is Laura and Vicki. The driver is waiting just outside the door, so let's get the show on the road."

The big black Limo was stocked with wine, champagne, fruit, snacks and stereo music plus a telephone. The driver took them east through Henderson along Routes 93 & 95, and as they approached Boulder City, Scotty told them how this city was formed when Hoover Dam was being built. It was first called Boulder Dam, but years later changed to Hoover Dam. The US Government built the well planned model city, Boulder City, to accommodate the thousands that worked on the Dam. As the Limo traveled downward to the Dam, they could see the vast body of water laying from the Dam going north. Scotty continued being the perfect guide by telling them that as the Colorado River backed up to the Dam, it formed Lake Mead, one of the worlds largest man-made lakes which has a 550 mile shoreline through towering canyons and rugged desert country. Fishermen come here from all over the country for the sport of catching bass, crappie, and catfish. The Hoover Dam is the highest concrete dam in this country. The driver parked the Limo and everyone proceeded to make the tour including going down the big elevators. It was a magnificent sight and it was enjoyed by everyone.

After the tour of the Dam, Scotty and the driver found an elevated spot on the way back that gave a breathtaking view of the Dam and Lake Mead. There they all enjoyed a nice picnic style lunch and Scotty opened some champagne. The girls were enjoying being with such handsome guys and before long, everyone was much better acquainted. The girls told how they enjoyed being in the chorus and how nice Scotty was as their employer, while Bucko told them of some of Gar's heroic adventures. When Scotty told how Gar had saved the lives of him and the crew, the girls were really ecstatic to be in the presence of greatness. Gar was getting a little embarrassed by all the fuss and wanted to change the subject.

Their tour ended by the driver returning back to the front entrance to the flamingo. The girls told the guys where they could find them and they hoped that they would invite them along on their next tour. After the girls left, Scotty asked if the guys would like to join him for dinner and to see the Jimmy Durante show to which they accepted, and they agreed to meet at the theater doors at 6 PM. Then they went to their suite to freshen up for dinner.

They enjoyed the show very much. Laura and Vicki were easy to spot in their beautiful costumes, Vicki with her stunning blonde hair and Laura was also pretty as a picture. Every time the girls came on stage, they had different costumes. The tiny stars that adorned their chests left nothing to anyone's imagination. Gar and Bucko thanked Scotty for the day, dinner and show and told him that it was time to play craps now.

"I wish you guys luck, but don't break us," said Scotty with a smile.

"We need all the luck we can get," said Bucko as they headed for the tables.

Chapter 59

All of the Casino games were busy as the show crowd flowed to every type of gambling. They did, however, find their spots at one craps table and each started with $1000 in chips. Both guys bet conservatively while waiting for the dice to come around to them. Bucko was next to the stickman, right side, and Gar next to him. These were their usual spots. When the dice came to the right end of the table, it would always come to the player in the far hook or curve in the table and move clockwise. Gar noticed that the hook player was rather tall so when he threw the dice, his body was leaning over the chip rack. The player next to him on his left, would very quickly slip his right hand under the shooters waist as he tossed the dice and remove a chip from the shooters chip rack.

Gar couldn't believe what he saw. It was so quick. Everyone's eyes were watching the dice land and no one saw him steal a chip. The shooter had quite a few chips and apparently didn't notice any missing. Gar left his chips in place and told Bucko that he needed to go to the men's room. Instead, he walked far away from the table and circled to where he caught the pit boss's attention he signaled him over and told him of the cheating that was taking place. The pit boss thanked him and asked him to return to the table, assuring Gar that he would take care of the problem.

Gar returned and Bucko,not knowing the problem, asked him if he was feeling OK. He told him everything was good, and whispered for Bucko to keep a lookout for the guy at the far end. When the shooter tossed the dice again, the player to his left snitched another chip. But this time the pit boss yelled, "No-dice," and grabbed the thief's hands was so quickly the thief dropped the green chip on the table. Security guards grabbed the thief and held him while the pit boss asked the shooter if he was missing anymore chips. Then the shooter realized he was short quite a few green chips.

Security hustled the thief away and the pit boss asked everyone to please continue with their play. The pit boss gave no recognition to Gar and later, when things calmed down, he slipped him a small piece of paper. He put it in his pocket and later he removed it and read it. The pit boss thanked him and stated in the note that the Casino Manager wanted to reward him. If he would stop at his office, it would be appreciated.

Bucko caught on to the scenario and told Gar, "Nice going, we'll talk later."

He knew the value of secrecy. He realized the cheater might have friends or an accomplice with him and if they knew that Gar had tipped off security, he might have a problem. Bucko and Gar were making a living playing craps honestly and cheating was not an option. They both detested cheaters and liars.

Gar and Bucko played for a couple more hours and stopped at Scotty's office on their way to their suite. When Scotty saw them enter the office, he came toward them with a big smile and his hand outstretched, eager to shake Gar's hand.

"That was a great thing you did, Gar. That guy was taken to our back room and the boys had him thinking that they were going to cut off his fingers when he admitted to other crimes. The Sheriff just called me to thank me for spotting him. This bird is wanted for other crimes also. Nice going, Gar. The Casino owes you."

"You don't owe me anything, Scotty. Bucko and I hate liars and cheaters, so we were only trying to keep out the riffraff. Besides, you have already paid us with comping us with that lovely suite."

"Well, okay guys, and stay as long as you like. I 'm having my secretary type off a memo to the owners about your good deed. It will not go unnoticed."

Chapter 60

After the two returned to their suite, there came a knock on their door. They both looked at each other, wondering who could that be this late. Gar walked over to the door and opened it slowly. There, standing in the entrance, were Laura and Vicki. They still had their makeup on and were lovely to look at. Gar stood there staring at these lovely creatures with his mouth wide open.

"Hi. boys," said Vicki. "We just happened to be in the neighborhood and wondered if you might want to buy us a drink."

Recovering from the initial shock, he stammered, "Huh? Oh yeah, sure. Forgive me for staring, but I was so overcome by such beautiful angels standing at our door, I forgot my manners. Please, come on in."

As soon as Bucko saw the girls, he said, "Hi girls, what a nice surprise. Please have a seat and I will fix us all a drink. Gar and I usually have a martini at night, what will you all have?"

Laura said, "I'll have a martini also."

"Same for me," replied Vicki.

"I'll put on Guy Lombardo music," said Gar.

The girls made themselves at home and before long everyone was dancing. Gar could see that the girls had already decided which one of them was their objective.

Vicki was paying alot of attention to Gar, while Laura was hanging on to every word Bucko said.

"I think I'll phone down for some hors d'oeuvres and snacks," Bucko said, "I hope you girls will help us eat some."

The girls said they would like that. The kitchen soon sent up enough food to choke a horse. After snacks and more drinks, each couple was engaged in their own conversations. Before long Gar and Vicki realized they were alone. Bucko and Laura seemed to have disappeared.

Gar talked a lot of his adventures and Vicki had moved close to him on the sofa and to his surprise, she slipped her hand around to the back of his neck. Then she leaned in real close and said, "If you don't kiss me now, I'm going to die right here in front of you."

"Well now, we can't have that," he said, and swiftly embraced her and softly pressed his lips into hers. She tasted so sweet and her smell was intoxicating. She was so receptive and as he started to unbutton her blouse, she stopped him.

"No Gar." She pulled him to his feet and said, "Let's go to your bedroom, please."

He led her to his bedroom, where they quickly undressed each other and made love.

This was Gar's first since leaving Debbie and afterward, he started to have second thoughts about what he was doing.

"Vicki, I have to tell you this. I'm engaged, and even if this were the most wonderful night of my life, I need for you to know. You are so beautiful and I care for you, but we can only be good friends."

"Gar, I understand, and I really appreciate your honesty, but I'm a big girl and I know how life is. I could easily fall in love with you, but I know too that I wanted to come up here tonight, regardless of the outcome, so yes, I want us to be good friends."

Gar walked her to the door and after their kiss goodbye, returned to his bedroom. He was still wondering if he was making a mistake. He wasn't married and he had needs. Why wasn't it okay? He wrestled with this for sometime before sleep finally came to him.

Chapter 61

Bucko was drinking his coffee when Gar came out of his bedroom the next morning. The desert sun had been shining through their gold laced curtains for some time. Bucko had ordered some strawberries and bagels along with the morning paper.

When he saw Gar, he hailed, "Morning Tiger, Did you have a good time last night?"

"Oh yeah, partner. How about you?"

"I would have to say, things went very good last night," Bucko said.

The two had more coffee and after breakfast, they talked about how stupid the guy was last night to steal another player's chips.

"Actually he was lucky," said Bucko. "I was at a Crap game in Chicago a few years ago, when they discovered this guy switching dice and they took him into the back room. They held his hand on the table and another guy swung a sledge hammer on it, smashing all four fingers like hot potatoes. He ended up having them amputated. These guys will kill you for cheating, I know for a fact."

"You're right, Bucko. I'm so glad we both agree on that."

Bucko took his final sip of coffee, "Oh, I almost forgot. I talked to Jerry Patterson earlier and he's agreed to come over next weekend. He is looking forward to meeting you and playing with us.

"Is he doing anything besides writing gambling books?"

"Yes, he's still working in West San Fernando Valley, in Canoga Park for Rocketdyne , the missile and space people, working on The Atlas Missile Project, writing some type of computer program to measure the flow of liquid oxygen and fuel to keep them even. He says he has also been busy studying and trying to develop a way to beat the Blackjack game. He says he is about ready to launch a strategy that Blackjack lovers will pay to see. Getting it into a book form is where it's at right now."

Gar was quick to ask, "Has he been putting on seminars or teaching new players about the controlled shooting that got me started. I know you told me before that he had some great ideas along those lines."

"He told me he has been working on those ideas and he's looking for the right person to be his instructor. Maybe you could be the one."

"Wow! That's great," said Gar, "I can't wait to meet him. In the meantime why don't we try some of the other Casinos for something different. We haven't been over to Dunes that just opened, or down the strip to the El Rancho. What do you say?"

Bucko took his time answering.

"We could do that, but would our friend Scotty get his feelings hurt if he found us gambling elsewhere, while we are accepting free comps here?"

"Shoot, that's right. You may be right, Bucko. I forgot how touchy the casinos can get. We sure as heck don't want to put Scotty in a bad light. I'm gonna go down, have some coffee with him and put it to him straight, and see how he feels about it. I may even ask him how he would feel if we checked into a different casino after while. If he wasn't my pal and shipmate we wouldn't think twice about it."

Gar was gone over an hour and when he returned, he reported to Bucko that Scotty understood that they might like to try other casinos.

"He even offered to call the casino where we would like to stay, to get us comped there also. Some guy, right? Anyway, I told him we would get back to him when or if we decided to make a move. I did find out what most casinos expect from a player if he expects to receive a room, food, and beverages. They refer to it as RFB and they expect the player to give the casino 4 hours of play per day with an average bet of $ 50 to $75. Of course we have no problem since we are way over that. Also if a player wanted less, then of course he doesn't need to bet that high. Interesting information. Anyway, Scotty also said that if we just wanted to play a few sessions at other casinos and still stay here, he wouldn't object, as long as we each give his casino two hours a day of table play, that way the owners couldn't have an objection."

"That might be better for us," said Bucko.

"This moving from one casino to another is all right, but staying here is a lot less complicated. We get first class service and the other amenities are not bad either."

With that remark, they looked at each other, smiling.

Chapter 62

That afternoon, the guys crossed over the street and walked south to the Dunes Casino. They went directly to the craps tables and found their favorite spots. They both took $500 in chips and again bet conservatively while waiting for the dice to come to them. The player to the right of Gar on the end of the table, had a considerable amount on chips in his tray, and Gar could see that he was a "don't" player. That is, he was betting against the shooters, hoping they wouldn't make their point and seven out. It looked like the table was cold and he was cashing in. They just hadn't had a shooter that was good. Gar just loved to knock these kind of players off the table. These type of players usually do not shoot the dice, but just pass them when it comes their turn. As the dice came to him, he waved them over to Gar.

Gar put $50 on the pass line, while the don't player put $50 on don't pass. Then Gar rolled a 6 for his point and put $100 behind the pass line for odds. He noticed the don't player also put $100 odds behind the don't-pass bet. By now, Bucko was watching Gar and hoping he would make his point, so the don't would lose. He, too disliked the don't- pass betters. There wasn't anything wrong or illegal about betting the don't, but most players did not like dont-pass betters. The third number rolled by

Gar was the 6, his point number. The don't player lost his bets and said ,"Hey, a lucky shooter!"

Now Gar had a 9 for his come-out pass line, with $100 bet and quickly put $200 behind for odds. He glanced over and saw that the don't player doubled his bets also. After 3 more rolls, bam!! He rolled a 9.

"Winner!" shouted the stick man and the don't player yelled, "another lucky," but he was not laughing.

Bucko and Gar picked up on this and started to slap hands and congratulate each other, something they rarely did. They did not like any attention put on them. They know that 8 out of 10 sessions, they beat the casinos, so the less attention, the more they liked it. A Casino could bar anyone if they so cared to, and they do, especially at the blackjack tables, if they recognize a professional card counter.

Gar bet $200 on the line and could see that the don't guy was also betting an equal amount again on the dont-pass. Gar set for the seven and hit the 5-2 for a come-out 7.

"Winner again!" shouted the stickman and the don't guy was furious.

He yelled, "Sh—," and picked up what chips he had left.

As he was leaving, he looked at Gar and said, "You're a lucky A—hole."

Then laughingly Gar yelled, "Yes I am, sonny."

The whole crew thought that was funny and told Gar, "Nice shooting, that guy was getting a little loud anyway."

Gar continued with a winning session, followed by Bucko's nice hand and after another hour or two, tipped the crew, and headed for the Cashier. They were both up about $ 600 winnings. They headed back to the Flamingo and got ready for a nice dinner at the Steakhouse. When they entered the suite, there was a note under the door addressed to Gar. He opened it and saw that it was from Vicki. She was asking if he would call her dressing room sometime before 6 P.M. She wanted to see him after the last show. She stated she had some important information for him and that Laura was hoping Bucko would be available also. If this was acceptable, just call her room and leave a yes or no on the answering machine, since she and Laura would probably be in and out with her busy schedule.

He discussed the note with Bucko, and they agreed to have the girls up again. He called their dressing room and she was there. They agreed to see each other in his suite at 11:00 P.M.

"Did she mention anything about the importance of seeing us?"

"yeah, she said it wasn't anything bad, but she couldn't talk about it over the phone."

"Good. I always worry when a dame says she needs to talk to me."

"I can't believe that. I've never seen you worried. "I know that you never talk about your past and I remember when we first met, you mentioned you were married once, but not now. I know better than to press you about it, but anytime you are ready to talk about it, I'm here, partner."

"Thanks, Pal. I'll think about it."

Chapter 63

After dinner, they found their favorite crap table and each bought in for $1000. The tables at night always had the high rollers or at least more money men. For some reason big crapshooters like serious gambling at night. The two players to Gar's right were heavyweights. They had several thousand in chips in their trays.

Gar poked Bucko and whispered, "Look at the color of chips."

They mostly had all black, which were $100 each, plus a bunch of pink $500 ones. They were cool as could be and gave the impression that win or lose, it's only chips.

When these players got the dice, they just bet, picked up the dice and threw them as if they were tossing feed out to chickens. Thus the term "chicken- feeders" was appropriate for this kind of shooter. They had no rhythm or style like Gar and Bucko had. Most players or Casinos had never seen precision shooters like Bucko and Gar, and that was another reason why they didn't want added attention focussed on them.

The dice came to the big money guys and both lost quickly. Then when Gar made his bets and started pounding out the numbers, the rich guys started saying, "Hey we got us a shooter here," and they started making big money.

Every time Gar would set the dice and toss that perfect pitch, the high rollers would yell with joy. They kept asking Gar how he learned to roll like that?

Gar shrugged it off and told them, "From the Navy."

They had each number covered with a $500 chip, while Gar had $100 chips on his bets. Bucko raised his bets to $100 each, also. Every time Gar hit a good number, one of the money guys tossed Gar a green $25 chip.

"That's your tip, shooter, and every time you hit our numbers, we are going to tip you."

Gar shook his head and said, "Lets tip the dealers also," and he put money on each number for the dealers.

The dealers were all making lots of money on tips and pulling for Gar to hit the numbers. The onlookers were starting to stack up behind Gar and the other players. The Pit boss had to call Security to make the crowd stand back, because they were starting to press against the players and Gar was starting to feel hemmed in. He knew the importance of staying focussed and tried not to let the crowd be a distraction. He knew from past experience if a shooter did not stay in the zone, the dreaded seven would be the very next number rolled. With thousands of dollars on the table, a seven would be devastating.

Gar tried to blot out all distractions and focussed on the back wall of the end of the crap table, where the hard rubber backing looked like green diamonds. He thought of his favorite picture, a large waterfall cascading from high cliffs. He concentrated on throwing the dice into this waterfall. This was how he usually put himself into the zone. He slowly set the dice, concentrating on the waterfalls, and tossed his winning point, the 8. He was focussed' so deeply that he did not hear the crowd cheer, nor fellow players congratulate him. He simply looked down at the table, put the winning chips in his rack, and as the stick man returned the dice to him, picked up the dice and concentrated on tossing the dice into that beautiful sparkling water.

Bucko was very much aware of Gar being well focussed, and made sure that no one touched him or tried talking to him, because he knew that would break his focus and the ugly big red would raise its ugly head. "Big Red" was regularly referred to by older players as the number seven. There is nothing worse for a player to hear than the stick man yelled "Seven-Out"

Gar kept hitting the box numbers and the players were all collecting big winnings . The crew had to change their token box twice, because thanks to Gar, the tips that went into it had filled up twice. They were yelling and pulling for Gar as much as the players were. The chips that the players put on the pass-line at the far end of the table, where Gar had to shoot into, started small and now they looked like mountains of chips, as each pass-line bet was backed up by lots of odds-bets. The casino allowed double odds, so everyone was taking maximum odds .

With so many piles of chips Gar had to throw into, it was becoming obvious that if Gar hit a pile of chips, it would be over, because the rhythm would be broken and he would seven out. Also Gar was telling Bucko the chips were breaking his concentration.

Bucko said, "Lets go down on all bets, OK?"

"Right you are," said Gar and told the stick man to take down all his and Bucko's bets.

They must have had $3000 each across the board. The only bet they couldn't take down was the pass-line bet of $200, because it's a contract bet and it cannot be removed after the come-out roll. The other players left their bets up, not realizing that it was nearing the end of Gar's monster roll. The very next roll, Gar hit a stack of chips and the dice came up seven.

"Big red, Seven Out," yelled the stick man, and a huge groan came from the players. They all applauded Gar for his fantastic roll. The crew also gave him a hand for they too made alot of money in tips.

As Bucko and Gar were coloring out for the walk to the Cashier, one of the High Rollers asked if they could talk to them by meeting in the lounge for a drink. The boys agreed and proceeded to the cashier. Gar cashed in $ 22, 000, while Bucko's was $19,555.

"Hey, are you ever going to slow down and give me a chance to shoot the dice?" Bucko asked.

They were both laughing at this.

"But I'm not complaining," Bucko quickly added.

"I don't know about that, but I do know we have to make another trip to the bank."

Chapter 64

They found their new player-freinds at a table in the Lounge. As Gar and Bucko came forward, they stood up to introduce themselves and shake their hands.

"My name is John Brigance and this is Jim Starner, we are both from Chicago."

Gar and Bucko shook hands with them.

"My name Is Gar Savino and my friend goes by just Bucko, and we are both from New York."

John, the apparent leader, exclaimed, "My, oh my, you sure can control those dice. We have never seen anyone have such success and control over the dice like you displayed tonight. Can you tell us how you do it?"

"Yes," said Gar, "We both have spent hours of practice, trying to perfect a method that could put us into a rhythm, whereby rolling repeating numbers and avoiding the seven. It doesn't always work, but usually it helps give us an edge. Tonight we were lucky, or I should say the odds were in our favor."

"Well, you may call it luck, Gar, but we've been around long enough to know a precision mechanic when we see one and you have a world of talent in your skill. We have been discussing you while we were waiting, and with your permission, we would like to offer a proposition."

Gar looked at Bucko, who hunched his shoulders, as if to say, lets hear it.

"Go ahead, let's hear what you have."

"We both love to play craps, and although we have enough financing to sustain a loss, we hate losing all the time. We would like to hire you, or go as partners shoot the dice for us. We will put up all the money, and you do the shooting. We will split all the money you win above the original cashing in amount when we start a session . Any expenses, if we go to another place or city, will come out of our half. You will not have to spend any of your half on anything except for what you spend for food . The split will be this: an even 50-50 split. We control all the bets. If we have a losing session twice in succession, then we either dissolve the partnership or we renegotiate the deal. How does that sound?"

Gar took a long time before he answered.

"That is an interesting proposition. It also is not the first time we have been offered this kind of proposal. Yours is similar but different. Before I give you an answer, I will have to talk this over with my partner. However, if we do go with your plan. We must agree on one important point, and that is we decide on where we play. We also insist on fair play, nothing shady or illegal. Give us some time to discuss your proposal, say two days, and we will meet you here in this lounge at noon, day after tomorrow, Okay?"

"That will be just fine," said John. They said their goodbyes and left.

"Doesn't this sound familiar?" Bucko asked.

"What do you mean. Oh, yeah. You mean that guy back in Windham. yeah, you're right. I had forgotten about that. It seems someone is always wanting us to use our skills to make them money," said Gar. "What do you think?"

"I think we need to give this some serious thought before we get involved with someone we just met. Don't forget that Jerry Patterson will be here tomorrow and maybe he will have some advice for us. Let's not make any decisions until we talk to Jerry, OK?"

"That's good advice Bucko. It's near eleven, so let's go up to our suite and make ready for the girls. They will be up around eleven thirty."

Chapter 65

Promptly at 11:30, there was a knock at their door. Gar moved swiftly over to the door and opened it to two beautiful ladies. After Laura and Vicki kissed each of their guy's cheek and a salutary hug, they proceeded to the sofa. Bucko fixed each a favorite drink.

After the usual welcoming banter, Gar said, "Now lovely ladies, what is this mysterious proposition that you have?"

"It isn't really mysterious," said Vicki, "It's just an idea that we had that involves you guys and we didn't think the phone would be the proper way to talk to you about it. I don't know how to say this, because we do not want you two to take it wrong , so I'll just come right to the point.

"You both know that Laura's husband died in the war and she owns a house in the suburbs. She was kind enough to ask me to move in with her over a year ago. Now here's where it gets delicate, but I'm going to come right out with it. We are crazy about you two and we have this big house we would like to share with you. We are not asking for any commitments, nor any ties or strings attached. We simply feel that since we work at the Casino and you guys play at the casinos, that it would be nice to get away from the noisy, bright lights and come home to a home cooked meal and all the homey environment.

Laura and I love to cook and we would love to do it for you guys. You don't need to give us an answer tonight, just think on it and let us know later."

"Holy cow," exclaimed Gar, "That is something. You girls hardly know us, but don't get me wrong, I'm flattered as can be. You don't know but what we might be murderers, Bank Robbers, or masochists."

Laura quickly said, "Oh, yes we do we maybe stepped over the line, but we asked Scotty about you and he told us all about your heroic deeds, Gar. He didn't know a quality person. So there."

"My, oh my, you girls have been busy," said Bucko.

"If it sounds like we were too nosey or we went too far, We're sorry guys, but we are being totally honest, fellows," Vicki said, "We have seen wise guys and jerks come and go and we have dated some big time fakers. Scotty has made blind dates for us and everyone was a disaster. When Scotty first asked us to meet you two, we at once went 'Oh, no, not again!' but Scotty told us that you were different and he was right . So, we know you, now we want you to know us, and what you see is what you get. We make no promises that we don't keep and we put no claims on you other than to always be fair and truthful."

No one said another word for a long time. They were digesting the moment. Gar finally spoke.

"That was one great speech, girls. We are speechless. Thank you for your honesty and sharing your feelings. We are not going to take this lightly. We are going to talk and think about this and believe me, we will get back to you soon with our answer. In the meantime let's have another drink, while I put on some Glen Miller music."

Everyone was "In the mood."

Gar and Bucko were waiting in the front of the Hotel when they saw this tall, 6' 7" guy walk in. "Here he is," said Bucko, and grabbed Jerry's outstretched hand.

"Jerry, this is Gar Savino. He has been anxious to meet you for a long time."

"Hi Gar, Bucko has told me a lot about you and it's my pleasure to finally meet you."

"My pleasure also, Jerry. Your practice box and your good instructions have been the key to my being as successful as I am. Of course becoming friends with my pal Bucko hasn't hurt either."

Happy to have everyone together, Bucko asked, "Would you guys like to go to the lounge or up to our suite for a little refreshment before we go to dinner?"

"Hey, that sounds great, I could do with a little splash of water on my face, so lets go to your room. Maybe I could leave my bag there also before I get a room."

"Get a room nothing," said Bucko with confidence "You're staying with us and you have your own private room. We're gonna take good care of you, my friend."

"Say that's great , fellows. I didn't expect that, but thanks anyway."

When they entered the suite, Jerry complimented them again on the beautiful room set up and the accommodations. Bucko went to the bar and yelled out to Jerry." you still drinking those Bombay Safire Martinis?"

"Hey, yeah Man you sure have a good memory."

"Well, you know they say a good man is remembered by his good drink not by his good deeds," laughed Bucko.

Gar intercepted, "I think there's something missing somewhere in that statement."

Bucko brought the martinis over to the coffee table just as Jerry came into the room after washing his face and ridding himself of that desert sand.

"Here's to new friends," said Jerry as the three touched glasses and took their first sip.

The three discussed everything that had happened in their lives over the last few years and how Gar had become such a good craps player. Jerry told of his new book about Blackjack that just came out and what his plans are for holding clinics around the country to teach craps players how to win with his new system on rhythm rolling. He told them that he was still looking for some good shooters that he needed to put everything in motion. He mentioned that he was looking forward to seeing Gar play . Then the subject came up about the two money men they had met recently who wanted to back Gar's play.

"You need to know who you are in partnership with," Jerry said," If you do not know someone for a long time, do not go into a partnership with them, especially in the gambling world. There are still alot of hoods and shady characters out there that might cause harm to someone with bad actions."

This was good advice and Gar was quickly deciding what answers to give to the two guys they were to meet tomorrow night.

Chapter 66

After dinner the three went to the tables, looking for one where all three could play. Jerry was stick left so they needed a table where both sides of the stick man was open. Fortunately the show crowd was not out yet, so they were able to find a table open. They cashed in $1000, each and put their chips in their chip racks.

The first to get the dice was Gar. He used the seven set for the come out and hit three sevens in a row. Then with a point of six , he placed each number for $50 & $60 each. He banged out several numbers and hit the six again. He set for the world and hit three boxcars in a row, with the second one parlayed for a big winner. His next point number was 4, so after rolling a few box numbers, he used the 2-V and hit the four again. After his third point number of 9, he hit a chip at the far end and the seven came up.

Bucko showed he was up to the task and held the hand for another 35 minutes or so before the seven came out.

Next Jerry took the dice and with his long arms he could almost reach to his right and just drop the dice next to the wall. He set the dice squarely in front of him and after looking at the far wall to his right, past the stick man, he took aim with his right arm and gently tossed the dice softly to the back wall bounced once and stopped side by side for his point of 8. He then set the dice for the hardway set and rolled two fours for his point. Showing that he was using the hardway sets, all three guys loaded up with $100 each on all the hardways. Jerry had a 6 for his next point and after a few box numbers, he came back with two threes for the hardway 6, his point. The hardway paid 9 to 1, or $900, to those who had bet it, and Bucko and Gar did. Jerry could see that the pit boss was watching him closely. He was aware that some Casinos were starting to balk if a shooter took too long setting the dice and the answer to that was to put up bets for the dealers. Jerry put an extra red chip on his odds and declared, "Dealers are on the line." The dealers all chimed in, "dealers are on the line." Now the tension was eased. Then Jerry threw 4 red chips onto the layout saying, "All the hardways $ 5.00 each for the dealers." Now they are really exited and start pulling for Jerry to hit the hardway numbers like double 2's, 3's, 4's, and 5's..

Jerry had 10 for his point and setting two 5's on top he took aim and hit the hardway 10. The crowd that was watching yelled, the dealers yelled, and Gar and Bucko let out a yell. Everyone betting on 10 were big winners. Jerry had the dealers all cheering for him. He could do no wrong. He continued to hold the dice for another 45 minutes, before hitting one of the stack of chips at the far wall. He too received a hand from everyone. Then the three signaled each other for a break and they each headed for the Cashier to change their chips back into folding money.

They went to the lounge to take a break and to dices the session. Gar was first to praise Jerry.

"That was impressive. You not only teach new people how to play your new system, but you back it up with your skills. I watched how you sensed that the pit-boss may have wanted to put a little heat on you for setting the dice, but by you making all those dealer bets, you had them eating out of your hand. I learned a lot tonight from you. That was great."

"Well, thanks Gar. It did feel right tonight and we all did good. I must say, though, you have a fantastic delivery. My system is fairly easy to learn, but you seem to excel in everything that I teach. I'm really impressed, Gar."

"I told you, Jerry," exclaimed Bucko, "He's a natural and he has a knack for keeping the dealers on his side like you and I do."

"Thank you, guys for all the nice compliments, but let me interrupt for just a second. Jerry will you be able to stay over tomorrow night also?"

"What's tomorrow? Oh Saturday! yeah, that would be OK. Why?"

"Well we want to have you take in a dinner-show with us and we want you to meet our host and maybe meet the loveliest ladies who have made our stay here so wonderful."

"Hey, I'm all for that ," exclaims Jerry.

"Fine. Now let me find the house phone, maybe Scotty is still available for a nightcap."

Gar excused himself and made a call to Scotty's office, then returned to tell them that he reached Scotty and he would be joining them shortly.

Fifteen minutes later, Scotty arrived and Gar made the introductions. Jerry found out that Gar and Scotty were shipmates and are great pals. When subject of dinner came up, Scotty told them that all three will be his guests for dinner and the show. After another round of Bombay Safire Martinis, they all said farewell and they headed off to bed . Bucko asked Jerry where he generally played whenever he came to Las Vegas Jerry said he liked both El Rancho and The Dunes. Then they all agreed to visit them tomorrow. They wanted to play a little Blackjack also.

Chapter 67

After a late brunch, the three headed over to the Dunes Casino. This was the weekend and they could not find a crap table where all three could play, so Jerry suggested that they play some 21-Blackjack. They found a $10 table and all three were able to play along side each other. Jerry cashed in with $200, while Bucko and Gar started with $100. He really needed to pick up some pointers from the best blackjack player in the game. He figured Jerry couldn't write about the game unless he knew alot about it. He was right. Jerry seemed to know when to fold, when to raise, and when to double up. Gar tried to follow Jerry's play, but this was fast and when in doubt, Gar played it safe by not taking a card. He was staying even while Jerry was winning almost on every hand that he played. Bucko was breaking even with the house. It was plain to see that Jerry was an expert at this game. Before long, Jerry's green chips were all becoming black.

The Casino started changing dealers often, but Jerry was a master at beating the dealers. Soon his bets were from $100 to $300 on every deal. Gar had decided to quit and just stand back and watch him play, but Jerry grabbed his wrist.

"Do not leave," he said, "Stay and bet light, otherwise you'll upset the rhythm of how the cards are played out."

Gar realized what Jerry meant, said, "OK, you're right," and stayed put. Bucko also stayed and marveled at Jerry's skill and good luck.

The Casino could see that Jerry was up on his game and moving into the $500 chips. They must have figured that Jerry was a professional card counter, because the Pit Boss came over and told all the players that this was the last shoe. After it was played out, this table would be closed. All three players, just smiled. They knew Jerry hit them too hard and the Casino was stopping any further loss. The three colored up and proceeded to the Cashier to make the change from chips to cash. The trio were slightly animated at Jerry's good fortune. Later, Jerry gave Gar some pointers on how to win at blackjack. Gar was learning from a master player.

When they exited the Dunes, they decided to take a taxi to El Rancho. They started playing Blackjack, and this time, Gar was doing much better. Bucko was on a hot streak also. In no time their cash-in went from $200, up to $500 and again the casino started changing dealers. Whenever Gar missed his card, Jerry would catch his, and the same with Bucko. After the first hour, all three players were betting black chips and catching the right card on doubling down. When they were up several thousand, Jerry told them It's time to call it a day. The bosses are starting to circle the tables. If we stop now, maybe we won't be barred. They figure we are too good at counting."

With that, they all colored up, tipped the dealer, and made the trip over to the Cashier's cage. Jerry was telling them that counting cards was not illegal, but the casinos can and will bar you from playing there if they so decide.

Leaving before that happened, was a wise thing to do. Everyone agreed.

They caught another taxi back to the Flamingo and headed up to the suite where they showered again and relaxed by relating the day's events and to get ready for the big dinner-show with Scotty.

While Jerry was showering, Gar took the moment to quiz Bucko on his feelings about leaving the Hotel and moving in with the girls. He had phoned them earlier and had asked them up after the show and bring along a third girl for Jerry. They asked him if he had reached any decision as yet. He related some of the activity that had transpired and that they needed more time to discuss the idea. He thought after Jerry left, things would be less hectic. He also told Vicki he and Bucko were expecting to reach a decision on the money High Rollers tonight . She said she understood and that there wasn't any hurry on her answer.

"I've thought about them alot, Gar, but I was just waiting to talk it over with you. It's not a bad move, but we need to do some more talking about this. By the way, we haven't decided just how long we are going to stay here yet, not that I'm anxious to leave or if I ever want to leave. We just need to consider our options. Speaking of options, what have we decided about those two money guys? We promised them an answer tonight."

Gar took his time.

"Bucko, if you want us to go that way, we will do it, but after hearing good advice from Jerry and watching your expressions while we were listening to him. I don't think either one of us care much for playing for someone else. What do you say we tell them we decline to accept their proposal, for now?"

"That's what I was hoping you would say , Gar. We don't need to answer to anyone but each other, and I respect your decisions more every day. After Jerry leaves, we must take a day off and do nothing but clear our minds and decide where and what we do with our lives. Right?"

"As usual, you are right, Pal."

Scotty was waiting near the showroom entrance when the guys appeared in their best finery. The ushers escorted them to Scottie's private table and the waiters took their order for drinks. Scotty brought his wife with him and she was relishing in all the attention that these handsome men were showering upon her. They were finishing dinner just as the orchestra began their overture. The show was another lalapalooza smash hit. When Bucko pointed out Vicki and Laura in the lineup of chorus girls, Jerry agreed they were beautiful ladies. Then Bucko told him that a party was being held in our suite after the show and the ladies were bringing a surprise for Jerry. He beamed with approval.

When they left the showroom, the three thanked Scotty and his wife for a wonderful evening and went straight to the crap tables. They were lucky to find an open table, as the show crowd was ready to gamble. Saturday night was a big night for gamblers and most expected to play all evening.

The three cashed in and after putting their chips in the chip rack, Gar was first to start the roll. He felt good and rolled six 7's in a row on his come-out. Then after he got a 9 for his point, he went across the board with $650, including the point number. He had $100 on each with $120 each on the 6&8. Every time he rolled a good number, the dealer pushed $140 to Gar. When he hit a 4 or 10, they pushed $200 to him. He held the dice for a good 40 minutes and when the 7 came, he had a nice stack of black chips in his tray. Bucko was next and he, too, had a very nice roll, with betting heavy on the 6 & 8's. When Jerry got the dice he went with betting heavy on repeating numbers. He called it his Signature Trend

Set, where he made come-bets. taking maximum odds, and he was cleaning up on those numbers that kept repeating. He said they were his signature rolls for this session. Jerry also held the dice for at least half an hour. They signaled each other to take a break and left for the cashiers cage. Then they headed for the Lounge.

They all seated themselves at a table and gave the waitress their order. Then Gar spotted John Brigance and Jim Starner seated in the corner, and waved to them. He excused himself, and went over to talk with them. He thanked them for their fine offer to partner with him, but he had decided not to accept their offer at this time. He told them it would be great to play with them any time they met again at the tables. They appreciated his consideration and wished him continued success. John gave Gar his calling card, and asked him to call him if or when he changed his mind.

Bucko, Gar, and Jerry returned to their suite and at exactly 11:30, the three ladies appeared at their door. Gar introduced them to Jerry, while Vicki introduced Anna to Jerry and the others. Anna was taller than the other two and she made Jerry feel as if they had known each other for years. Bucko was the designated bartender and he made sure that each lady received her favorite drink. Gar made sure that the dance music was slow and serenading.

After a few hours, each couple paired off to enjoy each other and do their own thing. In this big suite, stuffed with several sofas and chairs, one could get lost and no one would care. Gar and Vicki disappeared to his bedroom where they were engaged in serious conversation, among other things and she again asked him if they had reached any decision about moving in with her and Laura. He told her that they hadn't yet reached a decision, and asked her not to be impatient with him.

He was feeling a little guilty for not calling Debbie back in Windham. She had been on his mind a lot lately. He thought that he was in love with her and felt sure she was truly in love with him. So what was the problem, he asked himself . Why do I have serious feelings about Vicki? He knew that he had told Vicki on the first night not to become serious about him and that he was engaged. She said that she understood, and she would just be a good friend, but would being friends and moving in with her be something an engaged guy should do? Gar was perplexed.

The big weekend was over. Jerry told both Bucko and Gar they could make a good living gambling, but there were a lot of pitfalls to be wary of. Then he spent much time describing what they were. He also said that when he had most everything in order, he would be in touch to offer them a deal in his new program. They all agreed to stay in contact with each other.

The first thing on Gar's mind Monday, was a long talk with Bucko. They ordered up a late lunch and agreed this was to be a leisure day, no gambling, just serious conversation. They hashed over the deal about gambling together and talked about how long to stay at the Flamingo. They talked at length about Laura and Vicki. Bucko told Gar how he had only one love. She had died years ago with cancer and he would never allow himself to marry again, nor would he have any desire to. They talked about trying to invest in some type of business that would be a good diversification when gambling became boring.

The first complete decision was not to accept the invitation to bunk-in with the girls. The second was to return to New York for two weeks to visit friends and relatives. Then they would return to Las Vegas, but to stay only 3 or 4 days at different hotels, move around more, try the Bahamas, or wherever the mood carried them. They would always play together, watching each other's back. Gar told Bucko he was realizing how it was possible to become bored or to find gambling every night a way to become dull. He wanted to find a way to keep his mind active in the real world and still be a winner at the tables. Bucko had never indicated before that this was one of the hazards of gambling, but now that Gar had brought it up, he agreed they should try to find a compromise.

That afternoon, they scheduled flights back to New York. Gar phoned Debbie and asked her to meet him at Laguardia Airport. He also phoned his two pals Sammy and Sandy. He contacted Vicki and told her they would be returning to New York for personal reasons and he would be in touch when he returned. He indicated that they would put a hold on any decision about sharing their home.

Bucko and Gar thanked Scotty for being such a great friend and host. They said they would see him again when they returned, after a few weeks. He wished them well, saying they would always be welcome at the Flamingo. They were taken to the Vegas Airport by the limo provided by Scotty. The flight would be nonstop to Chicago, with a 3 hour layover, then straight to NY. This gave Gar an opportunity to phone Debbie during the layover. She told Gar she had a week off so, there wasn't any problem meeting him in New York. He told her to pack enough clothes for all week, because it's time he showed her the big city. He called the Grimes and asked if he could bring Debbie for a couple days. Mrs. Grimes was more than happy to have both of them.

When Gar exited the plane and came through to the waiting lounge, he spotted Debbie Morton waiting for him. She had shortened her lovely blonde hair and put on a couple pounds, enough to make her look stunning. The two wrapped their arms around each other and gave a lasting kiss. Gar whispered,"I love you, and I missed you very much."

"I love you, too, and I thought I would die waiting to see you again."

He introduced her to Bucko and they proceeded to the baggage area. Bucko had left his car there, so he said his farewell and left to pick up his car.

Gar asked Debbie, "Did you bring the Hudson ?"

"Oh, sure. It's parked in the short term area. Shall we go?"

"That can wait. Let's go to the Lounge and have a sandwich. I'm starved. Besides, I want to talk to you about your vacation."

She stared at him.

"My, this sounds serious. Is there a problem?"

"Oh no, sweetheart. We just need to make some plans about New York, that's all."

He told her about both of them staying at the Grimes' and that if she would like, he would get tickets for a Broadway show. She was eager to do all these things and became all excited as he revealed his plans. Then they picked up the new Hudson he had given her, and they drove to the Grimes' home.

Mr. and Mrs. Grimes were both home and showered Gar with love and made Debbie feel like one of the family.

"I took the liberty of calling both Sammy and Sandy on your behalf," said Mr. Grimes, "They both agreed to come over tomorrow evening for a cookout , so we will have a celebration or maybe we could call it a family reunion."

"That would be great," said Gar, "I can't wait to see those guys."

"Debbie, our daughter Rose is away at College," said Mrs. Grimes, "so I've arranged for you to take her room, if that's OK with you. Gar still has his room next to yours. He will always have a room in our home. I should have said his home , for he will always be a part of our family."

Mr. Grimes said, "After you all freshen up ,we are taking you out to dinner, but I need to know what you like to drink so I can get the cocktails ready."

The homecoming was enjoyed by all. Debbie was accepted and smothered with attention by everyone. Sandy and Sally were wonderful to her. Sammy and his wife Karen were also very kind to her.

The three men carried on like high school chums, hugging each other, punching each other lightly on the shoulders, telling jokes on each other, just like they used to years ago. The fact that Sandy had lost both of his hands was not an issue. He had become so dexterous by now that he could do almost everything by himself. He had become very important to the sales department at New York Life Insurance Company. He had wanted Sally to give up Nursing, but she still wasn't ready to give it up.

Sammy's wife, Karen was working at Empire Trucking Company along with all of the family. Sammy's parents were part owners and Sammy was now off the trucks doing dispatching duties.

They were all interested in hearing how Gar had become so successful in playing craps. He told them everything and he let them know that to him, gambling was a tough life. He enjoyed winning, but after a while, the bright lights and the noise of all the people shouting, along with the anxiety of trying to stay focused, took its toll. He told them he needed to become involved in something different for part of his time.

The next morning, Gar got up early and told Mrs. Grimes he was going for a neighborhood stroll. He enjoyed greeting neighbors as they were on their way to work. He came to a shop with a sign that read, "Joe Miller's Barber Shop."

He stood across the street staring at the shop. Finally, he walked over and opened the door. He saw the elderly gentleman sweeping the floor. He wasn't sure until he turned towards him, that this was Joe.

"Are you looking for a barber, Joe?"

Joe stood staring at the stranger. Then he recognized Gar

"That you, Gar Savino? You came back to see old Joe? My, oh my, just look at you. You sure are a sight for sore eyes," he said as he gave him a big bear hug.

"Nice to see you again, Joe. I was wondering if you still had the shop. It's been a long time. How are you, anyway?"

"Well, the arthritis has almost put me out of business. My right hand just doesn't want to cooperate. Believe it or not, I'm getting ready to sell the place. How about me selling the shop to you? What are you doing these days?"

"Joe, I've been doing some construction work and a little traveling. Right now I'm visiting with the Grimes. I decided to take an early walk and was hoping that you were still here. So nice to see you, but I'm sorry that you are selling. I hope you get your price and get to enjoy your retirement for a long time."

After having a nice chat, Gar returned home and found Debbie having her breakfast with Mrs. Grimes. Gar told Debbie he was taking her to Pier 83, on west 42nd Street at the Hudson River for a narrated, breathtaking sightseeing tour of New York's major sights, including the Statue of Liberty.

"Then we are having dinner at the famous Rainbow room at Radio city and see a Broadway Show." He could barely contain his happiness and excitement. "You are about to see New York City, my darling."

"Oh my, all that in one day?"

"yeah, and more the next day if you can stand it ."

Over the next three days, Gar took Debbie to all the major sights; Radio City Music Hall,The Empire State Building, American Museum of Natural History, Lincoln Center for Performing Arts, Rockefeller Center, St. Patrick's Cathedral, Ellis Island and The Statue of Liberty. They visited Broadway which is referred to as "The Great White Way," and saw two Broadway Shows, "Bringing up Father," and "How to Succeed in Business Without Trying."

At the end of the third sightseeing tour, Debbie was giving out vibes that she was getting worn out and this was harder than work. Gar realized he was pushing her too hard and asked her if she would like to return to the mountains or for them to return to Windham to catch their breath before doing more traveling and she agreed that would be nice.

The next morning, after bidding the Grimes goodbye, they drove back to the beautiful town of Windham. The massive green foliage from the hillsides was luxuriant. They stopped at one creek crossing and walked along the creek, listening to the spellbinding water as it made it's way across the rocks; the robins warbling their happy trills; the light breeze gently tossing Debbie's curls.

Debbie caught the moment in silence, then whispered to Gar, "Darling, you tried so hard to please me by touring that wonderful city, and I loved it, but nothing can compare to this. Mother nature is singing her overture. Her prelude to an orchestrated movement, just as we are in our first movement to marriage. Let's not ever forget this moment or place," as she tenderly squeezed Gar's hand.

Gar easily sensed this was, indeed, a cherished moment and swept her into his arms and as he softly crushed her lips to his.

"Will you marry me?"

She had waited so long to hear these words, and now, as the tears streamed down her face, she could hardly breathe. She embraced him with all her might and as she fought to catch her breath, the words came out with such velocity,"Yes, yes, yes, my Darling!!"

Debbie and Gar spent the next few days in Windham at her apartment. They were busy planning for their wedding. They had much to discuss. Gar knew that his life would never be the same. He would no longer be a loner. Every decision would have to include two people. He didn't want to give up his passion for craps playing, but they both agreed gambling was not the number one priority in their life anymore. Not if they were sincere about marriage and family.

Gar asked Debbie to call her employer and tell him she would not be coming back to work. The important project now was for Gar to find a career job, or find a business he could buy into. He had saved his money from the Oil Co. and had won close to $75,000 in gambling, so he had over one hundred thousand to invest. He could always go back to Socony Vacuum Oil Company, but he wanted to try his hand at owning a business first. They both knew that they would have to move to a larger city to do this, but they were willing.

"We will going to rent a U-Haul trailer and head back to Brooklyn, rent a house and have a talk with the families about our future. We will set our wedding date as soon as we secure our first home."

Debbie was very happy to get things moving in that direction. He also thought that they should start looking in the papers and want-ads under Business Opportunities to see what was available.

They were fortunate enough to find a large house for rent in the suburbs of Brooklyn and it was perfect for all their needs. The owner liked Gar and Debbie and told them if they liked the place, he would sell it to them and apply the rent towards the down payment. They told him that they liked the offer very much. They soon had the place furnished and they had the Grimes and Cross' over for a housewarming party. Then they all helped plan and arrange their wedding. The same Pastor that Sammy and Sandy had was chosen to marry them. He knew there were to be two best men, so he didn't try to be surprised at this. Both Sandy's wife, Sally and Sammy's wife, Karen were very helpful. The three girls liked each other.

The wedding was for the families only, however Gar's friend Bucko was invited and he came to wish them happiness. He realized Gar would not be available to play as his partner anymore. He told Gar to follow his dream and become a good business man. True happiness is with the family, not in a Casino.

Gar found several opportunities to buy into, but none that he cared to pursue.

One day Sammy called to say that his father had told him that a friend of his who owned a large Salvage Yard in Brooklyn had died.

"His widow was wants to sell low for a quick sale. It is on three acres and right next to the main road. The Salvage Company owns several Tow-trucks and is under contract with the city to be on call to haul away wrecks whenever they occurred. They also own a very large body repair shop next door to the Salvage Co. and it is leased out. This is an ongoing concern and the right person could be in business without starting from scratch."

He definitely had Gar's attention and he immediately contacted the Real Estate broker and set up an appointment. The next day Gar met with the Real Estate salesman and proceeded to "Best Auto Salvage," where they looked over the entire property. Gar had a thousand questions and he liked all the answers. He talked with the hired help and the foreman. Everyone was willing to stay on. Gar didn't understand everything about the business, but he liked being around autos and heavy machinery and knew that he could manage it after a short time. Besides that was what a foreman was for.

The asking price was three hundred fifty thousand dollars, which included all the equipment at the yard, including five large Tow-trucks. Gar had a third of this in cash and he made an offer of three hundred thousand to the broker, who took the offer to the owner. The very next day he asked Irving to accompany him to Chase Manhattan Bank, where he asked for a business loan. They were hesitant at first until Irving reviewed Gar's resume with them and about the Medal of Honor that Gar had. They agreed to take the matter to their Finance Committee and would get an answer to him in three days.

While Gar was waiting for answers, he revisited the Salvage Company and took notes as he watched how the company handled it's operation. This was truly a busy business. They had customers coming in all the time for parts of all kinds and they had crews dismantling wrecks and taking off parts to sell. They had acres of autos and trucks to choose from. This was the largest salvage company in the metropolitan area and he was wondering if it was too big for him to manage. He didn't think the bank would approve his loan, since he hadn't any previous experience and he was afraid his offer to buy would be rejected for this was worth more than his offer.

He toyed with the idea of calling the real estate company and upping the offer, but after talking with Sammy, he was convinced he was just getting the last minute jitters.

"If the company turns down this offer, you can always submit another one for more. Just sit still and be patient.

Gar was finding out how to be a business man. The longer he waited, the more he wanted the company. He started for the phone more than once. He was driving Debbie crazy with his edgy, itchy, impetuous, nervous anxiety. When the third day came, he was like a caged animal. When noon came and no phone call yet, he told Debbie this was a mistake, he wasn't going to get the place and he was going to take a walk

Just as he was about to close the door, the phone rang. He ran to the phone and after the third ring, picked up the receiver. It was the bank and he had been approved for his loan. When he finished with the caller, he yelled up the stairs to Debbie, to tell her the good news.

She whispered under her breath "Thank God."

It wasn' t thirty minutes before the phone rang again. It was the real estate company and his offer had been accepted. They wanted to close the deal with him within 15 days, if he was willing. Gar gave them his lawyers name and said that if the lawyer was willing, it would be all right. He was going to be in business!

Gar was very excited about his new business venture. He promised himself he was going to make this into the biggest and best auto and truck salvage repair company in the East. He spent every minute with his office people going over the books and having the accountant bring him up to date on all transactions.

He asked continuous questions and wrote down all the answers in his notebook. He spent time with the employees, listening to what each had to say. He often called Debbie to say he would be late getting home. Every aspect of the company was getting a close look. He needed to be on top of everything. He hated to be surprised by ignorance and bad judgments. Anytime someone had a better idea, he wrote it in his book. At the same time he was careful not to make any suggestions or changes until after the closing papers were signed.

He sought out key personnel like the body shop manager, the manager/dispatcher of the tow trucks, the parts manager, and office manager. He wrote down the duties of each division and what the managers expected from his employees. He then entered the salaries of each person in that department. After consulting with each person, Gar always asked everyone the same question.

"What is one thing that could be done to make this department better?"

The office manager was an elderly lady named Grace Livingston. Her husband died some years ago and she had been employed by the deceased owner many years ago. She practically ran the business, more so when the owner became incapacitated. Her name came up in many of Gar's questioning of the employees. So he decided to spend more time with her. If she was detrimental or overbearing to this company, he needed to be aware of it at once.

He asked her if he could take her to lunch this day. She abruptly informed him she always brought her lunch from home. He asked her if she would join him in the owner's office, where they could both eat their sandwiches together. She agreed and asked him where his sack of sandwiches was. He told her he was just going to get it, but then she said she'd had more than enough and she would share with him. This surprised Gar. This didn't seem like the actions of a tyrant. He heard about how she loved her husband and how much she missed him. They both wanted children, but they put it off until it was too late. After his death she threw all her energy into this job and now it was everything to her .

After she related her life, she wanted to know if he was going to replace her. Gar knew how to read people and he recognized quality in Grace. He stood in front of her and told her he wanted her to continue with her job. He told her she would be getting a raise and that he was depending on her to help him make this company grow larger. She promised him she would help him in any way that she could. He thanked her for saying that. He knew he knowledge was very important to this company. He felt if others had a problem with Grace, it was most likely she was right and others were wrong. Time would prove him right.

The day after he closed the deal and was officially the new owner he held a meeting with all the employees and told them what he expected from them and what they could expect from him. If anyone had a problem, they must take it to their department manager first. He told them that as the company grew, so would their salaries. He hired a sign painter to erect a new neon sign at both the Body Shop and the Parts place. It was now "Savino's Body & Paint Shop". The parts place was "Savino's Auto Parts." He had thousands of calling cards made.

Gar called on every auto insurance company and made a point of taking a different adjuster out to lunch every day. He visited the Highway Patrol and made sure that his wreckers were called and the rotation was fair, same for the police department, making sure that his company was first on their list. He quickly learned how to read the NADA. book, and he soon became an expert in evaluating buying wrecked autos and trucks. He visited every other body shop and made them aware he would be selling autos that had been totaled in value, but were repairable to sell again. He instructed his yard men that every vehicle he bought that was to be resold as a repairable unit be washed, cleaned, and polished. They thought he was crazy, but every unit cleaned and waxed brought top dollars to the firm. He sponsored softball teams, bowling teams, and marathons. He believed in advertising and had Grace buy ads in all the local papers.

He asked the parts manager to explain how he handled the parts off a unit when it was bought and moved to our shop. He said they simply took off each part, tagged it, and put it in the bin for sale. The motors were taken out and tagged and stored in the motor area and sold "as is". Then the rest was moved out into the field to sell as body parts.

Gar asked, "How many as-is motors do we sell in a month?"

The Manager replied, "Maybe three or four, they are not fast movers."

Gar thought on this for a while then said, "I would like you and all your crew who pull parts to meet with me at 7:00 AM tomorrow morning. We need to update our ideas."

The next morning,they were all there waiting for him.

"Good morning men. I'm glad we are all here. We need to make a few changes on how we treat these parts as we take them off each vehicle. Every motor we remove from a unit, I want us to check it for oil and start it. I want our mechanics to evaluate the condition of the motor. We will have two types only , good or bad. If he says it's good, we label it good, steam clean it, and paint it with the manufacturer's original color. We then place it in designated area and sell it with a 30 day warranty. If a customer wants to hear it run, we do it. Every part we take off to place in our bins, we wash off first, and tag it. The rest of the unit will be washed, tagged and placed in rows designated by the make, such as Chevrolet, Ford, Chrysler, and so-forth. I want the fields mowed weekly between the units and the roadways between them kept clean. I do not want to see someone going out to see a unit for a part, returning with sand spurs and cockleburs, or mud on their shoes. I know you're thinking, 'Hey, this is a junk yard .' No, it's not. It's an auto parts business, and we live here. So let's be proud of our place."

At first, he men grumbled, but after a few weeks, they could see the wisdom of all these changes. The customers remarked how much nicer everything was. The parts sold quicker and sales of motors went from 3 or 4 a month, to 10 or 12, and getting better. The workers also seemed to enjoy the changes.

At the end of six months, Grace told him sales were up in every division of the salvage yard & parts department. She had never seen such an increase in profits since she had been there.

"How are the body shop and wrecker department doing?"

She hesitated before she spoke.

"Well, in comparison to the auto parts over the first six months, I would have to say, not so good, but if we compare it to how it did year by year, it seems to stay about the same."

"You mean we haven't had any substantial increase in profits over our first 6 months?"

"Yes, that's correct, I'm sorry to say."

Gar told her to bring him a copy of the monthly status of the body shop for the last 12 months.

"Say nothing to anyone and try to have it to me in a couple days."

The next few weeks he concentrated on the goings and comings at the Body Shop. He made several phone calls to adjusters that he had taken to lunch in the past and asked them if everything was satisfactory with the quality of repairs that were made at the shop. Everyone said all the jobs were good and there were no complaints from customers. Gar asked Grace how the Body Shop accounts receivable and accounts payable were handled and who paid them.

"Jane, secretary to the Body Shop Manager, Bill Wolfe, handles all incoming checks to the shop, and paid all the invoices between the first and tenth of every month, from the shop checking account. On the tenth of every month, she brings me all the paper transactions for the previous month. After I review all of the papers, I send everything to our accountant, who keeps a record of everything and sends all the paperwork back in three days with the amount that we have to pay the state for sales tax, workman's comp, FICA, and Soc. Sec. taxes."

Gar thought about it for a while.

"Grace, I'm asking a hypothetical question. Could someone, if they are dishonest, charge for a job and get paid for it without you or I knowing about it , or could an insurance job run over an adjusters estimate and someone at the shop pocket the difference?"

"No. Jane's repair invoice would have to match the Insurance draft including the customer's deductible."

"Ah," said Gar, "Is it possible for a customer to pay, shall we say, two hundred dollars for his deductible, and the shop's invoice only show the amount of the insurance draft, which would be two hundred less?"

"Yes, but the problem with that is too many people would be involved. Bill, the shop foreman has to approve the estimate. He orders parts, the paint shop orders paint and does their part and everyone in the shop sees the estimate and work order on each car, because the work order stays attached to the inside of the windshield until everything is completed."

He thought over what she had said. "So you are saying that if it did happen, more than one person would have to be involved. Am I right?"

"Yes, I think that is the only way."

"Okay, Grace, thank you. Oh, one more thing. Has there ever been a problem in the body shop with a money shortage, or a problem with management?"

"Not that I'm aware of, Mr. Savino."

"Thanks Grace, you have been a big help."

He wanted to set her at ease. "Oh, it's all right to call me Mr. Savino in front of others, but when we're together I'd prefer Gar, if it's all right with you."

"That would be fine , Gar," she said, smiling.

Gar reviewed the profit and loss sheets, the payroll , and salaries of everyone at the body shop, including the wrecker drivers. Everything seemed to be all right, but the net-profit should be greater. He would have to keep searching for a clue.

One day, Gar got a call from a customer who complained that the body shop had charged him and his insurance company for 4 expensive wire wheel covers and there wasn't anything wrong with his. Gar said he would look into the matter and would get back to him. He went to Bill Wolfe, the body shop manager and asked him about it. He verified that all four wheel covers were off the car when it came in on the wrecker. Gar thanked Bill and left. After the body shop closed that night, he and Grace went into the office and looked for an invoice from the Cadillac company for 4 wheel covers, but could not find any. The next day Gar invited the customer to the parts office.

When he came, Gar told the customer he wanted to look at his new wheel covers. When he inspected them, he saw that they were not new. Someone did a nice job polishing them, but they were not new. Gar had Grace write a check to the customer for the wheel covers and told him a mistake had been made and he would take care of the matter. The customer accepted his apology and went away happy. Then Gar called the body shop and asked the shop foreman to please step over to the parts office as soon as he was free to do so.

Grace was with Gar when Joe, the shop foreman came in. Gar told him the shop had been under surveillance for some time now and that he was ready to send someone to jail. He told him someone had cheated the insurance company and the customer out of the cost of 4 wheel covers and he knew this wasn't the first time that this happened.

He looked the foreman straight in the eye. "You have committed a felony."

"No sir, I acted on Bills orders. He had me remove the wheel covers before the adjuster came, then after the estimate was written, he had me replace the covers. He does this quite often. Yesterday, we removed a $300 windshield we stored it in the parts shed. He told the adjuster it flew out from inside pressure and was demolished, and the adjuster believed him. Now he wants me to put it back. I'm no crook , sir, and I'm not going to jail for him."

"Okay, Joe, I believe you. Go back to work and keep this between us. If you tell anyone, especially Bill Wolfe, I will see that you get to spend some time in jail."

"Thank you, sir, and I will tell you the minute that he steals another thing."

Gar knew he would have to fire both Jane and Bill, and perhaps Joe, but he would have quality replacements ready first. Gar decided to ask a professional employment agency find a manager for him, someone with excellent qualifications and recommendations. He wanted background and credit reports. Gar was going to hire someone that could also teach him everything about the body shop repair business. He was going to make sure customers would not get fleeced from his shop. He stressed secrecy with the agency and agreed to pay their fee if they found his man.

They found a shop manager presently employed at the Baron Cadillac Company. The company had recently bought the dealership and brought several key men with them from another town. They had offered the body shop manager to stay, but with a substantial cut in salary. He was dissatisfied and looking for a change. His background met all the requirements and a meeting with

Gar went very well. At a second meeting he was hired and afterward Gar immediately fired Bill and Jane. He made them clean out their desks and vacate the premises at once. They tried to object, but Gar relayed all the forgery, lying , fraud, and stealing they had done. He gave them one hour to leave or he would bring charges and have them put in jail . They were gone in 30 minutes. Grace had their checks ready for them and resignation papers for them to sign.

Gar hired a new secretary/office girl for the body shop and devoted all of his attention to the body shop. The new manager was Benjamin Jamison and preferred to be called Ben. The new secretary was a nice black lady who also came highly recommended. Her name was Leandra Jackson, but she preferred to be called Lee for short. She was divorced and had one child in grade school. She was very efficient at bookkeeping, typing and a nice telephone voice. She and Grace hit it off very well. Gar decided to keep Joe as the shop foreman after Ben told him that he was well qualified, and so far seemed loyal to the shop.

In six months Gar had become an expert at writing estimates and he was enjoying all the activity at the shop. He also became better acquainted with the insurance adjusters and he took delight in taking them out for lunch. Ben and Lee were proving to be good assets for the company. At the end of six months, the profit from the body shop was far above his expectations. To show his appreciation, he took every employee and their girlfriend or wife out to dinner on a Saturday night. They all got to meet Debbie and everyone told her how great it was to work for Gar. The next month Gar did the same for the Auto parts shop. They also told Debbie the same about Gar. The business was becoming very successful.

Debbie was very proud of Gar and she became his sounding board, listening to all his problems, only offering suggestions when he asked for them . She felt as though she knew every part of the business just from listening to her husband tell how he handled these projects. She was getting bored sitting at home and asked Gar if it was time to let her come to work with him. She told him she didn't mind office work and would like to become active in the company. Gar balked at letting her go to work, but after she continued bringing it up, decided to allow her to try. He asked Grace if she would take Debbie under her wing and teach her a little about the office work and let her gradually become a needed asset. Grace was more than willing and found Debbie was not only helpful, but she soon became her close friend.

Gar bought a new Chevy El Camino pickup truck and had both sides lettered with the company name, "Savinos Auto Parts & Salvage." It was white and the red lettering made it a thing of beauty. He surprised Debbie by taking her Hudson and trading it for a new Buick Electra with all the extras. He had the ability to make deals with all the dealerships and he bought anything he needed at wholesale prices and, of course, brought every item into the company, thereby not having to pay a tax on it as his personal income.

The three close families set aside the first Sunday of each month to have a family type dinner, alternating between the three boys , and Sammy's and Sandy's parents were always invited. The parents of both Sally and Karen were also invited, but rarely came. Debbie's parents were not alive and she had been an only child. Each family was expected to bring a dish to pass , thereby eliminating the host doing all the cooking. Debbie was very good at playing the piano and there was always a sing-along before the party was over. Mr. Cross would always ask her to play and sing "Amazing Grace," while Mr. Grimes could be counted on to request "Danny Boy." The three Heroes always made sure she played their favorite Navy song, "Anchors Aweigh."

At least three times a year, both mothers never failed to ask when would they see some grandchildren, and each time the answer was "We're working on it Mom," and laughter followed after each guy would say he was working on it harder.

These three Heroes who had such a tough beginning, even if some of it was self-made, managed to grasp the gold ring as they rode the merry-go-round of life. In a world of give and take, nothing is given without a price. No one knew this better than Gar, for he had discussed this very topic with Debbie at length more than once.

His theorem, or proposition, was that life was cruel early on, and it had swung back in balance by him becoming successful, as it did for Sammy and Sandy. The big question in this equation now was, "Will the pendulum of life swing back to the beginning again?"

Debbie's answer for him was that the cruel part of life was influenced by cruel things such as, acts by man, acts by nature, and evil driven persons. However, as we become more cognizant of this, we do have the opportunity to counterbalance this by influencing our life with goodness. Good over evil will always prevail if we put our faith and trust in God. Gar knew she was right and when she told him it was time to attend and join the Baptist church, where they were married, he accepted her decision without question.

Gar invited Bucko to come and spend a day or two him , so he could show him his new company. They had talked many times by phone and Bucko was eager to accept the invitation. Gar asked Debbie if it would be all right if Bucko stayed at the house. She felt it would be nice to see him again. She knew he was one of his closest friends and it would be great for him.

Bucko couldn't believe how much the company had expanded and how much Gar had learned about the business. He took delight in giving him the grand tour, introducing him to all of his managers. Gar took him and Debbie out for lunch.

After lunch, Gar asked "Have you made any plans about going to work or are you going to try playing craps as a living? The last time I saw you, we were both thinking about doing something else and as you know, I did. I don't mean to interfere in your personal life, but since you are my good friend, I'm interested."

"Funny you should ask, because since I found out you had invested in your company and how much you liked it, I have been looking around for something also, but so far, nothing has come of it."

Gar let the conversation change to how well Debbie was enjoying her work and how she was becoming very important to the business.

To his great surprise, she offered "Gar, why don't you let Bucko come to work for us, or am I speaking out of turn?"

Gar and Bucko, both caught off guard, looked at each other, then back at her.

"Hey guys, I'm sorry. I never should have said that," she hurriedly exclaimed.

Bucko quickly replied, "No Debbie, you haven't said any thing wrong. It was just that I was thinking about something else, and my mind went blank."

Gar was quick to come to Debbie's aid.

"Say, that's a great idea Debbie. Actually, I have thought of doing that, but didn't know how to approach doing it. Thank you sweetheart, for opening the door for me. What about it, Bucko?"

Bucko, looking for words, finally said,"You don't have an opening in your business that needs me. Besides what do I know about parts?"

"I didn't know anything either pal, but I have some ideas that maybe you might like. Are you able to invest, or do you want to just be employed?"

"If an opportunity is right, I'd rather invest."

"Okay, let's finish our lunch and we will talk some more in my office when we return."

Gar told Bucko that there was money to be made selling automobiles. He had been thinking about buying or starting a good used car business, not a rinky-dink one, but one that dealt fairly with it's customers and only sold newer models. He wanted two or three mechanics to turn over the inventory fast.

Those that didn't move quick enough, would be taken to the auction. He discussed how he had the perfect arrangement for buying damaged vehicles by use of his wreckers and from the salvage buying from insurance companies. Then the body shop would repair the less damaged units that were deemed sale able. Then the used car dealership would sell them. Whenever the shop was slow, he would buy more repairable units, keeping everyone busy.

They talked about buying into a new car dealership, but Gar thought that they should just try the used car business at first and if things progressed as he hoped, they would expand later.

He explained that he wanted a partner who would be in charge of all the used car sales and it's employees. They would be equal partners but Gar would not take a salary or profit from the new business for two years, but Bucko would. Gar would use his experience and help him get started but all the management would be done by Bucko. This seemed to be a fair way to have a partnership. He told him if he didn't want a partner, he could buy the dealership by himself and they could still handle it the same way. He just wanted someone he trusted and Bucko was it.

Bucko was very receptive and when Gar offered him the chance to be an equal partner in the new venture, he said, "I want in. Let's do it ."

They decided on B & G Motors as the name of the new business and they found just what they wanted on Main Street, with lots of traffic because it was on a corner. It was for sale by the owner, who had gotten tired of the car business and his vehicles were not selling. He let the place get seedy and run down. He had two large buildings that could easily be upgraded for mechanical use and a better showroom.

Gar and Bucko negotiated with him and he finally accepted a deal that gave him a substantial down payment, and he would carry the mortgage over twenty years with the option of paying off ahead of time. The property had a nice long front that would allow for at least twenty cars shown facing the highway. They upgraded the lighting and soon it was like a shining beacon. They had a local Radio DJ broadcast the opening after everything had been ready. Gar invited finance companies to set up and offer on-the-spot financing at the opening. Bucko hired a sales manager and staff to handle sales. Bucko was learning fast but relied on his ability to hire quality personnel to help him make the right decisions. He hired three mechanics, and two detail men, plus a wash boy. Every unit sold had a warranty with it. Sales increased every month and was enhanced by satisfied customers.

In the partnership agreement was a clause that stipulated that each partner would carry a life insurance policy of one hundred thousand dollars with the other partner as beneficiary. In event of a death, the beneficiary must use this amount to buy out the deceased's half from his estate. Thereby the remaining partner would have full ownership. This would eliminate any unnecessary problems if a tragedy happened. There wasn't a partnership at the auto salvage or body shop, just a will drawn up, with Debbie as beneficiary.

Chapter 68

The success of Savino Salvage and Auto Parts, along with Savino's Towing and Body Repair Shop put Gar's name before many people. The television station called him and asked if he would allow them to televise a documentary about him and his business. They heard how fast his business had grown and in checking his background, discovered that he was also a Congressional Medal of Honor hero. They felt that he and his company were news, and worthy of a segment for TV. He was hesitant at first, then after he thought of all the free publicity this would generate for the company, gave his permission.

It was a very professional documentary and it did produce additional business for all of his companies. You would have to be blind or deaf not to see or hear something on the TV about the Savinos. He was constantly answering the phone from congratulatory well wishers. The Grimes and Cross families were thrilled with the successful exposure and had called him and Debbie several times. The segment covered the life of Gar and ended with him and his bride, Debbie.

The story was also seen by the inmates of the State Prison at Auburn,NY. One in particular stared at the documentary with such hatred that he yelled out, "That's him! That's the bastard that set me up. That's that damn Wop that caused all my problems twenty years ago."

His cellmate, Nick Garcia, said, "What's your problem, you better quit shouting or the guard will be over here."

"That's the guy that screwed me!" Tom yelled.

The guard came to his cell door.

"Quiet down Wysocki, or you'll lose your TV privileges. You 're due for parole shortly, do you want to throw that away now?"

"No sir, I'm sorry. I got carried away. I'll shut up."

Nick looked bewildered and asked, "What the hell's got into you, anyway?"

"That guy on TV, that Savino creep, he did something to me when we were at that reform school in Industry years ago."

He told Nick how he had put peas on Gar's plate and that he was most likely the one that planted those cigarettes in his bunk.

"So what? Now you're even. Why, after all these years, would you still hate the guy?"

"Because he's a dirty Wop Italian and now he's rich. When I get out, now that I know where he is, I'm gonna make him pay." His face was red with rage.

"Oh yeah, sure, then you'll be right back here doing more time. That's real smart, Tom."

"No, no, They're never getting me in here again. I'll think of some way to get him and the law won't know it's me."

"Yeah, yeah. I've heard that a thousand times before. Just listen to yourself. It's twenty years since you saw this guy and you want to hurt him over a silly cigarette. The

TV said that this guy served in World War Two and was a hero. Tell me where were you during the war?"

"None of your freaking business, Jerk-off," said Tom.

Tom Wysocki was released from Industry right after the war had started. Instead of volunteering for the service as most good Americans did, he and two of his pals robbed a liquor store in Buffalo and were apprehended after being spotted at a gas station. He was sent to Elmira Correctional Prison for five years. When he was released, he went back to Buffalo where he drove a taxi for two years until he was fired for drinking on the job and being abusive to customers.

He became an alcoholic and once more thought it would be easy to take whiskey and money from another liquor store. He was a hard learner. This time, the owner had a pistol near the cash register and when Tom came in late one night with his cap pulled way down, he knew this was trouble. Tom pulled out his gun and demanded the cash. The owner already had his hand on his pistol and in the blink of an eye, he brought up his gun and fired into Tom's shoulder, sending him crashing into a stand of beer and wine. He hit the alarm system at the same time and the police were there before Tom could even think of crawling away.

He spent a week in the hospital, then from jail he was sentenced to twenty years at the Auburn State Penitentiary at Auburn, NY. He behaved himself and was now up for early parole. He was determined Gar was going to suffer for that incident at Industry, even if he wasn't sure that he was the one that planted those butts in his bunk.

Chapter 69

Gar was an early riser and usually he was up long before Debbie. He enjoyed reading the paper with his coffee by six AM, and since Debbie didn't go to the office till nine, he would be at work by seven thirty.

On this particular morning. Debbie was still not at her desk by ten and Grace asked Gar if Debbie was taking the day off. He at once dialed his house and when no one answered after five rings, he became very worried . He told Grace he was returning to the house and he would call her from there. He didn't waste any time speeding back and silently prayed that she hadn't been involved in an accident going to work. He was somewhat relievedto see her Buick was still in the driveway, as he came screeching in. He shouted as he rushed through the front door.

"Debbie!"

Hearing nothing, he ran up the stairs still shouting, "Debbie, where are you?"

From the bedroom he passed the bathroom, where he saw her sitting on the floor next to the commode. She had just vomited again and the toilet was flushing.

When she saw Gar she cried, "Oh Gar, I have been so sick. I tried to call the office, but the nausea was so bad that I just couldn't leave the bathroom."

Gar picked her up and carried her to the bed, where he carefully laid her on the bed. After he put the ice bag on her head and got her calmed down, he asked her if she thought maybe she was food poisoned. She didn't think so, because it started before she had breakfast.

"Well, I'll help you get dressed and then we are going to the emergency room at the hospital. We are not going to take a chance that it may be serious. I'll call Grace to let her know, then I'll call your doctor to meet us there."

Debbie tried to protest, but Gar was not going to change his mind.

At the emergency room, they were expecting them and although her doctor was not there, he had told the ER to call him after they had run some tests.

Within the hour the doctor appeared. He told her and Gar that she was pregnant! Gar was shocked and happy. Debbie was also in shock. As she was crying with happiness, she was searching Gar's face for any sign that he might not want a baby just yet. She saw that Gar truly, really did want this, and he hugged her and kept saying, "Darling, I'm so happy for us. This is what I've been hoping for. This baby will never see an orphanage, by God."

The ER gang congratulated the couple and the doctor told Debbie to make an appointment with his office right away. They drove back home and Gar made her stay in bed for the rest of the day. He sat down and called all the families and friends with the good news. Bucko told him he was happy for him and that used car sales were up from last month. Grace congratulated him and assured him that she and Ben had everything under control, so he should stay home and comfort Debbie.

The next months were somewhat difficult for Debbie. She was always sick in the morning with nausea and discomfort. The doctor assured her that this was normal and prescribed tomato juice and saltine crackers before getting up in the morning. Gar would be sure to place both at her side of the bed before she awoke. She wanted to return to work, but Gar wouldn't allow it. He was overprotective of her and he made sure that she had everything that was needed to help her get through this. This was all new to him and he was a real worry wart. Having lost his parents early in life made him more cognizant of how frail were the ties that bind us together.

More good news came one evening from Sammy. He called to inform Gar and Debbie that Karen had just come from the doctor and she too was pregnant. He could hardly contain himself with the joy of becoming a father. Both he and Gar were joking about getting Sandy's Sally that way too. They were having their fun, but they also knew how badly Sally wanted children. Gar wanted a party to celebrate, but Sammy told him that wasn't a wise thing, because it would make Sandy and Sally feel bad so they didn't do that. Gar insisted that the two of them get together to talk about old times and some new ideas about Sammy's trucks. They agreed to meet Friday night at Vinnie's Bar & Grill.

Chapter 70

Sammy was all smiles when he arrived. He spotted Gar over at the corner table. They gave each other a brotherly hug and told Vinnie to bring a pitcher of draft beer over to the table. They brought each other up to date on all the current events and everyday business chatter. Of course they were crowing a little about the addition that was coming into their lives.

After a while, Gar asked Sammy if the trucking company had occasional collision damage to their units, and if so, where they were repaired? Sammy said that with the large fleet they had in service and the amount of other vehicles on the highway, there were damages every day. The long distance tractors weren't bad, but the city trucks were involved all the time. He told him that most all of them were sent to Liberty Truck Repair Company. They were big enough to do both body and engine repairs, including frame straightening. The problem was they were also so busy that it took forever getting a unit returned.

"Why do you ask? Your place isn't big enough to handle trucks, is it?"

"Well, right now it isn't, but I was thinking since I've got a lot of land that's not being used and we are already in the repair business, why not look into the rest of the collision world and do the trucks also. That is, if someone I know would send all their damaged units to me."

"Hey pal, if you go that route and decide to try it, I'll talk with Dad and I'm sure he will be glad to have you do it. Remember, he was the one that told you about the place that you have now, right?"

"That's right, and that's why I'm interested in expanding into the trucks."

"Okay, Gar, I'll talk to him tomorrow and give you a call."

Two days later, Sammy's father called Gar and told him that he would send all of his repairs to him if his shop would be large enough to handle his big rigs, including frame straightening. He emphasized that the parts costs on these big units were tremendous and he would need a much larger amount of working capital to carry him over until the unit was fully repaired and paid for. If he had several units in the shop at once and his working capital was inadequate, he could be bankrupt in no time. He suggested Gar search out a truck repair company that had been successful.

"Have an accounting firm go over their books, determine what capital would be needed, and either buy them out or use the information to have a shop built on your own property. Either way, be sure that you aren't under capitalized. When and if you do make the move to go for it, I'll send you my work."

The next few months Gar kept his watching the business opportunities section in the paper, looking for a truck repair company that wanted to sell. He also asked a few real estate companies to notify him if they had one for sale. Over a period of four months, he managed to find two. He inspected, investigated, interviewed, researched and made ridiculous offers, but he wasn't able to close one. All of the information that he gleaned from those companies was written down and stored for future use. If and when the right opportunity came along, he would be ready. He hadn't yet figured out how he was going to get his hands on enough cash to go big, but so far, none was needed.

Chapter 71

The parole board notified Tom that he was on the list of inmates to be interviewed for parole. They instructed him as to how he should dress and what basic questions he may be asked. They would insist that he had a proper place to live and have employment waiting for him if he was granted parole. Everything that he was to submit had to be typewritten and OK'd by the Warden. This was to be the second time that he'd asked for a parole hearing. The previous yeahr he was denied parole because of his attitude. They didn't feel that he showed enough remorse and that he might be inclined to cause bodily harm to society once again.

Tom's cousin lived in Port Chester, NY and guaranteed room and shelter for Tom. He had also secured a job for him as a taxi driver there. The Cab company had sent a letter to the Warden, confirming employment, when and if he was paroled.

Tom had rehearsed over and over what he was going to say at his hearing and just how to say it, shedding a few tears if need be. This would be the hardest thing he would ever do. He hated the owner of the liquor store and laid in his bunk many nights dreaming of how he was going to castrate him when he got out. His hatred was sent in a new direction ever since he saw Gar Savino on the television. He was searching for ways to put a hurt on him and still not get caught doing it. He promised himself if he ever was released, he would never be put away again. They would have to kill him first. Tomorrow was the day for his interview with the parole board.

Bucko had been accepted into Gar's family circle and was expected to attend the family dinners whenever an invitation was given. He was such a gentleman and his devotion to Gar was admired by everyone. He came across as a rather shy person to some, while others viewed him as mysterious. Gar had always hoped that Bucko would eventually open up and reveal his past or whatever mystery it was that created a cloud over his demeanor. He never tried to push him into any revelation, but rather patiently waited for him to come forth on his own.

This was not the case with the ladies of his new found family friends. Bucko enjoyed the light teasing that the wives gave him and he seemed to always be able to sidetrack the issue of his past. However, this day as they all gathered around the fireplace for after dinner chitchat and sing along, Sally boldly spoke up.

"Bucko, I can't stand not knowing who you are or what the mystery is about your past. All of us have accepted you into our lives with love and nothing you tell us will change that, so please tell us something and put me out of my misery."

Chapter 72

Bucko chuckled and he could see that everyone in the room was seriously waiting to see what his reactions would be. He realized it's time make a statement, good or bad, this family has taken him on face value and so what was the problem?

He cleared his throat and said, "You're right, Sally, and all of you. You have accepted me into your family with love and I want you to know that I deeply appreciate that, and I love you all the same way. There's no mystery about me. I see that some could think that since I've not been forthcoming with my past, and for that, I apologize.

"My name, as most of you know, is Robert Fullmer. Bucko is a nickname from school. I was born and raised in White Plains, NY and after my mother died, my father remarried. He owned a tool and machine shop and was fairly successful. I finished high school there and I had an interest in music. I learned to read music and often I would be seen or heard playing the piano at one of the taverns where alot of my school chums would hang out.

"That is, until my father found out about it. He demanded that I forget about pursuing music and come to work at his machine shop. I, of course, rebelled and we had several verbal fights." Bucko hesitated as he started to tell the next part of his sad story.

"One day he physically beat me after one of his violent tantrums. He was much bigger and a very strong man. One of his employees observed how he was treating me and tried to intercede on my behalf, but my father punched him away like one would brush off a fly. He then directed all of his attention on me. He was red with rage and utterly out of control. I was laying on the floor, partially dazed from his wicked slap.

"When he turned around towards me. He lost his footing on all the loose metal that was strewn around the floor from all the pushing and shoving and fell across a sharp, steel spike that he had been working on for a pick. He fell with such force that the steel shaft went clear through his chest and part of his heart. He died instantly. Witnesses easily substantiated that his death was by accident, absolving me from any charges, but I was traumatized. I felt that I was the cause of his death.

"My stepmother didn't help me. In fact, she never missed an opportunity to scream in my face, 'Murderer! You caused your fathers death!'"

He looked down at the floor. The emotional effects of this story were evident on his face as he continued, "It was so bad that my doctor placed me in a Care Center and I had to undergo much therapy before my mind could accept the fact that my father's death was an accident.

"My stepmother took over ownership of the machine shop. My father had set up a trust fund for me to receive when I became twenty one, which meant I had to wait three more years to receive it. My love for music vanished when I had mental problems about my father's death. My stepmother became so abusive towards me that I had to leave the house. She refused to give me a penny from the shop and later remarried one of her workers and then it was their machine shop. To this day I have never gone near her or the shop.

"My visions of college and a music career were gone forever. I found employment with Cummings Lumber Company. I was desperate to make enough money to tide me over for three years until I could receive my inheritance from my father's trust fund.

"The work was hard and as a beginner, I had all the "gofer" jobs, 'go for this and go for that.' After three years, somehow I was beginning to like the work. I had worked my way up from a yard bird to assistant yard foreman, and then the assistant buyer, accompanying the owner out into the field.

"Mary, the owner's daughter came to work in the office after she had graduated and we started dating. We fell in love and later we were married. My salary was more than sufficient by now and I put my trust fund into long term investments. My life was becoming more meaningful and I was happier than I had ever been in my life.

"We tried everything to have children, but nothing happened. After ten years we decided to adopt. Just as we were about to receive an adopted child, her doctor told us that Mary was actually pregnant. We were on cloud nine and so very happy. Then her father suffered a stroke and died before the baby was born. He had willed the company to us and I took over as the new owner . Mary delivered a beautiful daughter and we were, again, very happy.

"Things went well for another fifteen years. Our daughter had just gotten her learner's permit to drive.

One day, she and Mary were waiting at an intersection for the light to change. When it changed to green, she started across the intersection. A driver trying to run a red light and cross in front of them, crashed into the left side of our car. It struck so hard that our car rolled over and over three times."

Everyone in the room was watching Bucko as he said with defeat, "Our daughter's neck was snapped, killing her instantly. My Mary's back was broken and she was forever paralyzed from the neck down."

Sally screamed, "Oh my God!" and she started to cry.

Bucko, who had been telling his story nonstop from a stoic like trance, was suddenly jolted back into reality by Sally's outburst. He looked around to the others as if he was seeing them for the first time.

As he became oriented again, he said, "I am sorry if my life is too graphic, please accept my apology. I never should have given you all my grief at one time."

He lowered his head, apologetically.

Gar rushed over to him and hugged him lovingly.

"Bucko, you didn't do anything wrong. We asked you—no, we badgered you into telling. I am so sorry for you. We will never ask again about your life. If you want to finish your story someday, we would love to hear it, but I think for now it's too much of a strain on you. We need to let you relax for now. Besides, we haven't heard any of our songs played tonight."

Everyone tried their best to make the transfer to a happier mood, but Bucko's vivid tale held them in such awe, it was difficult to do. Debbie quickly realized their dilemma, went to the piano and softly began the families' favorite, "Amazing Grace." It was magical. Everyone gathered around the piano with their arms around each other, some with tears still on their cheeks, and sang that lovely hymn.

Chapter 73

The parole board should have nominated Tom for an Oscar for his role in how to act remorseful. He sold them a real bag full, and they bought it. He received their decision in writing the following day. His parole was approved and he would be released to the care of his brother in three days.

His brother was waiting for him as he passed through the iron gates to freedom. He went to work as a taxi driver the following week, just as he was ordered to do. He met with his probation officer the first day and he clearly understood what he could and could not do to keep from violating parole. He would not be allowed to leave the county or the state without permission. This was the one thing that upset him the most. His brother constantly reminded him this was his last chance, so do not blow it. Tom would have liked to slap him every time he said that, but he kept his cool, all the time putting together a scheme to travel to Brooklyn and find where Gar lived. Port Chester was only about an hour's drive northeast, so this was not that big of a problem. He would bide his time and put his plan in motion when the time was right.

Debbie was in the eighth month of her pregnancy and she had really blossomed out. Her morning sickness had left her months ago and other than being uncomfortable at times, she was doing very well. She was still driving her car and she hadn't any problems picking up any groceries that were needed for the house. Gar hired a lady to come to the house once a week to do the cleaning and the laundry. He insisted that she call him or Grace every morning by ten o'clock and every afternoon by three o'clock. Everyone at the office was put on alert to expect a call from Debbie. Everything was going well so far.

Rose Grimes, Sandy's sister, graduated from Colgate College and was employed at Bantam Double Dell Publishing Company on Broadway in New York City. She commuted from Queens, where she was still living with her parents, Irving and Mary Grimes. She usually was present at the family dinners and when Gar married Debbie, she was immediately drawn to her. They formed a bond of friendship and on her days off in the middle of the week, she would often drive down to see Debbie. They either shared some coffee and cake or they would visit the local diner for lunch. Debbie looked forward to those days and Rose delighted in sharing her free time with her new sister-in-law. Whenever a new boy came into Rose's life, even temporarily, they dissected him endlessly. She also helped Debbie do-over one of the bedrooms into a nursery for the expected baby.

It was during one of these visits when they were putting paper butterflies on the nursery walls, when they heard the front door chimes.

Debbie was pasting the backing. "Oh, now who could that be?" she asked. "I'm right in the middle of this. Rose, would you mind catching the door for me, and if it's a salesman, tell him we aren't interested?"

"Sure thing," said Rose and scurried downstairs and opened the front door.

The man removed his hat and said, "Good morning, Mrs. Savino, I'm with Encyclopedia Brittanica and I would like to show you our free trial publication."

"But I'm not Mrs. S——"

"Most people aren't interested, but if I may just step in for one moment, I'm..."

"Who is it ?" came Debbie's voice from upstairs.

"I've got it." said Rose. She turned back to the salesman, "I'm sorry but as I tried to tell you, I'm not Mrs. Sav.." but by the time she got to "Mrs." again, he had put his hat back on and walked off the porch. Rose closed the door and returned upstairs.

"That was strange."

"What's strange?" asked Debbie.

"That man. He called me Mrs. Savino and tried to sell me an encyclopedia. But when I tried to tell him that I wasn't you and he heard you call from upstairs, he left in a huff. Maybe he thought I was trying to tell him I wasn't interested instead of that I wasn't Mrs. Saravino. Funny thing though, he didn't sound like a salesman."

"Oh well," Debbie said, "We get salesmen out here all the time. Don't let it bother you."

Chapter 74

Tom briskly hurried down the street, where he had parked his car. He was cursing himself for not knowing that someone was in the house besides Gar's wife. He had painstakingly spent precious time watching the house over the last few weeks and was sure he had the perfect plan, but now he'd have to make some changes. Leaving Port Chester without permission, even this close, was a violation and also time consuming. His brother was always asking him where he had been if he was even five minutes late for anything.

He'd asked his parole officer for permission to drive to New York City to apply for employment with the transportation department of the Port Authority as a bus driver then talked with his employer about taking a leave of absence to have his gall bladder removed and told his brother that he had gotten permission to go to New York City to seek better employment. He found an abandoned warehouse where he was going to use to keep Gar's wife until he collected the ransom from Gar.

He pulled into a convenience store to get some cigarettes and to think about his dilemma. When returned to his car and as he was about to leave, he saw Gar's wife pull up, park and go inside. He told himself all was not lost. This was a better opportunity to implement his original plan. He pulled his car around back and parked it where it wouldn't be noticed. Then he hurried back to her car and got into the back seat, put a ski mask on and lay on the floor. When Gar's wife returned with a small sack, she put it in front, started the car and proceeded to drive away. When she stopped at the stop sign, Tom put a gun to the back of her head and told her to remain calm and not to scream. She was so startled that she instinctively let out a scream. When she did, Tom tapped her with the gun butt hard enough to knock her unconscious. He got into the driver's seat and tied her hands and put a blindfold on her head.

He drove to the warehouse, where he stored the car, and lay her on an old mattress he'd bought for the occasion. When he was sure she was going to be all right, and that she was securely tied, he left to call Gar.

Gar was at work and Grace answered the phone. She informed Gar that the call was for him. "Hello, this is Gar Savino."

"Listen up, Woppo, I'm only gonna say this once. We have your wife and if you want to see her alive again, you need to put two hundred thousand dollars in a sack and put it in a place that we tell you. We know you may think this a hoax, so when we hang up, you try calling her so you are convinced. We will call back in five minutes to give you instructions where to put the money. One other thing, my Woppo friend, if you call the police, we promise that your wife will not live to see you again. Like I said, five minutes."

Gar was stunned. He tried to ask who this was, but the person talked fast and hung up quickly.

Grace could see from Gar's face that something was wrong and came over to him and asked, "What's wrong, Gar?"

"Grace, that guy just said he'd kidnapped Debbie!!! I need to call the house, NOW!!!"

He dialed home and Debbie answered, "Hello."

Hearing her voice was a great relief. "Debbie, thank God. Are you all right?"

"Yes, I'm fine. Why are you shouting? It's not time to call you."

"Debbie, a man just called me on the phone and told me that they had you kidnapped and they wanted two hundred thousand dollars ransom and that they would kill you if I told the police. He's to call me back in five minutes. Are you sure that everything is all right at the house? He sounded so sure of himself."

"Gar, I assure you that I'm fine. Rose was here for lunch and I discovered that we were about out of milk and bread, so she went to the convenience store for it. She will be right back. Someone is playing a cruel joke on us, sounds like."

"Maybe so, but boy, he sure was convincing. When Rose comes back, ask her to call me, okay? I love you and I'll see you at six."

"Okay, Hon. Bye."

Gar turned to Grace and related to her what had just transpired. They talked about what a bad joke this was.

The phone rang and Gar grabbed for it ,"Hello, this is Gar Savino."

The voice on the other end said, "So now are you convinced?"

Gar's patience had run out, "Hey jerk, I don't know who you are, but you've got one sick mind. If you call here again, I'll have the police on you in no time."

"Hey, Savino, this ain't no joke. We have your wife!! You must not have called your house, wise guy."

"Yes I did. She is home and safe and this conversation is over!"

Gar slammed the receiver back into it's carriage.

"Can you believe th—" The phone rang again and he picked it up, "YES ?"

"This ain't no joke, you freaking Wop. You better check on your wife now. I'll call your house in thirty minutes. You better be there to answer it."

Gar related the story again to Grace. He told her he was on his way home and to call the police and inform them what had taken place. Even if this joke had gone too far, they needed to know about it .

Chapter 75

Gar didn't waste anytime rushing home and coming into the driveway he could see that Debbie's Buick was still in its usual spot. He ran in the front door and there was Debbie standing there in a bewildered state.

"Hi honey, did you find out why that guy told you I was kidnapped?"

"Thank God you are all right. No, not yet. Where is Rose? Did she leave without calling me?"

"No, she hasn't come back yet." She felt herself becoming tense. "I'm getting worried. I thought that was her when I heard you drive up."

The phone rang. Debbie answered before Gar could get to it.

"Hello," she said. Silence. Then she said again, "Hello?"

A deep voice on the phone said, "Is this the Savino residence?"

"Yes, it is. This is Mrs. Savino, may I help you?"

The voice asked with urgency," You are Mrs. Savino?"

"Yes, would you like to speak with Mr. Savino, he's right here?"

"Yes, I would."

Gar took the phone from Debbie,"Hello, this is Mr. Savino."

"Say, what's going on there, Pal? We have your wife and now you've got someone that says she's Mrs. Savino. You are playing with dynamite pal."

Gar said,"Look, whoever you are, this has gone too far. As you can see, my wife is here and you are not funny. The phone company will be onto you, so hang up." He started to hang up himself and had a thought Oh! Wait just a minute. If you have my wife, what does she look like?"

The caller hesitated, then said, "She is about five- ten, brown hair, I guess, and pretty."

"Sorry, you jerk. Now I know this is a hoax because my wife is big as a barrel and is eight months pregnant."

When Gar hung up the phone, he told Debbie about the conversation.

Debbie yelled,"Oh my God, they've got Rose! They think she's me, Gar. Someone was here this noon and Rose answered the door for me because I was detained upstairs in the nursery." Debbie told Gar about the salesman.

Gar called Grace to see if she had called the police yet. She had and told him to call Inspector Spicer, who wanted to speak with Gar. He called at once and told him everything.

A patrol car was at Gar's home in less than five minutes and Gar again told Inspector Spicer and the other policemen everything he knew. They determined that Gar was right. They must have taken Rose by mistake. A phone call to the Grimes home established that Rose was not home.

Gar repeated every word that transpired between him and the kidnappers. When he related how the caller kept repeatedly calling him a Wop and Woppo, a bell went off in his brain. Only one person ever called him that name. He told him about Tom Wysocki and the incidents that occurred at Industry.

Within no time they had tracked Tom's entire history. They talked to his brother, his employer, and his parole officer. He had to be their man. They found his car behind the convenience store and an all-points-bulletin was put out with his description, along with Rose's. They were also looking for the car that Rose drove. With all the good information coming in, the police spotted Rose's car at a service station. The driver was making a call at the pay-phone when the police apprehended him. Tom did not have a clue that they were after him. He hadn't any chance at all to run They cuffed him and after some persuasion, he told where Rose was. She was found and taken to the hospital for a checkup. She was released soon after.

Gar and Debbie went to the hospital and were waiting for her when she was finally permitted to leave. The nightmare was over and everyone in all the families were so glad when Gar phoned that Rose and Debbie were OK and the kidnapper was caught. Tom Wysocki would never see freedom again. A three-time loser!!

Chapter 76

Sandy and Sally had waited a long time before seriously committing themselves to having children. Both of them were in agreement that it was time to change that. Seeing both Karen and Debbie nearing termination only reinforced their decision. Sally had decided that a leave of absence would not hinder her career if she wanted to continue nursing after childbirth. Sandy was happy in his work and his salary was more than sufficient to warrant less income, if she quit working. So it was not unwelcome news when Sally informed Sandy one evening that she was expecting. Sandy was overjoyed and wanted to have a party to celebrate.

"Sandy, we can party anytime and that means having more people around. Not that I mind that, but I'd rather just have only you tonight. I want to share this special time with the one person I love and who makes my life worth living."

He was touched and wrapped his arms around her.

"Oh, sweetheart, that is the nicest thing I ever heard. I love you so!! We will have our own party right here. We have a bottle of red cabernet in the back of the refrigerator. We can have a pizza with all the trimmings delivered and I can cut some cheese to go with the crackers."

"Oh Sandy, can we? That would be so wonderful."

Sandy took the big NY Giants blanket from the foyer closet and spread it across the living room in front of the fireplace. He gathered all the candles, placed them in cereal bowls and wrapped foil around the bottoms so they wouldn't fall over. He lit the fire place while she made cheese cracker squares. He called and ordered a large pizza. He got the special wine glasses out of the cupboard and opened the cold bottle of cabernet wine.

When the pizza arrived, they put everything on the blanket, brought pillows from the sofa, lit the candles and turned out all the lights. The logs were crackling and as they raised their glasses for a toast, the room was no longer the front room, but a beautiful palatial boudoir fit for a king and queen. Shadows from the candles danced their soft ballet from curtain to curtain to their lovers delight. The touch from Sandy's artificial hand was as normal to Sally as breathing in and out. She had become so accustomed to these, that she could actually feel his tenderness flowing gently into her soul. True love can never be suppressed by a handicap. When she let her long flowing hair fragrant with lilac blossoms fall across his bare chest and the velvet softness of her lips tease the hardness of his nipples, he would nearly go out of his mind as he moaned with pleasure. This was how she felt when he took delight in teasing her. She sometimes would continue the foreplay until he begged her to stop, while loving the stimulating torture. Then they would lock themselves together as two combatant wrestlers and explode over the mountain of ecstasy. They soon drifted off to sleep wrapped in each other's arms . The sweetness of love!!

The firstborn in every family puts a strain on every one like no other event that ever happens. The doctors' appointments, morning sickness, night cravings, temper tantrums, anxiety, false alarms, and the cries of alarm when the mother sees herself in the mirror going from a beach blanket babe to a pear shaped milk factory. The father needs the patience of Job. He had to watch, listen and be her strength for her to lean on. At three AM, when she just had to have that ice cream and dill pickle, he gladly dressed and ran to the local convenience store.

Our Heroes were no different and over the next months they each had weathered the storms and were proudly boasting about how beautiful their child was. In 1947, Debbie was first with her eight pound boy that they named Timmy. Then Karen gave birth to a seven and one half pound girl named Holly. Sally was a few months later, giving birth to a seven pound girl named Sharon.

Chapter 77

The numbers gathering at the family dinners were increasing and the grandparents were in their glory. Nothing in the world can replace the euphoria of a proud grandparent. They buy all sorts of gadgets, toys, candies and spoil them rotten, then return them to the parents. They lovingly interfere with every training program that sounds too harsh and smother the little angels with hugs and kisses when they come running from a spanking for doing something wrong.

The civilized world gets its greatest strength from love of family. The Bible teaches that love is our greatest attribute. There is nothing more precious than the moment you feel that soft little hand slide into your palm when least expected and as you slowly turn, a tiny voice whispers in your ear, "Daddy, I love you" or "Mommy, I love you." It's whispered so carefully like the secret password that's offered as you enter into your lodge room. This is the ultimate best. Something hard to beat, unless it's later in years when that grandson catches the most fish and as they roast their sandwiches over an open fire at the campsite, he tenderly grasps Grandpa's hand and said, "Grampus, you're the greatest."

Bucko never thought that selling cars could ever be a satisfying vocation, but he soon found that good honest business practices can be rewarding, especially in the automobile world. The fast-buck Eddies come and go faster than the wind, but when the true blue entrepreneur backs his statements with actions, the buyers come running. His car lot had a large statue of a man in front with his right arm extended outward with the finger pointing towards an invisible person and a captioned sign that boldly read,"I WANT TO SELL YOU A CAR."

He never failed to be invited to the family dinners and by now was thought of as one of the family. He was coming out of his shell, able to discuss more openly of his tragedies of his past. He had that certain swagger to his gait again, like one has when everything is going well and you're feeling good. He was usually invited along when Gar, Sammy, and Sandy were going out for a beer at Vinnie's Bar & Grille. It wasn't that they needed a drink , it was more of a night out to shoot some bull and relax with friends.

Bucko had become friends with one of his customers and was dating her on a regular basis. They had met by accident, literally. She pulled into Bucko's lot just as he was about to leave. She had parked behind his auto. He looked behind him before he started his own. Not seeing anything there, he backed his car into her grille and headlights. It was a loud crash. She had just shut the driver's door and was moving away to browse around to see the autos on display. The noise from the crash caught her by surprise. She screamed and her heel caught as she started to run and she went sprawling onto the ground. He quickly realized his error and ran to pick her up and render aid if needed.

She allowed him to brush her off and accepted his apology. He repaired her vehicle and also had the entire unit repainted. He also had some mechanical work done for her free of charge. Over the next few weeks they got to know each other quite well and found they had a lot in common and started dating.

She was Edna May, a widow employed with the County Water Board as office manager. She had been there for nineteen satisfying years . She lost her husband from cancer. She had no children and no desire to remarry, or even date for that matter. There was something about Bucko that was different and she soon gave in to his charm and they became close friends. In a matter of six months they were engaged. They were invited to family dinners and she was accepted into the circle of caring people.

Bucko and Edna decided to wait until she finished her twentieth year at the Water Board, take her retirement , then marry and take a long honeymoon.

Chapter 78

Gar was a proud poppa and he would often find himself drifting into that dreamlike state all fathers enter into. They envision their son as President of the USA, or the famous doctor that saves the world, or maybe a Supreme Court Judge. Debbie also had dreamlike expectations of her beautiful child. Her ambition to have children and to make her husband happy was being fulfilled. She wanted so much to give Gar the family he never had.

Six weeks after Timmy's birth, Debbie noticed a bruise on Timmy's lip. She attributed it to maybe hitting it against his crib. Then she noticed in the following days he appeared somewhat less active, more fatigued or sleepy. Then when she saw slight ulcers inside his mouth one morning and he had a fever, she alerted Gar and rushed him to the emergency room at the hospital. The family doctor was called and after extensive testing, the diagnosis was Myelogenous Leukemia, a disease caused by malignant change in cells that produce granulocytes, one of the types of white blood cells made in the bone marrow. The resulting Leukemia granulocytes multiply and survive longer than normal cells. As their numbers increase, the Leukemia cells "pack", or fill up the bone marrow and disrupt the production of normal white and red blood cells and platelets.

The doctor ordered a bone marrow biopsy and the results were conclusive. Timmy was put in isolation and transfusions of healthy granulocytes were administered along with antibiotics intravenously .

Debbie and Gar were devastated and stayed close day and night, sometimes without sleep, hoping and praying for Timmy's well being. The doctor said it would take a few days to know for sure if Timmy could survive, but assured them he would leave no stone unturned and was contacting every specialist educated in this field for updated information. As the hours passed by the news kept getting worse.

Timmy's body was now producing a rash that consisted of tiny, bright red and dark red spots. The doctor told them that these spots were minute areas of bleeding in the skin and internally. He said that because of the Leukemia, he had Thrombocytopenia Purpura, which is associated with Hodgkin's disease, or Lupus. This is caused as the body forms antibodies (normally protective proteins) that attack it's own platelets. Healthy platelets are damaged and removed from the bloodstream at a very high rate. It was possible that some of the chemicals in the treatment for Timmy may have caused the reaction, so they stopped the antibiotics. However a well known specialist reported that there was, at this time, no known cause for Thrombocytopenia.

They had only two suggested alternatives, first prescribe a corticosteroid drug to decrease the destruction caused by antibodies, then if that failed they would have to prescribe a "splendectomy," an operation in which most of the spleen is removed. The spleen normally destroys worn-out red cells, but an overactive or enlarged spleen may also destroy platelets and prevent a patient's recovery. With Gar and Debbie's permission they administered the first plan. The parents waited through the night for a good sign. At two AM the doctors came to the waiting room and met with Gar and Debbie. With tears in their eyes, they had to tell them that the strain was just too much for little Timmy's heart and he had slipped away from them.

Debbie opened her mouth to scream out, "Timmy," but only a whisper came out as she fainted into Gar's arms. He gently laid her on the sofa as the doctors checked her pulse. Gar was also badly shaken by the news that Timmy had passed away, but he knew he had to be strong for Debbie. His thoughts and prayers of having a family were being taken from him, but he knew he had to get Debbie home and see to her comfort and welfare. The doctors gave Gar some tablets to calm Debbie and advised him to put her to bed and have a family member stay with her a few days until after the funeral. They quietly advised him not to try to suppress her grief. Grieving is a natural process that had to occur before she could move on with her life. Gar was gentle with her and after he finally got her into bed, he made the necessary calls to the other families, the Baptist Pastor and the Funeral Director. After he made the arrangements and he could sit down and relax, he started to cry uncontrollably. All his pent up anxiety and hurt flowed out in a river of tears. He was in this condition when Sammy and Sandy came in the back entrance and rushed to him and held him and softly helped him grieve. Then one by one every member of the families, including Bucko and Edna entered the house and took over the task of caring for the Savinos .

Chapter 79

The next few days, including the funeral, were the worst days any human being could ever go through. The parents assured the families they no longer needed their appreciated care and wished for them to return to their homes, but after they left, the quiet house was deafening. They were overly polite to each other and were trying to appear strong, but as a wave of suffering sorrow would wash over them, they would quickly go to a bedroom or bathroom, whichever was closest, and sob away the terrible hurt that never seemed to release its stranglehold. It was another three days before Gar could muster enough strength to return to work. He was fortunate to have Grace and his good shop managers. It was another week before Debbie returned to help Grace in the office. The work proved to help both her and Gar to move forward with their lives and their marriage. Gar threw himself into working harder and more aggressive. As each of his business projects grew larger, he was making preparations to expand to truck repair. He gave up trying to find a wealthy partner and decided to go it alone. He had decided to buy-out one of the smaller truck repair shops and move it to an area on his own three acres. To an area that faced the road and build the shop there. He put up everything that he had as collateral and with a mortgage payment that was scary, was ready to enter the truck repair field and take on the big boys. He stole expert mechanics and repairmen from other companies by paying higher wages and better benefits. He hired the most qualified shop manager and foreman. He romanced all the truck appraisers and adjusters and was not bashful about asking them to send their wrecked units to him. He invested in one of the largest truck wreckers made and added it to his fleet of tow trucks. He told Sammy's father that he was ready to handle all of Empire Trucking's repair work. Savinos was becoming a very large conglomeration. He then incorporated.

The first six months were the hardest. The jobs were starting to come in and the truck shop was very busy, but after buying those very expensive parts and waiting for each job to be completed, the cash from limited capital was putting a hardship on their working equity. Gar was expecting this and kept assuring Grace that things would get better, but we must not panic. He was right and after that first few months the cash started to build and soon they were solvent again.

Gar had become so wrapped up in his work that he and Debbie were distancing themselves from each other. It had become quite apparent to Grace and she asked Gar to take her to lunch one day. While at lunch, she told Gar to listen to her while she told him a few things and if he wanted to fire her when she finished, that would be all right with her.

She then gave it to him with both barrels blazing. She reminded him that he and Debbie were in love with each other and it was time for him to pause in his relentless drive for success and give attention to the one person that means so much to him. She discussed the sadness that they had to endure with the loss of Timmy, but now it was time to put their loss behind them and go on with their marriage. She told him how all of his friends could tell that they loved each other, but if someone didn't take the bull by the horns now, they might drift too far apart to ever find the way back. To Grace's pleasure, Gar listened and when she finished, he told her that she was right. He had been everything Grace had said and he promised her from that moment on he would apologize and be the husband that Debbie needed. True to his word, Gar took Debbie out for dinner at her favorite steakhouse and romanced her like never before. Once again the marriage became gloriously wonderful.

He rewarded Grace by making her one of the officers in his new Corporation and raising her salary. He knew she was nearing retirement age and promised her a nice pension whenever she felt that she wanted to take a rest and retire. That was when she told him that he and the Savino Corporation was her life and unless he fired her, she would work there until she died. It was quite a touching moment and Gar felt a big lump in his throat as he thanked her for such devotion.

Chapter 80

One morning after Gar had gone to the office early, Debbie called him and told him that she had forgotten to tell him yesterday of an appointment she had for a checkup and would be in later that afternoon. He questioned if she was sick and she assured him she was not and that it had just slipped her mind about the appointment.

Later that day, she called again to tell him everything was okay, but a good friend of his called and she had invited him over for dinner. She decided to stay home and get a few things for dinner at the market and let the guest be a surprise for Gar. He kept trying to get her to tell him who it was, but she would not give in. She really had him guessing and kept teasing him with silly answers. Finishing her little game, she told him that dinner was at seven and cocktails at six.

"Don't you dare be one minute early or two minutes late!"

He spent the whole afternoon trying to rack his brain, then he knew who it was. It had to be Scotty from his ship, the manager of the Flamingo Hotel in Vegas, out here on business. It would be nice to see him again. This would be a nice surprise.

At six o'clock sharp, he wheeled his El-camino into his driveway, walked in the front door whistling his favorite song. He set some papers on the desk in the foyer.

"Debbie, I'm home. Where are you?"

"Out here in the kitchen, Sweetheart."

He walked to her and gave her a kiss on the cheek.

"Where's Scotty?"

"Who?"

"Scotty, your surprise guest."

"I don't know a Scotty, darling, besides he is not the surprise guest."

"Well, who is it and where is he?" exclaimed Gar as he fixed a martini.

"The surprise guest is going to be late, but there is a message from him. I wrote it down and put it under your dinner plate in the dining room. If you don't mind, let's wait until you have your cocktail and sit down to dinner before you read the message. That way it will still be a surprise, Okay. Sweetheart?"

"But I thought..."

"Oh Gar, please trust me. It will be fine."

"Well, I guess there's no harm in waiting," he said, as he gave her a little hug.

They had some small talk, enjoyed their drinks and then Gar helped her take the meal to the dining room. They sat down and Gar turned over his plate. A large blue card is folded and as Gar opened it, he read the bold words, "Our surprise guest is a baby boy... arriving in seven months!!!!!"

Gar was shocked. Then his face went from a startled expression to one of profound happiness.

He yelled, "Oh Debbie, is this true?"

She nodded her head, "Yes. Yes. Yes. ."

They hugged and kissed each other and softly whispered, "Thank you, Jesus!"

They were so happy and Gar had a thousand questions to ask; how she knew, why she kept it a secret, how was she feeling, and when could they tell everyone? She told him about the new Sonar that lets parents know if the baby is a girl or boy, and theirs was definitely a boy. They both cried with happiness. Then they began calling all the families with the good news.

The Savino Corporation was growing at a fast pace. Gar had chosen a business that was always in demand. When the economy dropped a little and employment slowed, people repaired their vehicles and bought more used cars. When the economy was up, people bought new cars, but with more cars on the roads, they created more collisions and more repairs had to be made. He caught the cycle going both ways. It was the same with the trucking companies. When the economy was up, they bought more trucks, when it went down, they repaired more of the old ones.

Gar fine tuned his managers to a point where he was no longer the sole decision maker. He had hired the right people, gave them just enough responsibility and let them compete against each other as to who could make the highest profit . He rewarded them with bonuses and benefits. He had a manager for the auto repair shop, one for the truck repair shop, the tow truck fleet, the salvage yard and one for the auto parts department. Under each manager, he had a working shop foreman that had control of the laborers plus did small repairs as well.

Gar set the last Thursday of every month for a managers meeting at 6 AM. Grace was there with the monthly total of all the shops. Coffee and doughnuts were always available. At first, some were griping about the early hour, but when they realized how serious Gar was about this and the rewards that were made, they soon looked forward to being there. They got caught up in the spirit of competition and took pride in their departments.

Chapter 81

In 1948, Debbie had an easier time with her second pregnancy and the birth of her new baby was without incident. Gar wanted to name him Tommy but Debbie objected, because it was too close to Timmy. The memory of his short life still hurt very much. They settled on Mark as his christian name. His hair was not like his father's jet black, but a white, toe-head. This of course would turn blonde after he grew older. He was a large baby, eight pounds at birth, and the parents had him checked more times than needed for any signs of a blood disorder. After another ten months, the pediatrician told them Mark was healthy as could be and they only needed to check him on an annual basis from now on. When he was one year old, Gar took him to work with him and showed him off to all of his employees. Debbie couldn't go with him because she now was in her final days of her present pregnancy. The doctor had informed her that next month a baby girl would arrive at the Savino home. Both parents were very happy and excited with the news.

The happy event climaxed with the birth of a beautiful daughter that they named Donna. Debbie and Gar were very happy God had blessed them with a wonderful family. Just a few years ago they were going through trials and tribulations and thought they wouldn't survive the tragic death of Tommy. Now God had given them two precious lives to care for and raise with the Savino name. Gar remembered how he vowed that he would have a family one day and that he would never let his name be washed away without a trace. He remembered how it had hurt when he returned to Elmira and found that there wasn't anyone left but him in his family. He thanked God for all the gifts that he had been given.

The Savino enterprises continued to grow and expand and over the next ten years, Debbie and Gar had three more boys, David,Toby and Michael. They were were fine, healthy boys and were very athletic. By the time they reached teenage they were involved in all the sports as the seasons changed. The basement was full of all the sports equipment that they each needed. Gar would buy them practically anything they would ask for, but he demanded that they convince him that they truly needed each item and that they would not be wasteful. He also demanded that they were always respectful to their parents and other families. They had to have good passing grades and with all these criteria being kept, they hadn't any problem getting Dad to finance their little events. Mark and Donna, being the oldest, were always either the instigators or the leaders in schemes and projects, but as she became a teenager, she began to break away from boyish things and drift off to be with girls of her age. The big advantage that she had was an older brother and three younger ones that discouraged many would-be wise guys picking on her. In fact it became a problem getting dates, since every new boy had to pass being scrutinized by all her brothers. Sammy and Karen had one more child after Holly, a son, Richard. He was born without complications and was a joy to the parents. Sammy made sure a toy truck was always available for him to play with.

Sandy and Sally had a son after Shannon, named Douglas, and they too had not suffered any misfortunes. All three families still met once a month at different homes and maintained a close relationship. The elder parents were held in great reverence and respect by all the children. Gar insisted his children call Irving and Mary their grandparents just as Sandy's children did. This pleased the Grimes' very much.

The way that the births had happened created a phenomenon that no one realized until after they gathered together for family reunions. All three boys born to each family were the same age. The first children of both Sammy and Sandy were girls and their second were both boys. Gar's first was Timmy, but after his death came Mark, who was the same age as Richard and Douglas. Sammy's daughter, Holly and Sandy's daughter, Shannon were both one year older than all the boys. Since all three families lived in the same county, the children went to the same school. The three boys were fierce competitors and great rivals. At the same time they loved each other. Wherever one was seen, the other two would be nearby, and if one was threatened, the other two would be there for him. Much of the school referred to them as "The Three Musketeers."

Chapter 82

When Gar's children all became teenagers, he gathered them together and asked each one if there was a specific vocation in this world that they desired to be or do. He did not want an answer right away, but for them to think about it, dwell on it, and write it on a piece of paper and they would discuss it in a month. He explained this was not a commitment, merely a time for them to search their inner selves and to see if they were able to openly discuss how they felt. He had started them early on family discussions and they were never bashful about speaking their minds.

He stressed the fact that it was very important to accept criticism, because in the outside world they will face this more than anything else. They had to learn to accept it, expect it, live with it and be able to return it.

"In a Biology class they take a dead frog and dissect it and examine every part of its insides. Here we will do the same while we are alive and instead of parts, we will examine our characteristics like our traits, our qualities, our peculiarities, and our idiosyncrasies. If you can handle this and not give in to pressure, you will have a step up in your climb to success."

The children loved a challenge and the day came for them to give their report on a Sunday after church. Debbie made extra popcorn and pizza and had plenty of soft drinks ready. They were ready and eager to declare what they wanted for themselves from this world and expected plenty of negative discourse. They were not disappointed. Debbie and Gar were relentless in their role as "devils advocate," and even though there were moments when tempers were challenged, they came through it in magnificent fashion. With love as the underlying factor, the experiment was very successful. So much so that the kids requested another date to do it again. Gar and Debbie were amazed at the talent and stamina for debate their children had shown. These kids were going to be very sharp and unafraid to meet whatever life had in store for them.

Mark was first to declare his love for the airplane and the US Air Force became his objective. Donna was influenced by clothes and she was very good with her artwork, so it was easy for her to declare her interests in design, not ruling out marrying the the right tall and handsome stranger. David was interested in the mechanical engine and how to improve on it, so he wanted to be a mechanical engineer. Toby played with toy race cars ever birth and he declared that one day he would win the Indianapolis 500, so he would have no problem becoming a race car driver. Gar told him that an education in mechanical engineering or something similar was needed before he could ever pursue racing. Michael said he was going to follow in his Dad's footsteps and be a CEO in a large corporation after he became a successful lawyer. Gar and Debbie were very impressed with the high standards their children had set as goals and encouraged them to go for it. They promised them they would be their biggest supporters.

As the three musketeers, Mark, Erich, and Doug continued through high school, their school won their district conference championships in football, basketball and baseball. Mark was an excellent pitcher in baseball while Rich was at first base and Doug was at shortstop. In football, Doug was a star quarterback while Mark and Rich were his go-to running backs. In basketball, all three were star players and took their team to the top. That year theirs was the only team to win every game that they played. It had never been done before.

The oldest girls from the three families were also very caring towards each other, attending the same school. Donna was slightly more athletic, since she grew up surrounded by four brothers and excelled in both basketball and softball. She had shown an interest in art at an early age and her parents urged her to follow up on this. When she was about to graduate, she was accepted in a school of design. Her talent was leaning toward being a fashion designer for women clothiers.

Holly had always loved the water and was captain of her school's swimming team. They won several ribbons for the school and became state champions three years in a row. She fell in love with her high school boyfriend, whose father owned a large boat company. Every weekend, weather permitting, they would be boating or sailing or scuba diving. Sandy and Karen were insisting on her going to college, but she refused. She wanted to get married and help her husband take over the boat business. After many heated discussions, a compromise was agreed upon. She would attend one year at a college of her choice and if after that year she still wanted to marry, she could with her parents approval.

Shannon loved her parents, but she idolized her father. She was amazed at how he refused to accept adversities; how he taught himself to use those steel claws as delicate instruments and to do so in public without ever being afraid of being on display. He really was her hero. She became very interested in watching Sandy use these artificial prothesis and, as her curiosity peaked, she started reading more books on different types and went with her father to the VA when he had to return for adjustments or replacements. So, it wasn't a surprise when she announced that she wanted to attend a college that taught how to create artificial limbs.

Sammy and Karen's son Richard, known mostly as Rich or Richie, made it known early he wanted to go into the Marines . He and his comrades, Mark and Doug had talked about making a career in the military many times. Their fathers were very helpful in their advice and providing information on military life. As they matured and still showed eagerness for that lifestyle, the fathers would invite someone from each branch of the military to the house for dinner. Afterward, they would have a bull session of question and answers for the boys. Both Rich and Doug made up their minds to enter the Marines. They tried in desperation to talk Mark into going in with them, but he was adamant about flying and since the US had separated the Air force from the Army and Navy in 1947 and made it an equal partner, he would have to try for the Air Force Academy.

Chapter 83

After the three boys had obtained all of the information that was needed to make their decisions, they wanted to know the answer to the most important one of all. How do I enter the United States Naval Academy at Annapolis or the United States Air Force Academy at Colorado Springs? The answers to these came at a surprise dinner arranged by the proud fathers at the home of Irv and Mary Grimes.

The President of The United States, Dwight D. Eisenhower, sent the leading Senator from New York State to the Grimes' home with this official proclamation.

"Richard Cross, the son of a Congressional Medal of Honor Hero, Samuel Cross is hereby nominated by the President of the United States, to attend the United States Naval Academy at Annapolis, Maryland. Having passed an entrance exam and met the requirements for entrance, it is my pleasure to place your name in the next class of students known as Plebe," signed by President Dwight D. Eisenhower.

The same was delivered to Douglas Grimes. The same was delivered to Mark Savino, except it was for entrance to the United States Air Force Academy at Colorado Springs, Colorado. It was a wonderful surprise for the three and a night they would remember the rest of their lives.

The Senator's speech explained to the audience that to attend these prestigious and distinguished Academies, a student had to be at least 17 years old, and not older than 23. They must be single, of good moral character, and a US citizen. To be considered for admission to the US Academy, a candidate required a nomination from an official source. A majority of vacancies at the academies were filled by nominations from US Senators and Representatives or from certain other government officials. Some nominations were based on previous military service by the applicant or their parents. The President of the United States could nominate an unlimited number of children of career personnel or children of veterans killed or disabled in action and children of prisoners of war or personnel missing in action. The Academy could enroll an unlimited number of children of Medal of Honor winners.

The Senator went on to say that after a candidate had been nominated, an admissions board examined each candidate's school records and college examination score They also considered the candidates medical and physical aptitude tests and other evidence of character, leadership potential, academic aptitude, and physical fitness. Most candidates who were accepted by the academy ranked academically in the top 20 percent of their high school class.

He told his audience that after the midshipman or cadet had been admitted, the US government paid for their tuition, room and board, and medical and dental care. Each midshipman or cadet was paid $600 a month. From this salary, they purchased books, uniforms, equipment, and personal service.

At Annapolis the first year midshipmen are called Plebes. The program at Annapolis seeks to develop students for military leadership. The academy emphasized both academic training and the development of leadership, physical, and professional skills. During the academic year, midshipmen devoted their major efforts to academic studies. But they also must participate in a varsity sport or in the intramural sports program. During the midshipman's first summer, they learned the basics of military life, including how to shoot and sail. The academy required physical tests, drills, and athletics for physical fitness. During their remaining summers, the midshipmen spent time at sea and at various naval installations. There, they learned about ships, submarines, and aircraft.

The academic undergraduate program curriculum included mathematics, science, engineering, social sciences and humanities. It also supplied a background in leadership, navigation, weaponry, and other professional areas. Each midshipman chose an academic major that provided in-depth study in a field of interest. These fields consisted of aerospace engineering, oceanography, political science, and 15 other areas. Graduates from Annapolis received their diplomas and Navy or Marine Corp. Commissions at the end of Commissioning Week in May. They then proceed as Navy or Marine Corp. officers to specialized training before reporting to their first fleet assignment.

The requirements and nominations for the United States Air Force Academy were the same as the Naval Academy. The students were called Cadets. They went through the same curricula as described before.

A Cadets normal weekday began with reveille (wake-up call) at 6:30 am. Before classes, cadets prepared their rooms for inspection and ate breakfast. Classes were held from 7 am to noon and from 1 pm to 4 pm. After classes, cadets participated in sports or extracurricular activities. After dinner, they studied in the dormitory or library from 8 pm until taps sounded at 11 pm.

Cadets lived by an "honor code" stressed complete integrity in word and deed. The code stated, "We will not lie, steal, or cheat, nor tolerate among us anyone who does."

The cadets themselves enforced the code, and violation of the code can be cause for dismissal. The academy prepared each cadet for a leadership role through military training. This training provided basic military knowledge required by an Air Force officer and included flying instruction and field trips. All cadets, even those who do not plan a career in flying, must take aviation and navigation courses.

After completion of their academic studies they receive a Bachelor of Science degree and earn a commission in the US Air Force. When the students enter the academy, they agree to serve four years as a cadet and at least five years as an Air Force officer.

Chapter 84

The Senator covered all the bases and when he finished, everyone in the room knew everything there was to know about Navy, Marine, and Air Force Schools. The families thanked him for the wonderful informative speech and for their nominations. All three were very excited with the good news and looked forward to high school graduation and moving on to bigger things.

David, Toby, and Michael were very impressed with what they heard and realized these benefits could be for them also, if they chose to use them. They hadn't shown so far any indication that the military life was to their liking. Besides, they still had a few years to go before a decision would need to be made.

All three daughters from each family graduated and were attending college. They knew exactly what they wanted to do with their lives and felt they were right on schedule, with a planned program.

Donna hadn't any doubt her future was to be a fashion designer. She had already been approached by big name corporations to come work for them after she had completed two years of apprentice, but declined all offers, stating that she wanted to complete her education and maybe form her own corporation.

Holly could not wait to complete the year in college she promised her parents. She was engaged to Bob

Fisher, whose father owned a large boat building company and had a large retail outlet at his marina. They were making plans for a June wedding as soon as her year was completed.

Bob and Holly were on the water every weekend that the weather permitted. If Holly wasn't home, she was sure to be with Bob either scuba diving, water skiing, or deep sea fishing.

Bob got permission to use his Dad's 50 foot luxury cruiser for special occasions and gave permission to have the wedding on the boat. Bob's father registered the boat as "Compass Rose" and the big beautiful white boat had blue accent stripes on each side of her hull. The interior was a gorgeous red mahogany with blue leather trim. He arranged for a three man crew to take the married couple on their honeymoon to Bermuda, then to the Bahamas, returning back to Fort Lauderdale and up the east coast through part of the inland waterway to home.

Shannon visited VA clinics and hospitals with her father and showed a desire to know more about artificial limbs or prosthetics. This prompted Sandy and Sally to arrange a meeting with one of the professors at Northwestern University, when Shannon was about to graduate from high school. He was impressed with Shannon and her positive attitude and explained the requirements needed in the field of prosthetics. A person must have a bachelor's or master's degree in occupational therapy. These programs included courses in biology, psychology, sociology, and occupational therapy theory and practice. All programs required students to complete a period of supervised clinical training. However, if Shannon wanted to proceed to prosthetics and not be a occupational therapist , she could take a shorter course and become a occupational therapist assistant, and make a decision later as she worked through her studies. At the same time,she may find that being an occupational therapist would be enough. At least she would be headed in the right direction and a further decision could be made later.

After high school, she passed the entrance examinations and was enrolled at Northwestern University. After her first year was completed Shannon had decided to take the full four years and get her degree as a full therapist and not an assistant. She was having such satisfaction of knowing that what she was doing was so worthwhile and purposeful. Seeing patients recover from illness and disabilities and be able to improve their own physical and mental well-being by carrying out activities for themselves was a rewarding experience. She hadn't given up on going into prosthetics, but she wanted to get her full degree as an occupational therapist first.

Chapter 85

During the summers, Gar gave the boys the opportunity to earn extra cash by letting them work at the salvage yard. They could help pull parts from wrecked units, disassemble motors, wash various parts or anything the foreman asked them to do. Sometimes they would ride with the wrecker tow-truck as they were called to an accident.

David was always interested in motors and was happy assisting the mechanics as they pulled motors and tested each one for resale. He had decided to follow up his schooling in mechanical engineering, and be able to have early hands-on experience as this was a boost to his career. Besides that, he was getting paid while he was learning.

Toby was always eager to ride with the tow trucks and occasionally the driver would allow him to operate the winches or let him drive the truck after it came into the storage area, but would not let him drive on the highway. When he was older ,he liked delivering parts to various shops with the company pickup truck.

When he found out that the salvage company was sponsoring a stock car owned by one of his Dad's employees, he became great friends with the owner and soon was going every Saturday night to one of the tracks they were running on. Slowly but surely he managed to work on the owner, Bill Johnson, to let him drive the stock car. He was allowed to warm the car up, but not any hot laps. Bill saw that Toby listened to him and didn't try any funny stuff and the kid seemed to show some talent for racing, he let him take some hot laps while other cars went out for practice. To Bill's surprise, Toby usually was never passed, once he got used to the high speed.

Bill's driver, Tony Kole, was upset that Bill was letting Toby drive his car, even if it was only in practice. Bill had seen Tony run a few years earlier and liked what he saw, so when he built his first stocker he hired him to drive. They would be racing a B-class car the first year then move into the modified class the following year, if all went well. When Toby arrived and kept pestering to drive, Bill was afraid he might lose his Dad's Auto Parts as his sponsor. The fact that he seemed to be a natural only added more complications to the problem.

The night Tony got held up in traffic and was so late he missed practice was the night Bill told Toby he was putting him in the car for the heat race. He told him that Tony would be here later to run the feature, but for now just go easy and try to qualify the car for the feature race. As they lined up, he had to start dead last since he was a new driver and hadn't any points. This was to be only eight laps and the top four would qualify to run the semi-feature. Those not in the top four would have to run the consi race if they expected to get in the feature.

When the starter dropped the green flag, he was high on the track at full throttle. They went into the first turn and he dropped clear down to the bottom groove and as he let off to give the engine a breath of air, he nailed the throttle quickly and shot under three slower cars. He followed the rest of the field down the back stretch into turn three, where he again dove to the inside, bouncing off the side of one of his competitors as they charged out of turn four. Toby moved into sixth place and still had seven laps to go. Bill was jumping up and down and could not believe some of the moves he was making. The guys in front of him were seasoned drivers and had some of the faster racers.

At the halfway flag, Toby was still riding on the rear of the fifth car, unable to get by in the turn. Every time he would go for the inside, the other driver would squeeze him off. On the next turn, he faked a move for the inside and as the other driver went for a block, Toby shot passed him on the right side. Now he was fifth and needed to pass one more to put his car into the semi. With two laps to go, the fourth car went into the turn too hard and tapped the rear of the third car, causing both to slide up the track just enough for Toby to get underneath both of them for third place. He felt his motor was much faster or better than the cars in front, but he played it smart and just rode back there in third place to the checkered flag. He was very excited and the crew was all over him when he returned to the pits. Bill pounded him on the back and everyone congratulated him as he climbed out of the car.

Toby told Bill he felt that his car was faster, but just couldn't find a hole to pass. He asked him if he could drive in the semi and the feature, but Bill said he would have to wait until he talked to Tony. He reminded him that Tony was supposed to be the driver and he had to honor his commitment to him, but since he wasn't at the track on time, there were some issues that needed to be addressed before the next race. Tony had shown up and seen the last few laps of Toby's race. Bill asked him why he was late. He was still steaming to see Toby in his car and took the question as an affront to his character, was quick to reply.

"What difference does it make? You were just waiting for an excuse to put that kid in the car. As far as I'm concerned, we are finished. You keep the kid. I'll find a ride with someone else."

Bill told him he was mistaken, but if he felt that way, perhaps it would be better if they severed relations and go separate ways. Bill returned to Toby and asked if he wanted finish the season driving for him. Toby said he would like that very much. Bill told him his father would have to give him permission. He could drive the semi and the feature race tonight, but Gar's permission would have to be obtained for them to continue. Toby agreed to talk to his father right away.

He found the semi and feature races much harder to win, since the slower cars had been eliminated, but he finished fourth in the semi and with a good showing of eighth in the feature, was considered by Bill and the crew to be very good for a rookie.

Toby found the right time to ask Gar about driving the stock car for Bill and after he had convinced his Dad this would not interfere with college, Gar told him he could continue driving and he would talk to Bill about it. He wanted to be sure proper safety equipment installed in the car.

Bill satisfied Gar that all precautions were being taken to ensure that the driver was being properly protected. He wanted him to know that Toby had alot of natural attributes handling a race car and he would make every effort to see that Toby received the best training and coaching as he progressed into higher classes of racing.

Gar was surprised to hear that his son was that good. If Toby continued to show a talent for speed and a desire for the advanced class, he asked if Bill would come back to see him and perhaps they could talk about getting into a modified or super-modified class. Bill said he would keep him advised of his progress and thanked him for sponsoring the car, Gar did not tell Toby about the last part of his conversation. He wanted to see if Toby really had a talent for racing, or if this was just a fascination as he moved from one type of toy to another.

Chapter 86

Toby never asked his father for racing money. He used his own money from working at the shop and bought a nomex fire-resistant racing suite and a Bell helmet. He always tried to help Bill on week nights and was never late arriving at the track on race nights. Once in a while David would go with him to Bill's garage, since he was very interested in the motor. Toby tried to get Michael to go also, but Michael was never interested in cars or racing. He loved reading and always had his nose stuck in a book. It wasn't any wonder that he was always on the debating team and his head was full of trivia. He seemed to remember everything that he ever read.

Toby listened to everything Bill told him about driving the car and after Toby had a little more experience, he was able to relate what was needed in the car to make it handle better. Bill had informed Toby and the official he wanted his car lined up in last place in every race, until Toby had a little more experience. This was not what Toby wanted, but he bit his tongue and kept his mouth shut. He liked and respected Bill very much. He soon realized he was doing this for his own good. Toby never liked last place and he usually just rode there in the heat race and had to run the consi to get in the feature race. He knew fourth place or better in the consi would place him in the feature, so he always made it to fourth in the consi. Bill questioned if he couldn't do better in the heat races, but Toby would only smile and say he was getting experience. The second night that he was stuck at the rear, for the feature race, Toby had made his mind up that he would show Bill and everyone else he was ready to be noticed.

All heat races were 8 laps. All semi and consi races were 12 laps and the feature race was 25 laps. Most heats and semis had 10 cars while the consi at times might have 20 or more in it. The feature usually had 20 cars. It was harder to come from the back in a heat race because you would run out of time or laps, but in the feature you had time and more laps, but had to compete with the best cars. The track was 5/8, just under a half mile, on dirt. To negotiate the turns, a driver would come full throttle until he had to turn. He would let off on the gas and turn sharp left and actually threw the car sideways, and as the car went sideways into the turn, he would get back on the gas, turning the wheel to the right, and catching the rear as it was coming around to power the car through the turn. If powered too late or toss the rear too late, the car would spin out. By turning to the right and applying the gas, the car would float sideways through the turn and then by turning back to the left, the car would straighten up and head straight down to the next turn.

Toby was getting ready as all the cars took the pace lap. From the last place position, he kept his eye on the flag man. When the green flag waved , instead of flying into the first turn, as most did, he held back to wait and see what happened. Past experience dictated that everyone would be overanxious and storm into the first turn, causing alot of slamming into the sides of each other, sliding out wide . Toby was right and as the three cars in front of him banged into each other, he pulled his car way down low, then powered past them on the inside. Going up the backstretch his momentum carried him side by side with the 17th car, but he had the inside and in the turn he easily passed him coming out of turn four. Coming up the front stretch to complete the first lap, he had gone from 20th to 16th. He had to follow the herd now and try picking them off one at a time. The closer he got to the front the faster his competition would be. The next few cars were running the higher groove and Toby's car was working great on the low side, so each lap he was able to pass one more car.

At the halfway flag, Toby was in 10th place and his car was sticking like glue in the turns. The front cars were playing follow the leader. They seemed to be running at the same speed and didn't try passing for fear of losing a spot. They were hugging the low inside groove, so Toby was not waiting, he drove his car high enough as he went through the turns so that the right rear tire would get a nice bite about twelve inches below the peak, which let the car slide out if he should hit a slick spot. He was able to pass the next three cars by riding the top rim, but the next seven cars realized he was coming and they could see that the top groove was becoming faster and they needed to stay in front of him. The sixth and seventh cars broke away from the bottom and drifted up in front of him, but they left just enough opening underneath, Toby's speed allowed him to sweep under and draw up beside the fifth place car. The driver looked over at Toby and his blank expression seemed to say, "Who the heck are you and where did you come from?"

He was determined not to let Toby pass him and drove a little too hard into the turn. This caused him to drift up the track just enough that he surged down underneath and came out of the turn in fifth place. With eight laps left, Toby wondered if this would be enough to get by all four cars. He went to the high side once again and by running higher, he didn't need to let off as quick as the cars running lower in the inside groove. As long as the leaders followed in line at the bottom, Toby knew he had a chance to beat all four cars. Each lap he was knocking off one at a time and with just two laps to go he was in second place. The leader realized if he wanted to win this race he would have to try blocking Toby, so he moved up in front of him for the block. If Toby made a move to go lower, so did the leader. His rear view mirror was full of Toby's car. At the white flag with only one lap left to go and Toby practically touched the leader's rear bumper when they started into the first turn, he moved high for the pass, but so did the leader. This caused him to brake some to keep from hitting the other car. He wanted to win, but not by spinning the other driver out. He lost a little speed by braking, but as they went up the backstretch he was able to close back up to within a car length and as he made the same move to go high, the leader made the same move to block, but this time Toby was ready for that. He stabbed the throttle and took a sharp left and went under the leader as they came out of turn four. They came down to the checkered flag side-by-side. In what some called a photo-finish, Toby was declared the winner by six inches.

Toby came around the track to the flag man, who handed him the flag to carry in his left hand as he took his victory lap around the track one more time. He was so excited a tear or two ran down his cheek. He had never won a feature race before. After his victory lap, he drove the car into his pit area where Bill and the crew were anxiously waiting for him. They were just as excited as he was and they showed their affection for him by hugging, high-fiving, pounding his back and telling him what a great job of driving he did.

That night Toby emerged as their hero, showing everyone he had talent and would be a real contender for track champion before the season ended. His brother, David came to the track with him that night and could not believe what he had just seen. Both had something to tell the rest of the family when they went home. Bill told Toby he was very proud of him and together they would be going places. He didn't understand that statement, but he liked how he said it.

Chapter 87

Toby told his parents about his big night and they responded by congratulating him by joining in the backslapping and hugging. His mother expressed worry for his safety, but didn't let this dampen the fun.

Gar gave him his big moment, but as everyone was heading off to bed, he asked Toby to join him in the den. There he reminded Toby that even though there was no doubt he had talent for racing, he would have to finish high school, then four years in college. He told him he would support him and sponsor Bill's car in the summer, but he had to complete his schooling. If he wanted to continue racing after college, he would help him, but before that, he would be getting a college degree. He ended the talk by saying this was how it would be and was not open for discussion.

Toby surprised Gar by saying, "You are right, Dad. I will go by your decision. I love you, Dad."

He gave his Dad a hug and went off to bed. Gar was expecting Toby to be more argumentative about college since he had a taste of Victory Lane. Maybe the good moral standards and family discussions that were such a big part of all three families, were paying off in surprising dividends.

Gar bowed his head and silently said,"Thank you, Father, for my family."

The three sons of our heroes, Mark, Rich, and Doug entered their schools in the fall. Mark was at the United States Air Force Academy at the foothills of the Rocky Mountains, near Colorado Springs, Colorado. He was now an Air Force Academy Cadet taking four years of academic work leading to a Bachelor of Science degree along with professional training to earn a commission in the US Air Force.

Richard Cross and Douglas Grimes were Midshipmen at the United States Naval Academy at Annapolis, Maryland. They were now Plebes (first year) and in training for four years of academic work to receive a Bachelor of Science degree and to receive a commission as second lieutenants in the Marine Corp.

A major point of discussion was prevalent at the family brought up by the wives of our heroes.

"Are we raising these boys and sending them to Military schools so they can go off to war?"

The fathers would respond with consoling compassion. "Of course not, dear, this is what the boys wanted and these are the finest schools in the world."

Then the expected response by the mothers was, "What about the Vietnam war?"

The fathers would usually come back with, "That war would be over by the time they graduate, four years from now, so let's not worry about something that's never going to happen."

Chapter 88

Before the Vietnam War, the United States was involved in the Korean war from 1950 to 1953, a local war in Korea. The United States and other members of the United Nations aided South Korea, while the Soviet Union and China assisted North Korea.

The war brought the first dogfights between jet fighters. In November 1950, Air Force f-86 fighters clashed with Soviet-made MiG fighters near the Chinese border along the Yalu River. Air Force pilots called this area "MiG Alley." They shot down 10 times as many jets as they lost there . When the Korean War ended, the Air Force had downed 900 enemy planes and had lost 139 of its own planes in aerial combat. The Korean War ended with neither side winning a complete victory.

The year the boys entered the Military schools was 1966 and their fathers were certain the Vietnam War would be history by the time the boys graduated from the Academies.

The Vietnam War was actually the second phase of fighting in Vietnam. During the first phase, which began in 1946, the Vietnamese fought France for control of Vietnam. At that time, Vietnam was part of the French Colonial Empire in Indochina. The United States sent France military equipment, but the Vietnamese defeated the French in 1954, and Vietnam split into North and South Vietnam.

United States aid to France and later to noncommunist South Vietnam was based on a Cold War policy of President Harry S. Truman. The Cold War was an intense rivalry between Communist and noncommunist nations. Truman declared that the United States must help any nation challenged by Communism. The Truman Doctrine was directed at first towards Europe and the Middle East. It was also adopted by the next three presidents, Dwight D. Eisenhower, John F. Kennedy, and Lyndon B. Johnson, and applied to Indochina. They feared if one Southeast Asian nation joined the Communist camp, the others would also fall, one after the other like what Eisenhower called "a row of dominoes."

The Vietnamese Communists and their allies called the Vietnam War a war of national liberation. They saw the Vietnam War as an extension of the struggle with France and as another attempt by a foreign power to rule Vietnam. North Vietnam wanted to end US support of South Vietnam and to reunite the North and South into a single nation. China and the Soviet Union, at that time the two largest Communist nations, gave the Vietnamese Communists war materials, but not troops.

In 1964, President Lyndon B. Johnson approved secret South Vietnamese naval raids against North Vietnam. Just after one of these raids, on August 2,1964, North Vietnamese torpedo boats attacked the US Destroyer, Maddox which was monitoring the impact of the raid off the coast of North Vietnam in the Gulf of

Tonkin. Johnson warned the North Vietnamese that another such attack would bring "grave consequences."

On August 4, he announced that North Vietnamese boats had again launched an attack in the gulf, this time against the Maddox and another US destroyer, the C Turner Joy. Some Americans doubted that the August 4 attack had occurred, and it was never confirmed. Nevertheless, Johnson ordered immediate air strikes against North Vietnam. He also asked Congress for power to take "all necessary measures to repel any armed attack against the forces of the United States and to prevent further aggression."

On August 7, Congress approved these powers in the Tonkin Gulf Resolution. The United States did not declare war on North Vietnam. Johnson used the resolution as the legal basis for increased US involvement. In March 1965, he sent a group of US Marines to South Vietnam, the first American ground combat forces to enter the war.

Chapter 89

The time had come for Bucko's wife, Edna to retire. Bucko promised her that when the time came, they would both stop working and start traveling. He discussed with Gar the Auto sales business and they decided to sell it. The sales were good, but to keep it open, they would have to find an honest manager and train him to their way of doing business. Gar was very busy and he wouldn't have time to train anyone, so selling would be easiest for both. The sale was completed in about three months, Gar had a nice party for Bucko and Edna and everyone wished them happiness in their new traveling venture. Gar hated to see his best friend leave and he was going to miss him. He told Bucko that if he ever needed anything, all he had to do was call him. They promised each other to stay in touch and to never let their friendship drift away.

Toby continued to win races at the Saturday night dirt track and at the end of the season, he was number one in points and crowned "Track Champion." During the winter, he and Bill decided to make the change from dirt to asphalt. It was time to move up into the Modified class. Bill was building a new car and had been assured by Gar that Savino Auto Parts would continue sponsoring the car.

Toby had become a real favorite with the race fans. His brother, David came to most of his races and enjoyed puttering with the motor. Bill used some of David's suggestions pertaining the the engine and the carburetor.

David was graduating this spring and he was looking forward to starting his first year at Purdue University School of Engineering in Indiana. He didn't have a flair for driving a race car, but he did enjoy seeing and hearing an engine when it was purring like a kitten. He liked knowing how to put together a perfectly balanced motor and to see it perform flawlessly. He was always kidding Toby how one day he was going to build the fastest race engine in the world. They were very close in all of their desires and when David related how great Purdue was, Toby knew that he would be going there,too. Their youngest brother, Michael could not understand how anyone would want to mess around with greasy motors or fill their lungs with carbon monoxide at a race track all the time. He would much rather read a book about becoming president of some big corporation.

At 4 AM the phone rang, waking everyone at the Savino home. Gar answered and it was Irving Grimes.

"Gar, I'm at the hospital. Mary has had a heart attack and they took her up to the operating room. It doesn't look good, Gar. I called Sandy just before I called you, but I just can't call the rest. Will you call the rest of the families for me?"

"Of course I will, Irv. I am so sorry to hear about Mary. We will be right over just as quick as we can get there."

Gar told the boys not to come just yet and he would call them after he knew more about Mary's condition.

Gar called the families and he and Debbie drove to the hospital.

They found Irv at the waiting area with Sandy and Sally. After they had given each other a loving hug and wiped away the tears, Irv related the evening's events.

"Mary said she didn't feel like going out for dinner, so we had a light meal of soup and a sandwich. We watched some television, but Mary was complaining of indigestion, so I gave her some Rolaids and we retired to the bedroom. I asked her if the Rolaids helped and she said maybe a little. We put on our pajamas and she said she probably just needed a good night's sleep since she was very tired.

"I guess I must have fell asleep, because I awoke by hearing her calling my name.

"I turned on the lamp and I saw she was having a lot of pain. She was holding her chest and told me it was a dull, crushing pain. I immediately called our fire rescue unit and started getting us dressed. I unlocked the front door and left it open. Then I ran back up to Mary. She was complaining about the pain going into her neck and jaw, then she passed out, and I thought she had stopped breathing. By this time the rescue team was coming into the house and I kept yelling, 'up here!'

"They started first-aid with cardiopulmonary resuscitation (CPR) and they had her breathing again. I rode in the ambulance with them. The hospital ER staff and the doctor were waiting for us. They administered an electrocardiogram and found she had a blocked artery. The doctor said there was not enough time for drugs to dissolve the clot and with my permission they took her directly to the operating room and called in a heart surgeon. He told me if the paramedics had not arrived when they did, she would not be alive."

Shortly after Sammy and Karen came in with Christopher and Betty, the doctor came into the waiting area to make his report. He reported that the operation went well and they had given her drugs to dissolve any unseen clots. He told them he was very concerned about her heart muscle.

"It received some damage from the recent attack and if it does not pump enough blood, she could suffer heart failure. She has been moved to a specialized intensive care area, called a coronary-care unit and will be watched and monitored around the clock. We just have to wait and see how she responds over the next 24 hours.

She will not know you or be able to talk to you for quite some time and when she awakens, the nurse will come to you, but you can only see her for 15 minutes at a time. It's very important that you not tire her."

The family stayed and waited with Irving and his daughter Rose, hoping that these next crucial hours would bring a better prognosis. After three hours passed, the Nurse came out with the doctor and they reported Mary was still experiencing pain in her chest and was not responding the way he hoped that she would. He had called in another heart specialist and both agreed that unless a miracle happened, she would not survive the next few hours.

The news was devastating to all of them, and Irving had to lie down on the waiting room sofa. The nurse stayed and kept monitoring his pulse while the family tried to comfort him. When more bad news came later that Mary's heart had given up and she had gone to be with her Lord, extra nurses were in attendance to help the grieving family members. They gave Irv some pills to calm his emotions. Sandy and Sally helped take Irv and Rose back to the Grimes' house, where they stayed and helped them get through this terrible tragedy. Someone from the three families was always there to give aid and assistance during the next few days. It was weeks after the funeral before the families were able to cope with this and to go on with their lives. The Military Academies allowed the three students to return for the funeral.

Rose, who had been renting an apartment close to her Manhattan office moved back home to take care of her father. Irving tried to talk her out of this, but she was determined and he soon found that it really was nice to have her around. Rose dated several nice men, but no one had swept her off her feet as yet, so coming back home temporarily was not a problem. It took her longer to commute to work, but she felt her father's welfare was more important. Irv retired and had increased his golf game to keep busy. It was tough for both of them, but before long the sadness eased somewhat and they settled into the routine of daily living .

Chapter 90

Chris Cross retired and he and Irv spent more time together at the golf course. Sammy was taking over more and more each day at the trucking company. Little by little, the partners in Empire Trucking Company sold their shares to Sammy, and he was now completely in control. Sammy's mother, Betty still worked in the office and was training Karen to take over. The company had quite a few trucks for local hauling and several long distance units on the highway, and were a major contributor to moving products across America . Sammy was sending his repair work to Savino's. It was a smart move on Gar's part to start repairing trucks.

The three heroes met every Wednesday night at Vinnie's Bar & Grille for dinner and family talk. They frequented Vinnie's so much that Wednesday night was a bigger night than the weekend. Vinnie was a friend to the three heroes and he actually had a banner outside declaring Wednesday nights as heroes' night. Locals adopted the three guys as family and any night one of them couldn't make it, they were very disappointed. Vinnie would not let the boys pay for anything, but they tipped very generously. Vinnie had to enlarge the dining room to accommodate the extra business and hired extra help for that night. Our heroes loved this neighborhood.

Sandy's daughter, Shannon, was now in her third year at Northwestern University and she loved her work in occupational therapy. She seemed to eat, sleep, talk, and dream about it. Whenever she was home for the holidays, she had a long talk with her Dad about some of the new things modern medicine was coming out with and how new technology was replacing artificial limbs with such amazing results, she wanted Sandy to let the VA equip him with an artificial hand. He told her he had heard so many negative stories from Vets where the artificial limb never worked right and caused more mental anguish, he didn't want to try it. If it failed, he was afraid it might bring back those terrible memories and nightmares he and Sally fought when he first came home from the war.

Shannon was persistent and she finally did get a promise from her Dad that if ever technology improved where it would guarantee him no less than 75 percent normal mobility, he would try it. She was delighted and very sure it would happen.

Shannon was having lunch by herself at the school Cafeteria one day when Dr. Dudley, one of her Professors on his coffee break, asked if he could joined her. He recognized her from his class and saw how dedicated she was to her studies. Shannon invited him to sit down.

He told her about his work in the field of prosthetics. He was starting the new year as Director of the Rehabilitation Engineering Program and Prosthetics Research Laboratory along with Biomedical Engineering and Physical Medicine at Northwestern University. Shannon greatly admired Dr. Dudley and felt honored that he recognized her.

One thing led to another and when she heard him mention about Biomedical, she asked him what it was . He explained Biomedical Engineering health professionals diagnose and treat human disorders. They also research and design medical instruments, working with doctors to develop more technologically advanced medical procedures.

"There are too many aspects to this study to mention in this short of time. You understand that Biomedical engineering has produced lasers that make possible bloodless surgery on blood vessels, nerve fibers retinas, and corneas. They have led to artificial hearts, valves, kidneys and hips. In general, they develop devices and procedures to expand the capabilities of disabled people and to improve the quality of their lives."

Shannon brought up the subject of her Dad and the loss of his hands and Dr. Dudley convinced her a prosthesis of the hand has proven to be very functional and that it didn't make sense for anyone not to have it, especially since the US Government was willing to pay for it. Shannon was excited learning how her Dad could receive something so wonderful. Dr. Dudley said he would personally help her father receive new hands if he would agree to have it done. He offered to talk to the VA on her father's behalf.

That night, Shannon called her Dad and told him all about her conversation with Dr. Dudley. She begged him to contact the VA and get the paperwork started for the new prosthesis. She was relentless and reminded him of the promise he made. He finally agreed to talk it over with her Mother and if she agreed to it, he would make the necessary arrangements. He would call her back as soon as he had something to tell her.

Sandy had a long talk with Sally about the information Shannon relayed to him. She felt he should proceed with the modern technology and be fitted for new hands.

"Make the arrangements and if the doctors at the University Clinic are sure that it could safely be done, let's both take a leave of absence and fly there to check it out. If we find that everything is as Shannon said, we can rent a room at a nice hotel and just stay there until they are finished. If you are certain you want this, then we do it together, Darling."

Chapter 91

The VA was ready to help him. In fact , they always wanted to change his metal claws to artificial limbs, but Sandy never wanted to go for it. Dr. Dudley talked to the VA and after a few weeks everything was at green-light and go!!

Sandy and Sally flew out to Evanston, Illinois. Shannon met them at the Chicago airport and drove with them in their rented car to the hotel near the campus. Shannon told them that Dr. Dudley was expecting them at 9 AM tomorrow morning and he would have one of the procedure doctors there to explain everything and answer any questions. She told them she would see them in the afternoon and have dinner with them later in the evening . She hugged her parents and told her Dad that she was very proud of him and that this was going to be so great for him.

Sandy and Sally promptly arrived on time the next morning at Dr. Dudley's office and after the usual greetings, they were introduced to Dr. Bennett, who would fully explain the procedures and be in charge of their well being. Dr. Bennett started by saying that an artificial limb is a synthetic replacement called a prosthesis.

"This prosthesis must be custom made for each patient. In most cases involving an amputated limb, the remaining stump must heal and shrink before a permanent prosthesis could be fitted. For several weeks, the stump may be wrapped tightly with elastic bandages to help shrink to a firm, smooth surface. In some cases, the person wears a rigid plaster cast to which a temporary prosthesis can be attached. During this time, the person exercises the remaining limb muscles to preserve their strength and movement and to promote circulation. In this case, that would not be necessary since an artificial metal tong or claw has already been used for a few years.

"The next step in preparing a prosthesis involves making a plastic socket that will fit over the stump snugly and comfortably. A cast for the socket may be obtained by wrapping the stump with bandages soaked in wet plaster and letting them harden . After the bandages are removed, they form a mold. Liquid plaster poured into this mold provides a model of the stump. A plastic socket is then formed over the model. Then an artificial leg or arm is attached to the socket. Materials used in making artificial limbs include plastic, fiberglass, metal, and wood. Light metal supports attached to the socket may contain an artificial joint to replace an elbow or a knee. In this case, the prosthesis will be a substitute hand. In most cases the substitutes look like a real hand. This is, of course, what we will be striving for in this case. We will be happy to replace your metal hooks that look like tongs, but have served you so well over the past years.

"Most artificial arms are controlled by a cable that loops around the opposite shoulder. Movements of that shoulder produce movement in the arm prosthesis. Artificial legs are chiefly controlled by the body's normal walking movements. In this case we are going to going to use a prosthesis process that has been developed and controlled by myoelectricity - the electric current produced when a muscle contracts. Metal disks inside the socket rest against the skin of the stump. The disks pick up myoelectric impulses, which are then amplified and used to control an electric motor in the prosthesis. In this case, Mr. Grimes, the myoelectric hand, the impulses from one muscle will open the hand and impulses from another muscle will close it. These actions are somewhat like the natural muscle contractions in an arm.

"Mr. Grimes, we will do our best to replace those metal hooks that look like tongs but have served their purpose, with a prosthesis that will look like a normal hand and give you better mobility. Do you have any questions for us?"

"Only one. When can we get started?"

He crossed his arms and smiled a wide smile, "That's what we like to hear. Let's break for lunch and then we will proceed to the lab and have a plastic cast made for the socket. The best part of this is that you have been using the artificial tongs for a while and it will be easier and faster to fit the socket and prosthesis. We also will be sampling some colors so the new hands will have the same skin tone and texture as your arms."

After lunch, the doctor and his staff removed the tongs Sandy had used for so many years. They proceeded to form and make the cast. Then they made the model and formed the socket over it. This was enough for one day and the doctor asked the Grimes' to return to the hotel, relax, have a nice meal with their daughter and come back in the morning. By 10 AM, they could form the new hand.

That evening, Sandy and Sally had dinner with Shannon and they told her everything. Afterwards, Shannon drove them to various places and acted as their tour guide. They were impressed by the University and how nice everyone was to them. Later they agreed to see each other again tomorrow and do it all again. Sandy was very tired and the parents retired early.

At 10 AM the next day, they were at the clinic and the doctor and his staff started forming the new hand, making sure the metal disks and all of the components were properly aligned and adjusted. It took most of the day to be sure everything worked properly. After the Doctor and Sandy were absolutely sure that the right hand prosthesis was working well, they colored it and let it bake in the kiln overnight. The next day they started on the left hand.

After three days, they allowed Sandy to keep both hands attached and sent him back to the hotel to show his daughter and to find out if they did everything he expected. They wanted him to tell them everything that was both good or bad, and not hold back anything, no matter how small it may seem. Sandy was already saying they were better than he ever expected.

Shannon told her Dad how real his new hands looked and she cried with joy at the movement he was experiencing in just one day. Sally couldn't hold back her tears either as the three of them hugged each other with joy.

The next day Sandy reported to Dr. Bennett that his left hand was feeling some soreness and the staff made a few minor adjustments. The Doctor asked Sandy to stay the weekend because he wanted to see if anything else might need his attention before they sent him home. It would not be practical to send him home if other things needed adjusting, and have to fly right back again. They stayed the weekend and Sandy invited Dr. Dudley to join them for dinner Saturday evening at their hotel. After dinner Dr. Dudley offered Shannon a ride back to her dorm and she agreed.

When she saw her parents again the next day, she told them Dr. Dudley had asked her out for dinner and a movie.

"Don't you think you might be dating men too old for you, honey?" her mother asked with a questioning, concerned expression.

Shannon was determined to comfort her mother. "This is only a friendship, Mom, that came from helping Dad."

The matter was dropped and they all enjoyed sightseeing on their last day together. The following Monday, her parents had their last meeting with Dr. Bennett and Sandy reported that the new prosthesis felt very good. They scheduled a followup meeting in three months and then flew back home to New York that afternoon. Sandy was very thankful that his daughter pushed him into trying the new prosthesis. He was already doing things that he couldn't before. Life was definitely getting better!!!!!

Chapter 92

Mark, Rich, and Doug finished their first year in Military school with honors and were into their second year. David was going to College at Purdue, and Toby finishing his senior year of high school. He was still racing cars during the summers and was loving the modified circuit on asphalt. Michael was in his junior year of high school and enjoyed being on the debating team with all the controversy it produced. He could and usually did, argue about everything.

The Vietnam War soon became an international conflict. United States forces rose from about 60,000 in mid-1965 to a peak of over 543,000. They joined about 800,000 South Vietnamese troops and a total of about 69,000 troops from Australia, New Zealand, the Philippines, South Korea, and Thailand. The North Vietnamese and the Viet Cong had over 300,000 troops, but the exact number is unknown. Both sides developed strategies to take advantage of their strengths. The United States had the finest modern weapons and a highly professional military force. Their field commanders were General William C. Westmoreland from 1964 to 1968 and, afterward, Generals Creighton Abrams and Frederick Weyand. The United States did not try to conquer North Vietnam. Instead, American leaders hoped superior US firepower would force the enemy to stop fighting.

The United States relied mainly on the bombing of North Vietnam and "search and destroy" ground missions in South Vietnam to achieve their aim. They used giant B-52 bombers as well as smaller planes for its main air strikes against the enemy. American pilots used helicopters to seek out Viet Cong troops in the jungles and mountains. Helicopters also carried the wounded to hospitals and brought supplies to troops in the field.

In contrast, Viet Cong and North Vietnamese leaders adopted a defensive strategy. Their more lightly armed troops relied on surprise and mobility. They tried to avoid major battles in the open, where heavy US firepower could be decisive. The Viet Cong and North Vietnamese preferred guerrilla tactics, including ambushes and hand-laid bombs. Their advantages included knowledge of the terrain and large amounts of war materials from the Soviet Union and China.

The two sides fought to a highly destructive draw. The US bombing caused tremendous damage, but it did not affect the enemy's willingness nor its ability to continue fighting. North Vietnam concealed its most vital resources, and the Soviet Union and China helped make up the losses. American victories in ground battles in South Vietnam also failed to sharply reduce the number of enemy troops there. The US Army and Marines usually won whenever they fought the enemy, but North Vietnam replaced its losses with new troops, and often avoided defeat by retreating into Laos and Cambodia.

As the war dragged on, reactions in the United States divided many Americans into so-called "Hawks and

Doves." The hawks supported the nation's fight against Communism, but they disliked Johnson's policy of slow, gradual troop increases and urged a decisive defeat of North Vietnam. The doves opposed US involvement and held mass protests. Many doves believed US security was not at risk. Others charged that the nation was supporting corrupt, undemocratic, and unpopular governments in South Vietnam. The growing costs of the war probably contributed more in arousing public uneasiness in the United States than the antiwar movement did. By late 1967, increased casualties and Johnson's request for new taxes helped produce a sharp drop in public support for the war.

North Vietnam and the Viet Cong opened a new phase of the war, The Tet Offensive, on Jan. 30, 1968, when they attacked major cities of South Vietnam. The fighting was especially fierce in Saigon, South Vietnam's capital, and in Hue. This campaign began at the start of Tet, the Vietnamese New Year celebration. North Vietnam and the Viet Cong hoped the offensive would deal a serious blow to US forces and make the South Vietnamese people lose faith in their government and rise against South Vietnamese leaders. They also hoped the offensive would convince US officials to enter into peace negotiations with North Vietnamese leaders.

The plan failed to achieve all of its objectives. No widespread uprising of the population occurred in South Vietnam. In addition, the United States and South Vietnam quickly recovered their early losses, and the enemy suffered a huge number of casualties.

The Tet attacks stunned the American people and demoralized their war managers. Shortly before the offensive, the US commander in the field, General Westmoreland, had assured the nation that the enemy had already been largely beaten, but the "Tet Offensive" seemed to contradict this statement. As a result of the offensive, Johnson made a number of basic changes in his policies. He cut back the bombing of North Vietnam and rejected Westmoreland's request for 206,000 additional troops. He called for peace negotiations and declared he would not seek reelection in 1968. Peace talks opened in Paris in May.

The peace talks failed to produce agreement, and more and more Americans became impatient for the war to end. President Richard M. Nixon felt he had to reduce US involvement in the conflict. On June 8, 1969, he announced a new policy known as "Vietnamization." This policy called for stepped-up training programs for South Vietnamese forces and the gradual withdrawal of US troops from South Vietnam. The US troop withdrawal began in July 1969.

Chapter 93

In 1970, Mark graduated from the Air Force Academy as Second Lieutenant and was ready for combat. He was trained to fly the B-52, F-105, F-4, F-14 Tomcat, and TR-1. He had training in about every plane the Air Force had, but these were very special that were mainly being used in the Vietnam War.

The Air Force sent Mark overseas as soon as his leave from graduation was over. His pals, Rich and Doug had graduated at the same time from Annapolis as Second Lieutenants and all three were home together. Doug and Rich were also sent to South Vietnam when their leave was over.

Mark was assigned to the Air Force Air Wing Division Alpha and was making daily bombing runs into enemy targets. He was flying areas that President Nixon had just initiated. He ordered US and South Vietnamese troops to clear out military supply centers North Vietnam had set up in Cambodia. Large stocks of weapons were captured, and the invasion may have delayed a major enemy attack. This new campaign angered most Americans as they feared that this was widening the war and that the US should be withdrawing, not widening . The US Senate voted to repeal the "Tonkin Gulf Resolution," ending the Cambodian campaign.

Rich and Doug, second Lieutenants in the US Marines, were attached to the Third Amphibious Force, the largest field Command in Marine History, and were sent directly to South Vietnam, where they were assigned to Captain Lorgan's G-Company of the third Division. The US Marine Divisions were organized into three Regiments and Combat and Service support units . A US Marine Division had about 19,000 Marines.

Rich was in command of A-Platoon, which had three Squads and a Staff Sergeant. Each Squad consisted of 10 Marines, making a total of 30 men.

Doug was in Command of B-Platoon, which had four Squad and a Staff Sergeant, a total of 40 Marines.

They were in the same Battalion but rarely saw each other. Captain Lorgan had been using the two platoons to raid the Vietnam supplies near the Cambodian border until that had been discontinued. Now they were striking the enemy at every area spotted by US planes.

In March 1972, North Vietnam began a major invasion of South Vietnam. Nixon renewed the bombing of North Vietnam and used American airpower against the exposed formations of regular enemy troops and tanks. He also ordered placing explosives in the harbor of Haiphong, North Vietnam's major port for importing military supplies. These moves helped to stop the invasion, which had nearly reached Saigon by August 1972.

The renewal of bombing in the North kept the US Air Force very busy and Mark was now flying a TR-1, an American Reconnaissance aircraft that was used to locate enemy supply and troop movement. It was a very dangerous mission, but one that had to be flown.

It was on one of these missions that the enemy had gotten lucky and was able to hit Mark's plane with a missile sending it to crash into a hillside. He was able to eject himself from the cockpit and parachute to the ground. Unfortunately, he was immediately captured by the Vietnamese and they celebrated his capture by slapping him and beating him with their rifle butts.

They trucked him to Hanoi where he was paraded through the streets with his hands tied behind his back. Civilians repeatedly hit him with sticks as he was forced to walk tied behind a moving army truck . He was interrogated by the Vietnamese, but he refused to give them any information except his name, rank and serial number.

This angered his captors and he was put in a tiny cell and they refused to give him food or water for two days. After that, he was brought before the commander and once more he refused to give them information. They bound his hands over his head and tied them to an overhead beam. One more day of this and he still would not answer their questions. The next ploy they used was the good guy plan. A different officer demanded that he be cut down, given food and enough water to wash himself. He tried to be Mark's friend by telling him that he would make sure he would be fairly treated. All Mark had to do was to sign a statement that he renounced the war and that the US was wrong in bombing Vietnam.

This was not what Mark was going to do and he was defiant toward the officer. They tied his hands behind his back and pulled him up off his feet. In this terrible position, the pain was unbearable. They lowered him down after a few minutes and gave him one last chance to change his mind. The officer grabbed his hair and put his face right close to Mark's, he told him to recant or they would hang him there forever.

Mark spit in his face and yelled, "Never."

This, of course, made them mad and the guard hit him across the face with his rifle butt, badly breaking his nose. As he blacked out, they pulled him back up to the beam with his arms still tied behind his back. When he came to, the pain was unbearable. In short time, his shoulders were coming out of their sockets and he screamed in agony. The only relief he received was when he blacked out from the intense pain. He was left that way overnight. They wanted to make sure that his screaming would keep the other prisoners awake all night.

The next morning, his captors were convinced he was not going to renounce his country and he was lowered down and thrown into a small cell, not allowed to see or talk to other prisoners. It was weeks before he could move his arms again, even then they were painful to move.

Rich and his platoon were ordered to an area where the Recon plane had spotted a unit of enemy troops moving through the jungle. Still quite a ways from the target area, they were ambushed by enemy Viet Cong . He used three Marines taking point, the Staff Sergeant fourth in line, then Rich.

The first shots by the Viet Cong killed the front three Marines and severely wounded the Staff Sergeant. Rich ordered his platoon to retreat and take cover. He was pinned down between his Sergeant, who was about ten feet in front of him, and the rest of his men who were taking cover about twenty feet to his rear. Rich yelled to him, asking how bad he was hit. The Sergeant could hardly talk , but managed to say his right arm and left leg had been hit and was bleeding badly.

Rich yelled back ,"Hang on, I'll get you out."

He crawled to one of his dead men and took the hand grenades off his jacket. He yelled back to his platoon to give him cover. As they poured bullets into the enemy area, he threw a grenade as far as he could towards the enemy . He ran to the Sergeant and could see he was only minutes away from death. He pulled the pins from the other two hand grenades and threw them at the enemy. He put the Sergeant over his back and ran like he did when he was playing football, weaving left and right, jumping over dead branches. He reached the safety of his men, but not before a bullet tore across his back and into his left shoulder.

The medic was able to save the Sergeant and stop the flow of blood in Rich's wounds. The platoon surrounded the enemy and finally kill them. A helicopter was brought in and the dead and wounded were evacuated back to camp. Rich spent a few weeks in a hospital overseas before being transported back to the States. Rich was very despondent about spending so much time preparing to be a Marine officer and to fight for his country, then have it all go away after one bullet. The Marines gave him a choice of taking a discharge or staying in and being a teacher/instructor. He chose to stay in.

Doug's platoon was involved in one battle after another. He had a chance to see Rich before he was shipped back to the States and wish him a safe trip back. Then his platoon was called in to rescue one of the ridges that were being overrun by the Viet Cong. His unit was ambushed, also, but managed to kill the enemy and reach the ridge by early dawn, just as the enemy was staging another thrust and they would have been successful if he had been ten minutes later.

Doug's Commander, Captain Lorgan, was being promoted up the line and because of Doug's heroism, he was promoted to Captain and moved into command of G-Company and Battery.

Chapter 94

Mark was staying alive but lost so much weight, he would not have been recognized by anyone that knew him. He was issued one meal a day and even that was bad. Dysentery, flux, scours and pneumonia were taking it's toll. He was allowed one hour a day out of his pen/cell. He would have gone mad if he hadn't devised a way to communicate with other prisoners, using Morse Code. He repeated the names of everyone in the three families every day. If anyone had the least bit of news, it was relayed to each other before the day was over .

The high cost paid by both sides during the 1972 fighting led to a new round of peace negotiations. The talks were conducted by Henry A. Kissinger, Nixon's chief foreign policy adviser, and Le DucTho of North Vietnam. On Jan. 27, 1973, a cease-fire agreement was signed in Paris by the United States, South Vietnam, North Vietnam, and the Viet Cong. The pact provided for the withdrawal of all US and allied forces from Vietnam and for the return of all prisoners, both within 60 days. It also permitted North Vietnam and the Viet Cong to leave their troops in the south. In addition, it called for internationally supervised elections would let the South Vietnamese decide their political future.

Mark was coming back home. He was returned along with his fellow prisoners that had survived Hanoi Hilton.

He was skin and bones, but they failed to break him. He was truly an American Engendered Hero, one born of a Hero.

On March 29,1973, the last US ground forces left Vietnam. But the peace talks soon broke down, and the war resumed. Congress, responding to voters who wished to see an end to the war, opposed further US involvement. As a result, American troops did not return to the war. In mid-1973, Congress began to reduce military aid to South Vietnam.

The war ended on April 30, 1975, when North Vietnam troops entered Saigon and the South Vietnamese government formally surrendered to them. Saigon was renamed Ho Chi Minh City.

About 58,000 American military personnel died in the war, and about 300,000 were wounded. South Vietnamese military losses were approximately 224,000 killed and 1 million wounded. North Vietnamese and Viet Cong losses totaled about 1 million dead and 600,000 wounded. Countless civilians in North and South Vietnam also perished.

Would the United States enter another war without winning it? Does history repeat itself ? Will humans continue to strive to be inhumane to each other?

The Vietnam War was the first foreign war in which US combat forces failed to achieve their goals. This failure hurt the pride of many Americans and left bitter and painful memories. Americans most immediately affected included approximately 2,600,000 men and women who served in the war and their families. Most veterans adjusted smoothly to civilian life. But others, particularly those with psychological problems associated with combat stress, encountered difficulties in making the adjustment to postwar American society. These veterans suffered high rates of divorce, drug abuse, unemployment, and homelessness.

After World Wars I and II, the country viewed its soldiers as heroes. Americans who opposed the US role in Vietnam embraced those veterans who joined the antiwar movement upon their return from the battlefield, but some criticized or shunned those veterans who felt the war was justified. Many Americans who supported the war came to regard Vietnam veterans as symbols of America's defeat. Some leading hawks opposed expanding benefits to Vietnam veterans to match those given to veterans of earlier wars. These reactions shocked the veterans. Many of them felt that the nation neither recognized nor appreciated their sacrifices.

After the war, Congress and the public became more willing to challenge the president on military and foreign policy. The war also became a standard of comparison in situations that might involve US troops abroad.

Americans still disagreed on the main issues and lessons of the war. Some believed US participation was necessary and just. Many of these people said the war was lost because the United States did not use its full military power and because opposition at home weakened the war effort. Others pointed to the failure of the South Vietnamese government to develop popular support and to its over reliance on the United States. Still others viewed US involvement as immoral and unwise. Some of them felt US leaders made the war a test of the nation's power and leadership. Some viewed the conflict as a civil war that had no importance to US security. Since Vietnam, many Americans have argued that the nation should stay out of wars that do not directly threaten its safety or vital interests.

Mark, Rich , and Doug were back home in the United States after spending time in the war with North Vietnam. They were heroes just as their fathers were, but Americans were slow to give credit to returning veterans.

Mark would always have a problem with his shoulders and his back from the harsh treatment he received as a POW. He had to spend months in and out of he Veteran's hospitals before he was finally given a medical discharge and a monthly stipend from the US Government. He continued to live at home and Gar was always trying to get him to go to Vinnie's with him, but Mark preferred to be by himself and he shied away from people or parties . He had a ways to go yet before he would be over the effects of the war. The VA was very good with him and his doctors were monitoring him very closely. They told his parents that Mark will eventually be well, but it will take time and lots of TLC, tender loving care.

Rich and Doug stayed in the Marines. Rich had spent time in the hospital and after much healing and therapy, regained the use of his shoulder and was promoted to Captain.

Doug escaped being struck by enemy bullets and stayed in the Marines as Captain. None were married, as yet. Rich and Doug were living on base but they did get home often. They made sure they saw Mark every time that they came home.

1975 was the year that the Vietnam War was officially over. The US Forces were out of there in 1973. So, by 1975, Mark had almost regained his sense of humor and he no longer went every week for special therapy at the VA clinic. Donna was very successful in designing women's fashion clothes and had fallen in love with a male designer who had stores in New York, Paris and London. She married Paul Lamaar in 1974 and they traveled between their two homes in Paris and New York. David graduated from Purdue in 1972 and was hired by General Motors. Toby graduated from Purdue in 1973 and went to work as a mechanic in his Dad's truck repair shop. He had decided to work for his father so he could be closer to Bill Johnson, the owner of the Super modified he was now racing at Oswego, NY, on Saturday nights.

Michael was still in Harvard Law School at Cambridge, Mass. Shannon Grimes graduated from Northwestern and married Dr. Derek Dudley and together they were deeply involved in research work at Northwestern University Medical school, at Evanston, Illinois. Holly was happily married and enjoyed life with her husband, Bob Fisher, selling large boats and yachts. They held many family reunions aboard their 50 foot cruiser, the Compass Rose.

Sandy was conducting yearly seminars on selling insurance and Sally had continued to work at the hospital as nurse supervisor Sandy's new prosthetics were far better than those obsolete hooks-tongs.

Sammy and Karen were solidly in control of the Empire Trucking Company and their hard work was paying off in huge dividends. Shipping by truck was cheaper and more convenient than by rail.

Chapter 95

The Savino enterprises were doing nicely and this took up most of Gar's time and energy. Debbie had become very important to the company. She excelled in leadership as office manager. She had Grace as her mentor and right arm, while she had Leandra as her left arm. Lee, as everyone called her, was married to James and Gar found a spot for him in the parts department as their delivery man. Gar was so appreciative of loyalty and family ties. Whenever an opening came up, he would always ask his good employees if a member of their family needed work. He never hesitated in rewarding his employees for their faithfulness. His people were the highest paid in the auto repair industry.

Debbie and Gar spent many days and nights worrying about Mark. When the VA had told them that Mark would need a lot of TLC, tender loving care. That was what he got. They were so happy after nearly two years to see Mark coming around to being his old self again. Mark was dating now and then and when he told his father he wanted to find some kind of work because he was starting to get bored, it was music to his ears. But just what would Mark want to do? His physical condition would not allow him to do anything strenuous. He was a college graduate with schooling geared to military life. Gar decided to have a bull session with Irving, Chris, Sammy, and Sandy without Mark knowing about it. Perhaps someone might have a suggestion that would help motivate or maybe stimulate Mark's interest.

Irving and Chris had what they thought was perfect for Mark. With all the publicity and honors that he received from being a Vietnam Hero, he should get into politics. He might even run for Mayor of New York. Irv said he had lots of friends that would support Mark and back him financially. Everyone thought that would be perfect for him and they decided to approach Mark and get his reaction to being a politician. So the following day, Irv and Chris stopped over to talk to Mark and invited him out for breakfast.

He listened to everything they had to say and when they were finished, he told them he knew they worried about his future and appreciated all their fine ideas, but he was not the least bit interested in politics. He told them one of his good friends from the Air Force had recently gone to work for Delta Airlines as a Commercial Pilot and that he had been talking by phone with him and assured him he would not have a problem being hired. Mark said he was making preparations to arrange a meeting with the Delta officials.

Chris and Irv were surprised to hear that Mark had gone this far with his plans of seeking new employment. It showed that Mark may have turned the corner with his rehabilitation and that those terrible nightmares of his past experiences in Vietnam were finally letting him get on with his life. They congratulated Mark on his decision and told him that Delta was lucky to have him as their pilot. This of course made Mark feel real good and he related to these Grandparents how he had struggled with himself to take that first step. Once he had done that, his confidence was way up and for the first time in a long time, he was feeling good about life and making a difference in the world once more.

Later that week, Delta and Mark had their meeting and they hired him as one of their pilots. He was sent to Dallas, Texas and after two weeks of learning how Delta ran it's operation and getting the feel of those big passenger planes, he made his first flight from Dallas / Fort Worth to Hawaii by way of Los Angeles. He loved his new employment and to be able to fly once more was icing on the cake. He not only was thrilled to be in the air again, but the beautiful scenery of the many places he flew to, made him feel like an excited tourist. He soon found an additional bonus that had escaped him for nearly two years. Girls! These beautiful lady Stewards were creating a desire within his body that Mark had feared was almost lost. Life was starting to be good once more.

Gar and Debbie had worked very hard at raising their family. They made sure each one received the proper training in morality and spiritual growth, along with all the requirements to being a good human being.

Gar was having this very conversation with Debbie one evening when they went out to dinner. He seemed to repeat how both of them had sacrificed themselves and how they sent each one to college. Debbie sensed he had something on his mind, but he was tiptoeing around the issue.

"Come on, Honey. You've been giving off vibes all evening about something. If there is something bothering you, why don't you spit it out?"

"What? Oh, well, I have been thinking how we both have worked so hard raising our family, that we haven't done much together. I think we need to take a long vacation or what those TV actors call a hiatus. Let's just get away from all this money making madness for a while, or better still, sell it all and travel around the world for a few years. You know we deserve a break."

Debbie took a hard look into Gar's eyes and said, "Yes, it's true we need a nice long break, but Gar, are you sure you can handle being idle? You know how you are if you don't have a challenge. I can see us on vacation, maybe a long one, but I just do not believe that selling out is the answer to your uneasiness or itchy feet."

Gar didn't answer.

"Something just crossed my mind. Are you itchy about going back to Casino Gambling? Is this what all this is about? I don't mind you going to the Casino occasionally, but if you think I'm going to allow you to sell your great business and become a Casino Gambler again, just to fulfill your life's dream, you are crazy. It's never going to happen."

Gar had never seen Debbie so irritated before and quickly tried to calm her.

"No, no, baby. I won't do that if you think it's wrong."

"So you admit you were thinking along those lines?"

Gar found he had opened Pandora's box and he was in deep trouble.

"Debbie, I may have thought along those lines, but I was going to talk to you about it to see how you felt. Now I know, and it will not be mentioned again. We need a nice long vacation, so let's just allow our managers to do what we trained them to do and keep the business and let them make money for us. I think we should hire another office girl and promote our pretty black girl Leandra, to be an assistant to Grace. What do you think?"

"I think you got out of that real quick, you rascal. But yes, I think that would be very nice. Grace needs to slow down some and she loves Lee, so that would work out nicely. My, but you are the one," as she grinned and squeezed his hand.

"Where would you like to go when we start our long vacation, Debbie? A cruise, Europe, Canada or Mexico? Is there any place you have always wanted to see?"

"No, not really, but there are so many wonderful places right here in the good ole USA, that if I have to choose now, I vote to see all of America first."

"That sounds great to me, Sugar. I'll pick up some brochures and maps from our Auto club tomorrow. We no doubt will be going by car, since it will give us better access to all of the places."

Chapter 96

They both spent the next few weeks making sure all the department managers did not have a problem with their absence and to sweeten the deal, Gar promised an increase in bonuses if they had an increase in profits by December. Every department manager told him he need not worry about the business. After all, he hired the very best and they were eager to show him that all of his training would not be wasted, or be in vain. They wished only the very best for Gar and Debbie. Gar was not only a very respected employer, but a real Hero to each and every one of them.

Most every evening Gar and Debbie could be found with their noses in maps, books and brochures, planning places to visit. To them, it seemed like more fun than Christmas. They decided on driving across America and stopping at all the places that they had always read and heard about.

"Gar, there is one place that I really would like to see and know more about."

"Oh? Where would that be? Let me guess. It either has to be the Grand Canyon, or maybe the Canyons of Utah. Am I right?"

"No. I do want to see them, but they aren't the place I'm referring to." She had a smile on her face.

"Well, don't keep me in the dark. Where is it, Honey?"

"OK, it's that place where you grew up and where you lived in that awful Orphanage. I remember you telling me once how you went back there looking for anyone that could help you find someone who might have known your parents. You remarked how beautiful the town and the area were."

"Oh, you're talking about Elmira and the Finger Lakes area. Hey, that could be our first stop. I had no idea you were interested in that place. I do know that they had a bad flood in 1972 and they are in an economic struggle to keep the city prosperous. You'll love the mountains and lakes the Southern Tier has to offer." He remembered the beautiful rolling hills there.

"OK then, I'll finish packing and be ready when you are."

As she headed toward the closet for the suitcases, he headed for the door.

"I made arrangements at work and the boys will take care of the house, so we should be able to leave in two days."

The drive up through Route 17 in the spring was a beautiful sight. The lush new green leaves on the hillsides represented a velvety cushion of soft feathers gently waving in the morning sunshine. Gar and Debbie got an early start and escaped from the City before the morning rush had a chance to begin.

"My, isn't the countryside beautiful," said Debbie, "I had almost forgotten how mother nature makes everything look so gorgeous after the snow melted. I guess living in the fast paced Metropolis has a way of making us forget just how wonderful the rest of the world can be."

"You're right, Honey, I too sometimes find myself being caught up in the act of being too busy. The guy that wrote or said that we need to, 'stop and smell the roses,' sure did know what he was talking about. We've only gone maybe a hundred miles and already. I feel like a big load has been lifted off my shoulders and I'm beginning to see and appreciate things that I had taken for granted. We sure did need to get away and forget about all that work. The way I feel right now, maybe we will just stay retired and sell the business or let the managers run it. What do you say?"

She felt sure and excited at the prospect. "Hey, Sugar, I'm ready for anything that you want to do. We have earned the right to a nice retirement and the business will pay for it."

Chapter 97

As Gar drove into Elmira, off the Water Street exit, he could see that the flood of 1972 had made significant changes to the City. He saw where every store on the south side of Water Street to the river from near Main Street down to Madison Avenue, were gone and the city had landscaped it and turned it into a narrow park.

"Holy Cow, that flood sure did mess up my old town. I can't believe how most everything has changed. Say, how about us going back to that Holiday Inn that we passed coming in on Water Street to get a room and take a look around more in the morning. Maybe the Hotel Manager might know someone who could tell us more about that Flood, OK ?"

"That sounds good. Besides, we aren't in a hurry, anyway."

After breakfast the next day, Gar was asking the Hotel Manager if he knew anyone who could tell them about Elmira and the flood of 1972, and he told him about the Chemung County Historical Society and their newly renovated building just up ·the street near Lake street. He said a member was always there to answer each and every question about Chemung County. Gar thanked him, then He and Debbie proceeded to the Historical Society building. They were met by Mr. Boyd, who went to great lengths to show photos and explain in detail how

Chemung got its start as well as how the "Flood of '72" drastically changed Elmira.

Mr. Boyd referred several times to the Star Gazette Souvenir booklet that was printed after the flood to remind visitors and residents of just how cruel Mother Nature can be. His opening monologue reminded the listeners of the opening of the Bible. He started with,"In the beginning there was rain."

For most residents it was merely an irritant. Inconvenient and uncomfortable but not startling. As the first day of rains were pounding and five inches was reported, other counties were issuing flash flood situations. To Chemung, residents this was a temporary condition. They said that the Chemung River was still at low level and there was no immediate threat. They even declared they could handle another five inches of rain, no problem. So as they went to bed on Wednesday night, June 21st 1972, it was just another wet, summer day. Thursday, June 23rd, the rains from Tropical storm Agnes was not letting up. The heavy sound as if hundreds of typewriter keys were all hitting at once was what residents woke up to. The Dam was holding at Hornell, northwest of Elmira, but it was apparent conditions were rapidly deteriorating. The Conhocton River had risen 27 feet. The Canesteo River was already 7.7 feet over the flood stage at Addison. The Toga and the Cowanesque Rivers broke through the dikes and swept the residential areas of Lawrenceville, while the Susquehanna River invaded Towanda, PA.

Evacuation started in Elmira and the outlying rural sectors. Flood officials were still hopeful that the river in Elmira would not go over the 23 foot top of the dikes, but as they watched, the Main Street bridge washed away. The third day brought the full realism that nothing was going to be spared. Elmira's South side and downtown areas were under water. The National Guard came, as well as the Army Reserve. The schools and churches were used as evacuation centers. All bridges were either destroyed or damaged and all of the south side of Elmira was cut off from the north side. Helicopters were used to ferry food. Some areas were reported to be 12 feet deep in water.

By midday, the river had crested and mid afternoon, the water started to recede . The immediate danger was lifting, but now other problems would take over. Health and sanitation problems were bad. The National Guard patrolled the area to protect against looting. Devastation was everywhere. The musty smell was overwhelming. Debris and mud littered every street and yard. It was the aftermath of the greatest flood in Twin Tier history. Elmira and Corning were more like armed camps. Military personnel, carrying fixed bayonets on bullet less rifles, were everywhere. Food began to arrive in quantities and water tankers brought in water after trips of over 100 miles . The clean up was now underway. Coordination began on storage and distribution of food. There was despair, depression, relief and prayers of thanks. The fear of typhoid brought thousands to makeshift clinics for shots. Elmira and the Twin Tiers fought back, but so many buildings were lost that eventually the bulk of Elmira's business community moved up to the mall in Big Flats.

Gar and Debbie thanked Mr. Boyd for his time and Gar made a nice donation the Historical Society. They were feeling down as they left the building and decided they had seen and heard enough about how Elmira had been torn apart, even though Mr. Boyd assured them that Elmira will be like that bird, Phoenix, and will rise up from the ashes and live again.

Gar and Debbie drove to Woodlawn Cemetery and visited the grave sight where Samuel Clemens, Mark Twain and his family were buried. Then they drove over to the Elmira College campus where Mark Twain's Study had been moved from his Quarry farm some years ago in order that tourist could see where Mark Twain had written such books as "The Adventures of Tom Sawyer," "The Adventures of Huckleberry Finn," "The Prince and The Pauper," "Life On The Mississippi." The study was shape octagon and had windows on all sides.

The next day, the Savinos continued on their westward journey to see the many sights this great country has to offer. They visited the Arches in St. Louis , the Grand Canyon, the Boulder Dam, all of the beautiful Canyons of Utah, and a few shows in Las Vegas before they decided to return to New York.

Debbie had been noticing lately that Gar had become somewhat edgy and at times was easily agitated. She noticed this coming on before they had taken their trip but she'd felt it was because he had been working very hard and needed time away from his work. Now she could see it becoming more noticeable. She knew it wasn't about money matters, because Gar had turned his repair shops and Salvage yard into a very successful conglomeration. She finally decided that Craps playing was at the bottom of this and with such passion for the game, she should let him go back to it as a relief valve to his disposition.

When were almost home, she told him, "Honey, I've been thinking. Maybe I have been wrong by not allowing you to visit the Casinos and play the Craps game that you love so much. Maybe you need to do that occasionally. So, if that is what you would like to do, do it with my blessings."

Gar was taken by surprise and exclaimed, "Baby, are you sure? How did you know I had been thinking about that? You sure are a sweetheart if it's true."

"Oh it's true, Gar. I realized you needed to do something that you like and it wasn't fair of me to hold you from it ."

Gar stopped the car, pulled her to him and said, "I love you more each day. Thank you, baby".

Chapter 98

The following day they arrived home and they both remarked how nice it was to be back. They had driven over five thousand miles and were somewhat a little car weary. Debbie seemed much more tired than Gar.

Soon after they had unpacked she told Gar, "I'm just too tired to fix dinner Darling, do you mind if I shower and hit the hey, I'm beat."

"Sure thing Sweetie, I'm not very hungry anyway. I'll just fix a sandwich. You get some rest and I'll be up a little later. I'm going to wait until morning to call the office."

The following morning, Gar was up early and after talking with Grace and his shop foremen, he was relieved to hear everyone was on the ball and each department was functioning properly. Grace reported that each shop had an increase in production over last month.

When Debbie came downstairs, she complained again of still being tired and she told Gar she had made an appointment with her doctor. Gar looked surprised.

"Are you sick, Honey?"

"Oh no," she quickly remarked, "I just remembered I put off my last appointment to go on our trip, so I thought since I need to see him about my decreased energy, I'd get the annual checkup also."

That seemed to put Gar at ease somewhat but he still was concerned.

Later that day, Gar made the rounds, checking on all of his departments and was quite pleased at how well everything was going. He felt proud of how well he had trained his managers, and how Grace seemed to have everything in control. He decided to just stay behind the scenes for awhile, as long as things were going so well.

Gar stopped at Vinnie's, his favorite bar, for a beer and called Bucko, who had also just returned from one of his trips with Edna. Bucko picked up on the first ring.

"Hey Bucko, how was your trip?"

"Hey, yourself, stranger. We got back a few days ago Gar, we had a great time. How about your vacation?"

Gar told him how much they enjoyed the West and all the canyon lands. Then he asked Bucko to meet him at the bar for a beer. When Bucko arrived, they gave each other a bear hug and a pat on the back. Later, after some small talk and another round of beer, Gar explained to Bucko why he asked him out.

"I have this itch to get back to shooting Craps again, Bucko and it's starting to affect my mood. Debbie has seen it and she says if I want to start playing again, she would not try to stop me.

"You know, it's not that I want more freedom from Debbie. It's just something inside that keeps gnawing at me. It's an itch that won't go away until I scratch the heck out of it. Do you understand?" He hoped for an answer that would help.

"Yes, I do, Gar. I have had that itch myself a time or two. As a matter of fact, Edna has asked me more than once if something was bothering me. She hasn't ever been around gamblers like us and she hasn't a clue how it gets in your blood, and the only way you get relief is to get in a good crap game."

"I needed to have this talk, old friend," said Gar, "because I'm seriously thinking of going back to playing dice, but I can't jeopardize my marriage or hurt Debbie."

"The same with me, Gar. I wouldn't want to hurt Edna either. I'd like to make a suggestion, that is, if you are asking me to join you, we do some playing, close by in Atlantic City at first. If things go well, we can go to Las Vegas later for some big money."

"That was my thought, exactly. You know, of course, that I want you to join me, but I do not want to be the cause of any problems with Edna, Pal."

Bucko looked Gar in the eye.

"Edna will be no problem, Gar. We both have lived independently and understand there are times when we both might need some space for ourselves."

"OK, Bucko. I'll make sure everything is being properly handled at my shops and the timing is right, then I'll get back in touch with you. I may even sell my business to the right people, now that the kids do not need me for support anymore. I sure am happy Mark is flying again. He told us recently flying with Delta has been a lifesaving move on his part and he was very happy."

He and Bucko left the tavern together and after the usual goodbyes, each drove to their respective homes. Debbie was in the kitchen preparing dinner.

"Hi Sugar, how did it go at the doctors today?"

"Well, he took some blood and some X-rays and said he would call me with the results in a couple days. He seems to think I overdid myself on our vacation. What were you doing today? Did you bother your foremen and Grace at work?"

He moved to help set the table while she was placing some vegetables in a bowl. "Yeah, maybe a little. They don't need me anymore. Grace keeps them on the ball. I did see Bucko over at the Tavern and we had a beer together. I think he's getting a little bored doing nothing. Maybe the four of us could go out to dinner sometime soon. What do you think?"

"Sure. That would be nice. Maybe I'll call Edna later and set a date for Friday evening. Wash up, dinner is about ready."

Later that evening Gar called all his children and was happy to find that everyone was well and that they all liked their jobs and their lives. He always took great pride in how great his kids turned out and how they respected their parents.

Chapter 99

The following day Debbie had a call from her doctor who asked if she would mind coming in again, as he wanted to go over the X-rays with her. He also asked her to have Gar come with her. She, of course, wanted him to explain more, but he told her he would explain everything when she came in. This raised many scary questions and the doctor told her that she must not worry over what he had said, and basically he wanted her to have another mammogram and c-scan.

The next morning, after a restless night, she and Gar proceeded to join the heavy traffic and make the drive to the doctor's office. Both of them were quiet as they waited at a very busy intersection for the light to turn green on a six lane road (three each way). Gar was in the lane next to the curb. This obscured Gar's vision of traffic crossing from his left. He relied on the traffic light to tell him when he could proceed. As they waited patiently to go, they were both thinking about the doctor's request that they come in this morning . Debbie was trying not to show much emotion so as not to worry Gar, while all the time he tried to appear calm so as to not let Debbie become afraid of what was the reason for this urgent call to the office. At times like these the mind tends to allow a person to picture the worse case scenario and unpleasant thoughts tend to flood the speculating brainwork.

These thoughts were in Gar's mind as he watched the signal light go from red to green. At that instant, he started across the intersection. He suddenly realized the two lanes on his left did not move out as he had. Then suddenly he knew why, as he saw the auto hurling toward him at a very fast pace. It was later found this vehicle was driven by a school teacher who was running late and tried to outrun the red light that T-boned Gar's car.

Gar saw the teacher's car but the speed at which it was traveling, he could not take any evasive action to avert the horrific crash. His car was broad sided on the left side and tossed several feet before it rolled sideways for three or four times coming to rest in the median. Both he and Debbie were unconscious. The fire truck and rescue unit was on the scene in a matter of minutes and with the help of their jaws-of-life equipment, they had them both in two ambulances in quick fashion. Both vehicles were apparent total losses.

Gar came to as the emergency doctor concluded his careful inspection. He told Gar how lucky he was to only sustain three fractured ribs.

Gar was not interested in himself and kept repeating,"How is my wife?"

The doctor told Gar.

"Another doctor and team were taking care of her and as soon as I can, I will find out and come and tell you. In the meantime, we will have to wrap your chest and ribcage in order for them to heal properly. We will have you checked in at this hospital for a few days, just in case something else might show up."

In the another part of the emergency room the doctors tried to revive Debbie, but she sustained a broken neck and a very bad hit to the right side of her head bringing instant death to this wonderful lady. They now had to inform Gar his wife did not make it. This is the hardest task that all doctors have to perform, of notifying a person that their loved one has died.

This was news that Gar was not prepared for. He suspected something as the doctor stood beside his bed with a pale, ashen face and having a difficult time bringing forth his words. When he finally finished and that terrible word "dead" hit Gar's ears, his scream of, "No... No... Oh God, no!!", could be heard throughout the entire hospital. His wail was so bad the doctor had to sedate him for fear that he might injure himself further by one of his fractured ribs puncturing his lung.

Gar's family was called and with a saddened heavy heart they took over for their father and arranged all of the funeral and burial arrangements. The doctors insisted that Gar remain in the hospital, but Gar demanded that they tape his ribs and that he was going to his wife's funeral "come hell or high water."

He did promise to return to the hospital after the funeral, but since some of his family had told him that they would stay home with him until he was well, he called his doctor and told him he was not returning to the hospital. Sammy and Sandy's families and all his friends came by his home during the next few days to express their sorrow and wish him well. Gar felt like he was in a dark hole and no way to get out. His heart was broken and seeing his friends coming by each day did not ease his pain. Bucko was aware of his good friend becoming more and more reclusive and drawing himself into a hard shell to protect himself from facing the grim reality.

He decided that something needed to be done immediately or Gar might not ever return to normalcy. Bucko called Gar's doctor and related his fear that Gar was in need of either a psychiatrist or psychoanalyst. The doctor told him he agreed with him, but Gar refused to see another doctor and that he had tried more than once to persuade Gar to seek help and got nowhere. The doctor told Bucko that if he could get Gar to leave his house and do things to get his mind on something besides his bereavement, it could possibly snap him out of it . Bucko decided he would somehow convince Gar to come with him over to Vinnie's Tavern. Everyone knew them both and if he succeeded in getting him there, maybe, just maybe, it would make a difference.

t had been three weeks since Debbie's funeral and Gar had hardly left his house, except to visit his shops. All of his managers told him they would take good care of his business and Grace had assured him everything was going smoothly and he need not worry about that. The problem was that every time he visited the shops, he would lose control and break down in front of the employees. His managers finally had to tell him not to visit his shops until he was feeling better because it was not good for his employees to see him weep in front of them.

Bucko either called Gar every day or stopped at Gar's home to check on him. Gar's children, by now, had returned to their respective jobs and were trying hard to get past their terrible tragedy.

Bucko was being very patient with Gar and when the time was right, he would mention that they needed to get out and go here or there, but Gar was always putting him off, declaring he was too tired. One day, Bucko made a statement that was between asking and telling Gar that he needed to come with him to Vinnie's Tavern.

"Why tonight?"

"Well, as you know, you sponsored Vinnie's bowling team and they just finished the season by taking first place in their league. Now Vinnie and the team have decided to have a banquet in your honor to show their appreciation for everything you have done for them. I stopped there the other day and they were working like beavers, sprucing up the place. It would break their hearts if you didn't show up, besides I sort of promised them that you would be there. So, what do you say, partner?"

Gar stared at Bucko for what seemed an eternity. Then as the tears started to flow, he slowly sobbed, "I can't go Bucko, I just can't get over losing Debbie."

Bucko took his time as Gar was gathering himself and getting back under control.

"Gar, we have been best of friends for a long time and we have always been truthful with each other. I love you like a brother and will always be at your side in times of trouble. So, from that aspect, I believe that I have the right to enter into your unhappiness and speak to you from my heart. But......"

Gar was waving his arms.

"Stop Bucko, I'm just not ready for people."

Bucko again waited on Gar to settle down and he continued, "This has to be said, Gar, because the doctors and I are afraid that unless you snap out of this, your health will start deteriorating. If Debbie were here, she would want you to get on with your life. You owe it to your family and friends, but most of all, you owe it to Debbie."

Those last three words jolted him into reality.

"Oh, my God, Bucko, you are right. I never thought about that before. I do owe it to Debbie's memory as well as to my family."

Bucko silently watched as Gar seemed to be getting control of his emotions. He felt that if he was to speak just now, his efforts might be lost. Gar needed to make the next move if he was going to get well.

Gar stopped crying and after he dried his face with his handkerchief, he sat there with his face in his hands, looking at the floor. After while he cleared his throat.

"I feel much better now, Bucko. Thanks for all your help. I am starting to get a grip on things. I'd like you to stay while I get ready and I will go with you to Vinnie's, unless you need to go home first?"

"No, I'm fine. I told Edna I was coming here and that I might be going out to dinner with you."

Chapter 100

They arrived at Vinnie's later and as soon as they came in the door, shouts rang out, "Here they are! Here come Gar and Bucko."

Bucko saw that Gar had a big smile on his face as they shook hands with everyone . This was the first time Gar smiled in a long time.

Vinnie was quick to place a Scotch and water in Gar's hand and before long Bucko heard Gar talking and then came laughter. Bucko was seeing him return to his old self again and he silently thanked God for that .

About midway through the evening Gar touched glasses with Bucko and said, "Here's to you, my best friend. I'm moving forward from here and I'm in good health."

He raised his glass to Gar's and said, "I am proud to be your friend."

Then they gave each other a bear hug with the usual pat on the shoulder. After the banquet, Bucko drove Gar home and as he was getting out of the car he asked Bucko to give him a call tomorrow.

"I have some things to talk to you about ."

Gar's health continued to improve over the next few months and he was able to talk with people much easier. He spent more time at his office and was again having weekly meetings with his management team. He hated doing laundry, so he hired a maid to take care of his house and do the laundry. Someone who was highly recommended by Grace.

He made an extra effort to visit Sandy and Sammy more often and to call his children every week. After several months, he began to think that he might be making a pest of himself because it appeared to him that everyone seemed to be trying to get rid of him by saying that he needed to get out more, go here or go there. Go see this or that. Of course, they were hoping that he find a little more fun out of life. They were hoping he might find someone to share things with, but they would never suggest it openly to him even though they were aware of him being very lonely. His destiny would have to come into play in due course.

He and Bucko saw each other almost daily over coffee at Gar's home. Gar asked if Edna objected of him coming over so often and Bucko let it slip that things were not working out with he and Edna. It seems that she never wanted to do the things that Bucko did and Bucko didn't want to do what she did. They decided that maybe they should separate for a year and see if things changed. If not, then they would get divorced.

"When will this separation start?"Gar carefully asked.

"Oh, I guess as soon as I find an apartment to move into."

"Apartment my eye! You just get all of your gear and move in here with me. Why didn't you say something before, Buddy? You know you're always welcome here."

"Shoot , I couldn't do that to you, Gar. This is yours and Debbie's pl...... Damn, I'm sorry, Gar. I forgot myself for a minute ,"

"That's OK, Bucko. No harm done. I'm able to handle the reality more each day. But getting back to us, I would like very much if you would move in. It would be so great to have you. Besides since you sold your car business, you could maybe help me in some of my decisions about my shops. What do you say?"

Bucko paused.

"Are you sure Gar?"

"I was never more sure. I promise to give you space and not be in your way. You take one of the bedrooms and the extra bathroom. We have the maid to do the housework and she will cook the evening meals, if we want her to do so."

"Then how could I refuse such a deal? I'll take it ."

With that, they shook hands and Gar took Bucko on a tour of the house.

Having Bucko living with him proved to be good for both of them. They enjoyed each other's company and whenever a problem came up, they would openly discuss it and arrive at an agreeable answer. Whenever there was a family gathering, Bucko was always invited. Everyone knew he was good for Gar and how close they were and in time Sandy and Sammy and their families felt the same way about Bucko.

Gar took Bucko with him whenever he had his weekly meetings with his managers and before long Bucko was made Gar's assistant. This made it possible for Bucko to attend meetings and to stand in for Gar whenever needed. Gar was spending all his energy concentrating on every aspect of his large operation. He had toyed with the idea of selling everything, but he was not eager to leave his people unemployed. He wanted to take care of his faithful workers that had stood by him and were honest employees.

He discussed this with Bucko and they agreed that if he was keeping the business, it would require a "Hands-on" management by Gar. He would not be able to take off all his time to play craps, as he was planning to do. He and Bucko spent many hours going over plans to once more hit the Casinos. They agreed that Gar needed to bring in a corporate lawyer to find a solution fair to his employees.

The lawyer suggested that Gar either sell everything, or set up a profit-sharing agreement and have the managers become co-owners. Then after x -amount of years they would have the option of buying his remaining interest. This way they maintain and operate the business with their jobs secured, and later he would be paid off in full. He would receive a monthly profit check and would always be the owner until it's paid for. Gar liked that much better.

He and Bucko held several meetings with the employees and after everyone understood how this would become a win-win solution for them, it became real and they all signed on. Each department had a manager who reported to Grace, who was CEO. Any major changes had to be ok'd by Gar.

It was a done deal. Gar couldn't believe how quick and smoothly everything had taken place. He removed all of his excess cash from his business and only left enough for Grace to operate the business. Past records made this . Gar received a substantial amount from Debbie's Life policy and had a very large savings account. He was ready to form a partnership with Bucko, who had saved his money wisely also.

Chapter 101

Gar and Bucko had decided that if they were going to play craps for real money they needed to establish some ground rules and a workable plan. They made a point that it had to include having fun because if it was not fun, it would be like going to work. That was not what they had in mind.

Their priorities were:

1. Have Fun!

2. Practice on a crap table or box if a week goes by without Casino play.

3. Establish the amount of money to take into the Casino as bank money.

4. Establish the amount to start the game with, such as the buy in or session money.

5. On all other shooters, we use the five-count system before we bet on them, but we do not count a craps number in the five count. The five have to be five place numbers.

6. If we have two session losses in succession, we leave that table or casino.

7. We never argue with dealers or a pit boss. We leave the table if they are intentionally wrong. They practiced every day in Gar's basement where they had set up the practice box he had purchased from Jerry Patterson.

Gar also talked with Jerry over the phone and they agreed to meet in Atlantic City. He asked Jerry which casino had the best tables and he advised them to see him in person before they started going to the casinos again. He mentioned that he and his coaches had discovered a new and better way to play the game. Gar told him that if he had a better method than the one that he sold him before, that he would buy it. Jerry had agreed to show it to both of them if they came down to his home. Gar and Bucko drove down to Jerry's home and after a reunion, Jerry got down to business.

He explained to them others were taking his ideas and going their own way and teaching others without any consideration for Jerry.

So he had discovered a new method that no one could steal and the casinos could not tell what he was doing. It's not illegal or cheating. It is simply a new method that has been validated with several recorded sessions and everyone that buys into it has to sign a disclosure agreement.

"I defy anyone to figure out what we are doing because it looks like we are randomly just picking up the dice and throwing them. Here is how we do it !!"

After the demonstration both Gar and Bucko agreed that he did have something good and were willing to buy it and to sign a disclosure agreement. Jerry advised them to practice it until they got it down pat before using it for real. They agreed that this would be wise, so they left and drove back to Manhattan. They were fired up with this new method and they were committed to serious practice for the next few days.

Gar had seen an ad on the internet for a used crap table and after negotiations, he bought it and had it installed in his basement. This gave them the same results as playing in a real casino. He had several lights installed and a stereo system that made it as noisy as a casino. They tried to get the same effect as being in a casino.

Within a week they were ready to once again try playing in a casino. They got their money together and headed down to the newest casino in Atlantic City, The Taj Mahal.

Chapter 102

They drove south on the Garden City Parkway, then left onto the Atlantic City Expressway. Both men remarked how many changes had been made since the first Casino, The Resorts, had been built. It was nice to see how the city was cleaning up from the dark atmosphere that it used to be. Dark and dingy was coming down, replaced with bright and clean. They swung east on Virginia Avenue and drove to the Valet parking. As they walked in, the splendor of all the glass and the beautiful glass chandeliers caused Gar to say, "This is the nicest Casino that I have ever seen. Mr. Trump didn't spare much, he went all out on this one."

"I have to agree with you on this," replied Bucko.

Gar was about to ask where the crap tables were when he heard that familiar phrase,"The dice are out," and knew which way to go .

He and Bucko approached one of the $25 dollar tables and found both of their favorite spots open. They cashed in for a grand a piece and the dealers welcomed them and the pit-boss asked if either had a players card? Both answered no.

"No problem. I'll have cards made up for you. Just give me some identification."

Bucko was at stick-right-one and Gar was at stick-right, next to the stick man. Bucko got the dice first and tossed a 9 for his come-out number. He placed his odds and made a place bet on both the 6 & 8. He bet light, since it usually takes a few tosses for a player to know if they are zoned-in. He threw a couple crap numbers and rolled his 6 & 8, then sevened out. His loss was minimal.

The dice now were moved to Gar. He rolled a 4 for his come-out number, then told the dealer to put $440 inside (5-6-8-9). Bucko whispered this was too early for big bets, but Gar shrugged his shoulders, took the dice in his right hand and rolled an 8. Then he rolled a 7.

"Seven out," yelled the stick man.

Gar glanced toward Bucko, who was also looking at him. He knew he had made a rookie mistake and Bucko's silence was louder than any word.

The dice went around the table and Bucko had a fair hand and soon it was Gar's turn to shoot. This time, after his come-out number, he only bet the 6 & 8. As he started making numbers he raised his bets by using the casino's money. This is the correct way to play. Bucko had told him many times not to raise a bet until you have your initial bets back in your tray. Soon the inside numbers were up to $100 each and Gar was in his zone and the numbers were coming for him. It wasn't long before he won back the loss that he had on his first time with the dice.

About halfway through his roll, the pit-boss tried to break his rhythm by asking him if he and his friend would like a room and dinner comped by the Taj. Gar had been warned by Bucko that the dealers would try to disrupt a good shooter if he was taking good money from them.

Gar paused before he rolled again and told the pit-boss, "Sir, I will talk to you about after I finish my roll."

Then he remembered what Bucko had taught him. He put down the dice and picked up some red chips and declared, "I want a $ 5.00 bet on each of the place numbers for the dealers."

Immediately the crew all yelled, "The dealers are on the line."

From then on, Gar could do no wrong. The pit-boss also left him alone. He was having a monster roll and all the placed numbers had $200 or more on them. From time to time he would glance at Bucko who would smile and show him a thumbs-up salute. By the time the 7 came out on him, he succeeded to take several thousand from the casino. The entire dealer crew applauded him, told him it was a great roll and thanked him for the bets. Gar and Bucko thanked the pit-boss for the dinner but they didn't want the room. The boss told them the next time they came, just call ahead and a room would be waiting for them, fully comped.

They proceeded to the cashier and changed their chips for cash and after going to the rest room they took the escalator up to the second floor where they visited The Mark Anthony Steak House for a gourmet dinner. After dinner they picked up their car from the valet parking and headed for home.

The next day they had a late breakfast and as they were drinking their coffee Gar said, "You know, Bucko, I've always wanted to play craps in some of those exotic island casinos like Aruba or Freeport or Nassau, places like that. Have you ever been to those places?"

"Yes, I have. As a matter of fact, most big cities have franchised dealers that have junkets that fly you to their casinos."

"What's a junket?"

"That's just a classy name for a trip or excursion sponsored by companies or in this case by Casinos. They only charge a small fee to get you to come to them and gamble. I have found that Fort Lauderdale Florida area has the best Junket dealers mostly because the Bahamas are straight across the water from them. Plus that area draws huge players from the Miami area also."

Gar let that information soak in before he asked, "Do you still have a connection with those people and how do you feel about both of us going over?"

Bucko was quick to respond.

"Hey, partner, I'm always ready to go wherever you want to go. As far as contacts go, that was long ago and new people are in now, but all we need to do is fly down to Florida , buy a paper and call them. It's as simple as that. When would you like to go?"

"Shoot, I say let's pack some clothes for a couple weeks and leave in a couple days . I think we should rent a room or hotel in Ft. Lauderdale and use it for a base until we find out if it's plausible to stay over on the islands."

"Then that's a go, Buddy," said Bucko. "Oh, by the way lets be sure we pack our birth certificates, driver's licenses or positive ID's. Customs are very strict."

The next two days both were busy packing and getting the best price on the airlines. Gar told Sammy and Sandy he would be out of town for a few days. He had always told his family that Sammy & Sandy would know where he was.

Chapter 103

They flew to Florida and rented a room for two weeks at the Fort Lauderdale Holiday Inn. They bought the local newspaper and in no time Bucko was on the phone, calling for reservations on junkets to the Bahamas.

"I have the info on Freeport and Nassau, Gar. Which would you like to try first?"

"Let's go to Nassau. I've heard that their Crystal Palace Casino is a nice place."

"OK. I will make the deal." said Bucko, heading for the nearest phone.

After his call he said to Gar, "OK, here's the deal. We have to be at the airport no later than 8:30 AM. The plane leaves at 9 AM for Crystal Palace, Nassau . After going through Customs inspection, we are bussed to the Casino. We are offered snacks and unlimited drinks while on the plane and when we arrive with a full dinner after 5 PM. All this for only $98.00 each. For high rollers, it's half that."

"Say, that's a great deal Bucko."

The next morning they were at the airport on time and their Host was a guy named Sol, who welcomed them and explained everything again. Each was given a white badge about 1 inch square and on it was written "Crystal Palace," with a number underneath. Sol told them he had a manifest with everyone's name on it which would be given to the casino Host. That way they matched a face to the number and name so they always knew how much was bet. Another huge benefit was that the Casino did not deduct taxes on any amount won either on the slots or table games and the IRS was not notified.

When they boarded the plane, a pretty Hostess welcomed them aboard and asked each passenger what kind of drink she could get them. It seemed most everyone was having a screwdriver, so Gar and Bucko had that. The orange juice was very good, especially with Vodka.

After they were airborne, the seat belt sign was turned off and the Hostess brought refills and set up the first two seats into a poker place by turning the seats backward, placing a plywood sheet between them. Several of the regulars helped and in no time, the poker game was going strong. After each pot was won, a $1.00 donation was given to the Hostess. She made out just fine. The flight lasted 45 minutes and as they started their descent, the players looked out the windows at the crystal clear waters that were green and blue. The island was a beautiful sight.

After they departed the plane, they were ushered into the airport into two or three lines and took their turns going through Customs. Once through, they were asked to board the shuttle bus for the ride to the Casino. As they were boarding , Gar noticed a few players getting into a big stretch limousine. He asked Sol about it.

"The limo is for High Rollers. You too can ride in one if your bets are big enough. The Casino rewards the big betters, believe me."

The ride to Crystal Palace Casino took about twenty minutes and offered everyone a nice, scenic view of some of Nassau.

The driver stopped in front and again their doorman welcomed everyone to beautiful Crystal Palace. They ushered everyone to the escalator that led to the second floor mezzanine where they were given a free lunch. There was a nice balcony and bar where players could come for a break and be able to watch the entire Casino floor. Gar noticed that almost all of the workers and dealers were black.

"Most of the employees are black because this is their home," Bucko reminded him, "We are their visitors . You will find they are very proud people and take great pride in everything they do. Watch the dealers. See how fast they make change and keep accurate notice to the game."

Gar and Bucko were not able to find a table with their favorite positions, so they went to the right end of the table where they found room to play together. They both bought-in with $1000 each. When the box-man counted the money and sent chips to each, they were welcomed by their last names and he wished them luck.

Gar turned to Bucko.

"I am trying Jerry Patterson's new method from here since I'm out of position here on the end," he said softly.

Gar was given the dice first, since he was standing to Bucko's right. His first roll was a 10 for his point or come-out number. He decided to play the "Iron Cross" strategy by place betting only the 5-6-8 and the field. That way every number is covered. As long as he didn't roll a 7, he would collect on very roll regardless of whatever number came up. He held the dice long enough to roll about 25 numbers and remarked he liked the new system. Bucko continued with his usual soft touch method and keeping all the hardways on axis.

After a come-out of 5, put $25 on each of the hardways plus placing the same. Before long, he hit a hard 8, played it and came right back with a hard 6, which he parlayed that also. Now he had $250 on both the 6 & 8. He proceeded to hit some more good numbers until he hit the hard 6 again, that paid him $2,250.00.

Gar was cheering him on and he also started betting the hardways. Bucko was finding the groove and was cool and relaxed. After a few more good numbers he hit the hard 8 and again collected $2,250.00. The dealers and pit-boss were watching him closely, but he wasn't doing anything wrong, just shooting good craps.

After he held the dice for about an hour, the 7 came out and he was done. The dealers gave him a round of applause and he asked them to color him up. They counted the chips and gave him larger amount chips so he didn't have so many to carry to the Cashier. They told him that the total was $ 6,540.00 . Both he and Gar had decided it was time for a break and look over the rest of the casino.

At the rear of the casino, you could open the glass doors and be within 50 feet to the waters edge. There was an outdoor bar, a steel drum band, swimming, boat rentals and lots of ski-boats and lots of bikinis to feast your eyes on. They both relaxed in a nice cushioned chair and ordered an Oriental drink. This casino had much to offer to the player that liked sunshine,warm weather, and clear ocean waters. It was properly named The Crystal Palace.

"There is another casino on this island a little further down that is owned by Merv Griffin," Bucko said, "I think it's called Paradise Island. I have never been there, but I've heard of it. I never wanted to go there because I rather liked this place and they make me feel right at home. It's like the slogan, 'If it's not broken, why try to fix it?'"

"You are right about that. I like it too."

Gar and Bucko played another session at the craps table and were able to keep their winnings. Then they headed for the Seaside Steakhouse, where they enjoyed mouth watering steaks and seafood. This was included in their junket fee.

Bucko noticed Sol, their host, as they were seated, caught his eye and waved him over to sit with them. He came over and shook their hands.

"Hi, guys, I see that you had a few nice rolls at the table. That's good. We like seeing our members do good. By the way, from now on you ride in the limo whenever we come or go to the airport.

Bucko smiled and casually glanced at Gar.

"Thanks Sol. We appreciate that. We also would like to have you book us for a return trip day after tomorrow if possible."

"Sure thing, guys. Consider it done. Hope you become one of our regulars."

"Maybe two of your regulars," smiled Gar.

Sol was slow to react.

Wha..? Oh, yeah. Two regulars

After dinner, they both worked their way back to the craps table where they continued in having some nice winning sessions.

They continued until it was time to catch the limo back to the airport. After going back through American customs, they boarded their plane for the return flight to Ft. Lauderdale. The lady stewards served drinks of choice to those who requested them and in a short time the plane touched down in Florida. They located their rental car and drove back to their hotel.

As they were coming down the hallway, they noticed the door to their room was not closed.

"I guess the maid is cleaning our room," Gar said, "but its rather late to be doing that."

At that instant the door flew open and two sleazy characters ran out, knocking Gar and Bucko to the floor. Bucko was quick enough to reach out and trip one of them and as he fell, he noticed a tattoo of a skull and cross bones on his left forearm. Bucko was getting up as the intruder was also getting to his feet, cursing at him.

Before Bucko could grab him, the intruder pulled a gun and shot him.

Look out, Bucko yelled Gar, as the intruders were getting away. He was more worried about Bucko as he gathered him up in his arms.

How bad is it, pal?

I'm ok, I think. He only grazed my left arm. I just need to have it sewn up.

By this time the Security guard and room neighbors were running to them. Gar told him what happened and asked him to see if the bad guys were outside, getting away. The room clerk said he called 911 and a rescue unit was on the way. While someone was wrapping a cloth around Bucko s arm, Gar made an inspection of their room, but could not find anything missing, except for an old Navy ring he had acquired years ago. He seldom wore it, but he kept it as a memento of good times long ago. He always kept it under his shorts and t-shirts.

The police came together with the fire-rescue unit and after the usual questions, they had Bucko taken to the nearest hospital, where they agreed he was very lucky the bullet missed the bone and passed through the flesh of his left upper arm. They bandaged him and said to see his own doctor in a few days, then released him.

After they were back in their room, Bucko related to Gar that he could identify the robber if he ever saw him because of the tattoo.

Did you tell the police about the tattoo?

No, I didnt, Gar, because if the paper were to write about that, we would never see that guy again or his arm, and I am going to find that ba—one of these days."

Hey, Im with you, Pal. Have you got a plan, or are we just going head hunting?

He thought quietly for a moment, staring at the table in front of him.

The plan is we stay here, start visiting some of the night clubs and look into some of the night life around here and Miami. If it looks like we are on a losing mission, we will give up and get back to craps. Besides, we need a rest, while my arm heals, anyway, he said as he rubbed the sore muscles.

Right you are, Pal. This change might be good and Im dying to get my hands on those rats. I think I will get back to my morning walks again. Ever since Debbie died, I have been lax in my exercises.

Thats good, Gar. That way we both can sharpen up our muscles and get back in shape.

Chapter 104

They spent the next few days walking and exercising until Bucko was strong enough to start with the night life of going to night clubs and looking for the two intruders. Gar had formed the habit of carrying a roll of quarters in his pocket, from the days when he was always getting into fights. He now makes sure he has a roll with him everywhere he goes. He probably didnt need it since he had grown to six feet and weighed in at 250 pounds. Bucko was about the same, but much older.

Gar called Sol and canceled their trips to Nassau. Sol was sorry to hear of their misfortune and assured him that he would take good care of them when they were ready to go again. Gar also called the police to see if they had any leads on the robbers. They told him they hadnt found them, but they fit the description of the Gomez brothers, known hoodlums who had been involved in numerous altercations. The police were on the lookout for them for questioning.

"Sooner or later well get them. They are night demons. They are seldom seen at daylight. They steal for drug and gambling money and usually work together."

Gar thanked the police and said he would stay in touch. He related the information to Bucko.

Thats good info, Gar. That tells me sooner or later they will show up at one of the casinos and if were lucky, maybe they like shooting craps."

Gar and Bucko frequented the night clubs and beer joints around Ft. Lauderdale and northern Miami, but they failed to find their foe.

Finally Bucko was completely healed and they agreed to get on with their crap playing. They called Sol and he was able to go the next day to the Crystal Palace in Nassau. After Customs, they were seated in the limo and driven out to the Casino.

They had several light sessions at the craps table and a very nice meal. They were about to leave the craps table and go cash in their chips, as it was nearing the time to leave, when something caught Gars eye. There was a gold ring hanging on a gold chain around the neck of one of the players at the Roulette table straight across the aisle from Gars table.

Hey Bucko , he said softly See the guy at the Roulette table with the green polo shirt?

yeah, what about him?

See that ring hanging from the gold chain?

He tried to look without being noticed. There were too many players and too much activity making hard to see

No, I dont see that.

Well, let's walk slowly over that way. Be sure not to make eye contact with him.

They came closer and as everyone was making new bets and leaning into the layout of the Roulette table, the man in question leaned in to place his bets and the gold chain and ring dangled from his neck. Gar immediately recognized his Navy ring. He hurriedly ushered Bucko down the aisle to the Cashier and cashed in their chips.

Did you see the ring? asked Gar.

yeah, I did. Was it yours?

Oh yeah, thats my ring. Lets get closer and watch behind one of the other tables so we can fix the faces in our mind. There is someone with him that may be our other rat.

After they made sure they could recognize them, they went to the limo.

They had to be on our plane," Gar said, "I think we should make sure we board the plane before them so we keep track of them. We can talk about a plan after we get on board. Doing anything now would be futile."

Bucko and Gar were able to board before the suspects and took seats further to the rear. The Gomez brothers took seats midway and immediately requested two drinks. It was apparent they didnt have a clue they were being watched.

After much thought and strategy, Bucko and Gar devised a plan to even the score . When the plane landed and the hatch door swung open, the players started to leave. Gar and Bucko quickly closed in right behind the suspects. As they were starting down the dark, steep steps of the rolling gangway, Gar gave the suspects a hard shove. They started cursing and falling forward. The one with Gars ring hit the bottom first, while the other went sprawling to his side. Gar was on him quickly and tore his chain and ring from him. The robber was starting to get up, when Gar smacked him senseless with a sweet uppercut. He went to sleep quickly. Bucko had grabbed the other one and threw two punches to the nose and forehead that rendered the robber senseless. They left the scene before anyone knew what happened.

Revenge is so sweet , said Bucko.

Amen

Both Gar and Bucko returned to their hotel and after a good night sleep, started packing to return back to New York. They had decided to return home, check their mail and see if anyone was needing them. They had also decided to take some time off from gambling for a change of pace. They talked about what happened at the airport.

"The bad guys would never call the police," Bucko said, because they would never want to involve the police in any of their affairs . They already have a past record. Sooner or later they might put two and two together and figure that we probably were the ones, but they only saw us as they tried to run out of our hotel room. They saw us at the Crystal Palace in Nassau and didnt recognize us, so they have to chalk this one up as a bad deal.

Bucko was right .

Chapter 105

Bucko and Gar spent the next few weeks in Manhattan catching up with their mail and phone messages. Gar made calls to all of his family and when he called the Grimes home to talk with Irving , Rose answered.

After the usual banter, Gar was talking about all of the free time on his hands and thought he might take in one of the Broadway shows. He jokingly asked Rose if she would like to go with him.

Sure."

This quick response caught Gar off guard.

Uh, Oh, I mean I, hey you wouldnt want to go with an old guy like me and you dont have to go just because we are family friends.

What do you mean old guy? You are only four or five years older than me. Besides, I have been so busy at Bantam Books, Im ready for something different . This working seven days a week has gone on long enough . Are you serious?

Well I, uh, well yeah, I guess I am, stammered Gar .

After they made a definite time and place, they continued talking for another thirty minutes. Gar was relating the trips to Nassau and Rose was telling him how she had moved up to an executive position at the book company. She never married and never met the right guy.

She would have loved to tell him how she had always been in love with him and she had always measured her dates by him. She had purposely avoided most of the family gatherings because she never wanted Gar or Debbie to see in her eyes, how she felt towards Gar.

Gar told Rose he was reluctant to date again and he knew that no one could take Debbies place. He was quite adamant about about preserving his faithfulness to Debbies life by not seeing other women. He felt that even in her death he should be obligated to keep a standard of faith. At the same time, Rose was listening with great compassion and assured Gar that she, as well as he, loved Debbie very much. She convinced him that going to the theater with her was not because he was pursuing her or that he was seeking companionship.

Gar picked Rose up at her house and after he chatted for a while with Irving, he drove to Broadway and they took in the much publicized production of Cats. They stopped for a nightcap before he took her home. She had become quite beautiful and wore very expensive clothing. It was very hard for Gar to keep his mind off her.

Rose could see he was having some attention problems and asked him, Are you uncomfortable going out with me?

Does it show that much? Its not that Im uncomfortable, Rose. Its just that Im still getting over Debbie and having been a faithful husband, I feel like Im cheating on her.

She took his hand.

Listen to me. I do not want you to feel guilty about tonight. You have spent time mourning for Debbie and now you must get on with your life. That doesnt mean that you shouldnt think or talk of her while we are together. She was loved by us all, Gar and I want us to always feel free to discuss her without feeling guilty.

Thank you, Rose. You are very kind as well as beautiful.

She started to blush.

"Thank you, Gar. I wasnt sure you noticed.

Oh, I noticed all right. Its quite something to see you so matured. I still am overwhelmed by your success and all this time unmarried. Are you turned off by men?

Of course not, Gar. I like men. You have opened up a subject I was hoping we could talk about another time, but maybe its just as well that we get it out in the open now instead of later.

Oh my God. Please dont tell me that you are gay?

No, Im not gay or lesbian, Gar. So dont think thats why Im single. I do not know how to say this, so Ill just come right out with it. I love you, Gar. I have always loved you, ever since I first met you and you lived at our home after coming from that reform school at Industry.

Gar sat up straight, I never knew that, Rose.

I know that, Gar. I tried very hard not to let it show. I knew it would hurt Debbie if she ever knew. I loved her also. I stayed away from most of the family gatherings so that no one could see how I felt when I was around you.

Gar could only repeat to himself, I never knew.

I know, Gar. Do you hate me for telling you now?

He took her hands.

No, no, Rose. I would never hate you. Just let me get my breath and let this soak into my brain. I think its great and I want to thank you for having the courage to tell me now.

He softly touched her hair, moved his face closer to hers and whispered, You are so pretty."

He pressed his lips to hers and gently gave her a long, loving kiss . It seemed like fireworks were going off in both of their bodies.

Rose was murmuring, Gar, Oh, Gar .

Gar was murmuring, Rose, Rose, Rose.

They both suddenly sat up in their booth at the restaurant.

After a brief moment Gar said,Rose, I am feeling quite attracted to you and I want to be sure its not just some impulse of the moment, so I want to take you home and then I want to call you after I get my emotions together. If you and I still feel the same, I would like for us to have more dates and really get to know each other's bad habits and good ones as well. How does that sound?

That sounds wonderful and romantic, darling. I like your ideas

Chapter 106

Gar took Rose home and after a goodnight kiss he returned home. He could feel the excitement in his body and a quickness in his step that had not been there for a long time. Could he really be falling in love again? Was God allowing him a second chance at being happily married? He had loved Debbie with all of his heart and soul. Could it be possible to love someone else? He had to sort all of this out before he could go any further. He would not allow something to happen with Rose unless he was one hundred percent truthful and absolutely sure it was real.

Gar thought about Rose every minute during the next few days, but he deliberately held off calling her, because he needed time to sort things out. He also had conversations with Bucko about her after he had asked him what was wrong with him. He could see Gar was always deep in thought and was not his usual self. Bucko told him this was one problem that he had to work out by himself.

Finally, he decided that the only way to solve this was to see more of Rose, so he called and arranged another night of theater and dinner. In fact, they had several more dates that convinced him that their love for each other was real and there was no reason not to marry. Roses father and Gars family all thought it was wonderful they had fallen in love and approved of their wedding.

The wedding took place at Rose and Irvings home and everything was catered by only the best. Rose was so beautiful and her gown was elegant. They waited one full year from Debbies death to marry and not one person ever thought that it was too soon. The fact that Rose was known and loved by all certainly was a good thing. Everyone agreed they both deserved a chance at happiness.

Gar told Rose that he did not want to live in his old house anymore and wanted to buy closer to the city. She knew he felt uneasy taking her into the house where Debbie lived, but she would not embarrass him by making any comment. They found a home they both liked and closed the deal. Gar offered his old house to Bucko and financed it himself. It was such a great offer that Bucko could not refuse.

Gar told Rose about his craps playing but had not made any effort to go to a Casino. She kept her job at the book company and as she came to hear more and more of Gars experiences, she suggested he write a book of all his adventures. She said she would help him get it published through her work. At first, Gar just ignored the idea, but as she kept being persistent and pressed him, he relented and started to jot down an outline. His mind would recall this and that and before long, it started to come together. Each morning he and Rose would waken at the same time, have breakfast together, then after she left , he would take a pot of coffee into his den and start writing ideas onto his legal pads until he had it like he wanted. Then he would type it into a form the publishers wanted and the book kept getting bigger each week. For a break, he would either drive over to Buckos place or call him and they sometimes spent time at Vinnie's bar, shooting darts and shuffleboard.

Rose and Gar traveled often, visiting several tourist attractions in USA and in Europe. Rose loved France and the romantic places. She was madly in love and thanked God every day for her wonderful husband. All of Gars children accepted her and were glad to see their father happy again.

When the book was finished, Rose used her influence at Bantam and had it published. It truly was a great book and Gar was invited to appear on many talk shows, including The Larry King show. It soon became a best seller, and Gar was overwhelmed by its success. He was living in a strong feeling of happiness and the euphoric sensation reminded him of how he felt the first time he held the dice for over an hour and the large applause he received from the Casino dealers and players . Gar tried to be humble, but he was so very proud.

He never forgot to look into the heavens and say, "Thank you, God, for allowing me to love and be loved. "